A Healing Divorce

Transforming the End of Your
Relationship with Ritual and Ceremony

A Healing Divorce

Transforming the End of Your
Relationship with Ritual and Ceremony

by

Phil Penningroth

and

Barbara Penningroth

ISBN: 1-58721-793-7

This book is printed on acid free paper

Cover design by Takigawa Design
Cover photo by Marty Takigawa

1stBooks - rev. 12/26/00

About The Book

A Healing Divorce is unique. There is no other book devoted solely to rituals for divorce and ceremonies of parting. Written by a formerly married couple who have remained friends, this compassionate and practical book discusses significant issues to do with the process of separation and divorce and demonstrates how ritual can transform and heal the end of a relationship.

Based on the authors' personal experience, as well as interviews and extensive research, **A Healing Divorce** offers a way to diminish anger, alter destructive patterns and end a relationship with truth, love, care and forgiveness. It features inspirational stories of individuals who have created and performed parting ceremonies, either alone or with a partner. It offers model rituals drawn from a variety of spiritual and religious traditions. It includes a discussion about religious issues concerning divorce, and divorce and ritual, in both the Christian and Jewish traditions. There's a special chapter about the healing benefits of a parting ceremony for children. Several chapters, including a step-by-step guide, are devoted to the how-to of creating and performing a divorce ritual. The appendix includes both recommended reading and a list of contributors to the book, lay and clergy, prepared to offer the reader advice and counsel about parting ceremonies.

A Healing Divorce shows how ritual and ceremony can transform the tension and pain that arise during this difficult time into the emotional energy needed to gain new awareness, initiate the delicate process of growth and effect a positive life transition. It's for everyone — individuals, couples, families, clergy, lawyers and counselors — all who believe that the more conscious a parting and the more healing a divorce, the more life affirming the end of a relationship will be for individuals, families and for the world.

The purpose of ritual is to serve as the active door through which one passes into the larger life, from one stage of life into the next ... Like all real art, including the movement of sacred dances, ritual expresses the organic order that is already inscribed in our DNA. It is a dynamic pattern through which energy can flow in an evolutionary process toward a larger meaning or new stages of life.

Jean Houston
"Ritual as a Passage"
Quest, Winter 1998

Perhaps we are ready to dump our old models of isolation and separation and replace them with kindness, caring, intimacy and lifetime support. Because we are spiritual beings, it is not so much what our bodies do that determines the quality of our life, but the state of our spirit. Though our bodies may go in different directions, we can remain whole and joined in the heart. The end of a marriage or relationship does not mean the end of love. True love spans far beyond the boundaries we have laid over it, and it does not die; it simply goes on gathering force until everything we look upon is blessed by our appreciation of it as a gift of God.

Alan Cohen
The Heart of Parting, 1998

An event of divorce is too momentous in the life of individuals to be left in the hands of a judge and civil court. It cries out to be ritualized in a Christian context, to be "acted out" as a way of perceiving, a way of being, that will provide a point of reference for the future (as does the marriage service), which grounds its participants in "the way it will be."

Jeanne Audrey Powers
Rituals for a New Day: An Invitation, 1976

Acknowledgements

This book has been compiled as much as written. As you will see, it includes the creative work of many people over many years.

First and foremost, we would like to thank everyone, lay and clergy, who so graciously shared their stories and their ceremonies and rituals with us.

A special thanks to Scott Small, Lee Borden and Dorothy Scott, who opened the door to alternative liturgy in the Christian tradition, which led us to the Jewish tradition. From the Christian tradition of alternative liturgy, we want to express particular appreciation for the past work and current counsel of Rev. Jeanne Audrey Powers and Rev. Hoyt Hickman. Years ago, with a few other dedicated souls in the United Methodist church, they created one of the first books that offered rituals of divorce as an acceptable option for Christian couples: *Rituals for a New Day: An Invitation*. Our book stands on a foundation they helped to build. We also want to thank Rabbi Harvey Fields for his tutelage about the history of divorce in the Jewish tradition, and Rabbis Eliot Stevens, Earl Grollman and Alan Maller for sharing their contemporary visions of divorce rituals.

In the publishing world, we'd like to thank Ann West for her counsel about agents and publishers and for her editing, Joel Fields for his referrals, and Angellique for proof-reading the manuscript. We appreciate the expertise, patience and genial professionalism of Jim Sturgeon, Teri Watkins and the staff at 1st Books Library.

And last but not least, we'd like to thank our friends and helpers for their encouragement and support: Stacey, Norbert, John, Masha, Dan, Russ, Joel, Ann, Deborah K., Deborah A., Paul, Brian, Telase, Leslie, Marvin, Joanne, Sue and Larry Kramer, and Mike McCarthy and the writing group in San Diego. A special thanks to "Chris" for allowing us to discuss our shared experience with candor even when she may not always agree with what we say.

Contents

1

A Love Story About Divorce

Our Story

This is a love story about separation and divorce: how we parted after twenty-five years of marriage in a way that allowed us to honor what we had shared, forgive each other the pain we had caused and still remain good friends.

We met in the late '60s on the South Pacific island Territory of Guam where we had arrived with other partners from the opposite ends of the earth. We worked together in a cross-cultural mental health center that we both helped to develop and, as sometimes happens, mutual respect and admiration turned into love. We did our best to be kind and considerate when we decided to leave our other relationships to be with each other. However, looking back, we now realize that our partings from our partners were not as conscious as they could have been. Both of us vowed to do our best to never cause such pain again.

We moved back to California in the early '70s and found mental health jobs in Bakersfield, California, where we lived and worked during our entire marriage. Barbara created one of the country's early innovative psychiatric emergency services and then moved on to teach psychiatric nursing at a community college. Phil developed and administered alcohol treatment programs until he achieved enough success to change careers and work full time as a freelance writer.

For the first ten years of our marriage, we lived an ordinary and traditional family life. Though we could not have children of our own (after our child died as a newborn on Guam), during summers and holidays we coparented Phil's children, a boy and a girl, who lived with their mother in South Carolina.

In 1983, our life together began to change with a renewal of vows to celebrate our ten-year anniversary. What began as a sentimental reenactment became a searching re-examination of our relationship and marriage. We discovered that in critical

1

areas of our lives — work, spirituality and sexuality — we had drifted apart. Although it was impractical to work together as we had in the earlier years, we wanted to find more creative ways to enhance sex and share spirit. Thus began a journey of personal growth as a couple that we continue separately even today. For the next fourteen years, we explored many traditional and non-traditional forms of spirit, growth and change. These included Christianity, psychotherapy, Jungian analysis, 12-step self-help groups, couples work, Tantra and Quodoshka (disciplines combining spirituality and sexuality), Marriage Encounter, shamanic work, Buddhist Vipassna meditation, workshops with prominent spiritual teachers (such as Richard Moss, Stephen and Ondrea Levine, Jean Houston and Carolyn Myss), energetic therapies and the Pathwork of Transformation. We also experimented with other relationships and even lived for a time apart, across the swimming pool in the same apartment complex. For the last four years of our marriage, we purchased and created a home together as a reflection of the best we had shared.

We're often asked why our marriage failed, given the quality of our relationship. The simple answer is, it didn't. Even though its ending was painful, our marriage to us was a success. We relate with noted anthropologist Margaret Mead who, when asked why her three marriages had failed, replied that, to the contrary, all three had been successful, each in its own time. We believe in relationship and marriage as a path toward wholeness, Self and Spirit. In all the years of our searching and experimentation, our relationship was characterized by a commitment to do our best to love each other's desires as our own. This commitment is epitomized in a quotation by Jungian analyst Marie Louise von Franz: "Fidelity is loyalty to the true essence, the inner heart of the other." Even in the midst of the grief and pain of our parting, when loving the other's desire ultimately meant letting go of our marriage, we did our best to remain faithful to each other's true essence. Both of us wanted to part as consciously and lovingly as possible, and from that intent we created a parting ceremony which proved an expression of the very best of our union and helped us heal and remain good friends.

2

A Healing Divorce

We've all read the statistics: "Every thirteen seconds, someone gets divorced. Each year, in the United States alone, over one million families experience divorce. Every year, for every two couples that get married, one couple gets divorced" (Ahrons 1994, p. v). This 50% divorce rate is often interpreted as evidence of the failure of marriage as an institution. We disagree. Many reasons account for the increased divorce rate, including the fact that most people live — and find themselves living together — decades longer than they did even a century ago. Regardless of why so many people divorce, however, we would argue that if half of the couples who marry, sooner or later decide to divorce, then divorce can no longer be described as "abnormal." And, if divorce has become "normal"— as normal, say, as second marriages—perhaps we shouldn't be surprised that people who divorce are trying to find ways, including ritual, to make a painful process less destructive and more healing.

Not everyone believes this is possible. When you think about it, such skepticism really isn't surprising. Ours is a happily-ever-after world where songs, books and movies overwhelm us with fantasies of romance. Love is expected to last forever and, when it doesn't, hurt and disappointment suggest that somebody must have done somebody wrong. Just as we've all come to expect certain feelings and behaviors as part of romance, so we expect that if a love affair or a marriage ends, it will result in what we call the ABCs of separation and divorce: accusation, bitterness, conflict; acrimony, blaming, contempt.

We also live in a society where an adversarial legal system promotes an "us vs. them" mentality. In the context of divorce, this usually becomes "me vs. him or her." Conflict and contempt typically lead to court, where one side must lose for the other to win. There may be a momentary satisfaction in winning. But when you "defeat" someone you've lived with and loved for many years, who may be the mother or father of your children, is it any wonder that such a "victory" feels Pyrrhic, and that the guilt and regret that follow may have a crippling effect on the rest of your life?

3

Consider also the effects of such conflict on your children. Research over the last decade has shown that while divorce may be a relief to one or both partners, children suffer from the break-up of a family. They're never really prepared for it. But it is unbearable from a child's point of view when the conflict between parents doesn't end and may even escalate. In a separation or divorce, marital anger is often difficult to contain and sometimes spills over onto children with potentially devastating effects. Some of the most poignant responses to our parting ceremony came from adults who had been children of a divorce. One wistful college student we spoke to said, "I wish my parents had been able to do something like this; my life sure would have been different." (See more about children in Chapter 6.)

If all this isn't difficult enough, because we're only human and live in a tabloid culture, many of us also fall victim to *Schadenfreude*. This German word describes the perverse pleasure people sometimes get from the suffering of others; misery loves company and, hey, my divorce was hell, so how could yours be any better — why should it be?

Taken all together, the disappointments of romance, the conflicts inherent in the adversarial legal system and our temptation to *Schadenfreude* have combined to create what we call The Myth of the Bad Divorce. That is, all divorces are by definition acrimonious. We are to expect the worst of each other, accept the worst of ourselves, and consider wounding, destructive conflict as normal. Unfortunately, when people in marital crisis buy into this myth, it often becomes a self-fulfilling prophecy. But it doesn't have to be.

A lot of evidence — not as well known yet as it might be — suggests that many couples manage separation and divorce with a minimum of conflict. In *The Good Divorce*, Constance Ahrons (1994) noted that 50% of divorced couples she interviewed were either "Perfect Pals," for whom "the disappointments of a failed marriage didn't overshadow the positive elements of a long-standing relationship," or "Co-operative Colleagues" who, while not close friends, "co-operated quite well around issues that concerned [their] children" (p.5). In his unique book *Lost Lovers*,

4

Found Friends, Scott Nelson (1991) found that many couples after divorce continued to be friends or desired to establish more friendly relations with their ex-partners.

Why such a discrepancy between the Myth of the Bad Divorce and the real-life experience of so many people in post-divorce studies, not to mention the people we interviewed for this book? Could it be that many separating and divorcing couples are already doing their best to part with a minimum of conflict and a maximum of healing? We believe so. We also know that a number of them are using ritual and ceremony as a way to help facilitate that process.

The fact that you now hold this book in your hands is proof that some people believe a healing divorce is both desirable and possible. We disagree with those who insist that this runs counter to human nature, which during divorce, they believe, is likely to turn unconscious, selfish and brutal. When we show skeptics the video of our parting ceremony and tell them about others who have brought healing to their own divorce, they insist that all of these are special cases involving special people; that is, educated affluent folks, with years of therapy behind them. Surely, normal everyday people cannot do this. What we suspect, however, is that they, or someone they know, has suffered through the ABCs of divorce and cannot imagine another, different way. We hope that the stories in this book told by people who have used ritual and ceremony in the service of a healing divorce will change this attitude and encourage partings that are gentler, more creative, humane and life affirming.

Some people we've talked to have even suggested that helping people create and perform parting ceremonies might actually encourage divorce by making it easier to bear. We disagree with that, too. No parting ceremony can spare a divorcing couple the inevitable pain of loss and grief. We find it hard to believe that the anticipation of a ritual, no matter how healing, would make anyone's decision to divorce easier. On the other hand, once such a decision has been made, wouldn't it be more constructive for everyone involved if couples could part with a minimum of conflict and a maximum of healing?

Because of the many negative attitudes about divorce prevalent in our society, a healing divorce may seem like an oxymoron. If you're skeptical, or cynical, or even feel a bit angry, that's all right. The Myth of the Bad Divorce is mighty powerful. But its power is waning. Here's our advice: ignore the nay-sayers and follow your heart. It's true, divorce can be a harsh and painful reality. Sadly, we've all been conditioned to expect the worst. But even if you feel like the walking wounded, divorcing doesn't have to imitate *The War of the Roses*. Our experience, and the experience of others whose stories you'll read in this book, leads us to believe that, with the help of ritual, you can end your relationship with truth, love, care and forgiveness. No, it's not always easy, but we believe that you — and your children — will find it worth the effort. As you try to decide if a healing divorce is worthwhile for you, here are some questions to ask:

Did you love your partner?

Did you share a life together?

Was some of it wonderful and worth remembering?

Do you grieve his loss, or hers?

Do you care about your children's emotional well-being?

Do you care about your own?

Do you want to go on with your life? Learn from your experience? Bring more consciousness to a new relationship?

Do you prefer healing over conflict, peace over power, forgiveness over vengeance?

Despite the pain and anger you may feel, if you're like most people you probably answered "yes" to all of these questions. Doesn't it make sense, then, to do what you can to bring healing to the end of your relationship? Certainly, you may feel grief, fear, anger, jealousy — all the familiar emotions that make divorce so painful and difficult. But if you're willing, ritual can help end your relationship with integrity and honor in a ceremony that often proves as meaningful as the wedding that began the marriage.

Sound too good to be true? You bet, but only in the context of a culture that promotes the Myth of the Bad Divorce. Instead of *Schadenfreude* and legal battles where there are ultimately no winners, imagine a world where we could genuinely celebrate ceremonies of parting in which the goodness of a past relationship is carefully honored, difficult present feelings are truthfully shared and the future is gracefully accepted.

You Can Do It, Too

First, let's consider a harsh reality. For all those who will divorce, it's important to remember that your parting is already destined to end in ritual. Whether it's a two minute conversation or a full-blown hearing, divorce court is the ritual way we end marriages in our society. Despite the fact that this is about your life, you will probably have little or no say in the matter. Most likely, only your lawyer will be allowed to speak. This cold, impersonal legal routine too many times devolves into another ritual — bloody combat. True, you may arrange to escape the unpleasantness of court, but don't fool yourself. Even if all you do is sign the papers your lawyer puts in front of you, you are participating in a ritual. The question isn't *if* you'll end your marriage with ritual — law and society have decreed it to be so. The only question is what kind of ritual will it be?

Contrast the way things are now with an ideal we share with Ahrons (1994), presented in *The Good Divorce*.

> Couples would have a brief, quiet gathering involving the children. They could speak about the good things the marriage brought them, and the necessity for parting now. Each person could say what they wanted from their new situation, if this were possible to do without too much bitterness, and pledge that they will try not to bad-mouth one another. The children could be told that this was not their fault. Most importantly, these parents would say to themselves, their children, their friends and extended families, as well as to the community around them, that they are committed to continuing to raise their children in a healthy family,

7

albeit one in which they live in a different household.
(p.70)

We first thought about writing a book when we couldn't find anyone to advise us about creating a ritual like this to help end our own relationship. Oh, there are lots of books about the emotional and legal realities of break-up and divorce, many of them cynical, nasty and flip, some quite thoughtful and helpful. (We've included the latter in the Appendix.) But we could find virtually nothing about divorce rituals or ceremonies of parting. Our friends, many of them healing professionals, thought a ceremony of parting sounded good in principle but had no idea what it might look like. Even Stephen and Ondrea Levine's (1995) *Embracing the Beloved*, where we first came across the idea, only mentions a parting ceremony in passing and offers few specifics. We have since found more complete examples and models, which we'll share with you (see Chapter 11), but during the emotional throes of parting, we had neither the time nor the energy to do extensive research. We could certainly have used guidance and examples of how others had accomplished a healing divorce.

Separations and divorces usually proceed from the decision of one partner to leave (often by an announcement that the relationship is over), through pain and conflict to some form of parting, usually a legal proceeding in a courtroom. We have organized this book to reflect that common sequence of events.

As you read the personal stories people have shared, you will have an opportunity to reflect on how others have used healing ritual, either with a partner or individually.

We believe all concerned, including children, benefit when both partners participate in a divorce ritual, so we emphasize parting ceremonies created and performed by a couple. Yet we also know from both personal experience and our research that this ideal is often difficult to achieve — though not, perhaps, as difficult as the Myth of the Bad Divorce would have you believe. Remember, you can do a ritual or ceremony by yourself. Many rituals included here have been performed by one partner, usually with friends. If that is your circumstance, you can easily adapt what you'll read here to your own needs. Even if your partner chooses not to participate, you can still bring consciousness to your parting and healing to your divorce. We believe this is especially important if you are a single parent with children.

In Chapter Two, we describe conscious parting and discuss the process of parting through divorce, a "crazy time" filled with wild, fluctuating emotions and gnawing ambivalence. Your experience, perceptions and feelings about parting will differ depending on whether you see yourself as the one leaving or the one who has been left. We suggest different ways partners can work with their feelings to keep an open heart. We talk about the confusion caused by the involvement of a third party and offer some suggestions about how to deal with such a difficult situation. We also talk about shadows, those aspects of ourselves we dislike and have disowned — rage, jealousy, deceit, revenge, and other "negative" emotions — which often erupt from the unconscious during the stress of separation and divorce. How can you deal with the temptation to blame your partner to justify the parting? What value is honesty-with-discernment? We also describe the advantages of slowing down the process of divorce and why both partners need to take 100% responsibility for their part in the break-up.

In Chapter Three, we discuss divorce in the context of the Christian and Jewish traditions, offering reflections from clergy on the question, "is divorce a sin?" We present alternative points of view and describe how rituals of divorce and parting ceremonies are currently used in church and synagogue.

In Chapter Four, we explain how to prepare a parting ceremony, with or without your partner, using our own experience and the experience of others to decide about right timing and different practical matters — place, making time and space sacred, whom to invite, music and clothing.

In Chapter Five, we discuss performing the ritual itself, including how to develop a tribute to your relationship, how to let go of the past with gratitude, how to let go of the future of the marriage with acceptance and how to work toward and express forgiveness. Finally, we suggest ways to symbolize the parting, as well as vows and commitments you might make for the future, either individually or as a couple.

In Chapter Six, we talk about the effects of divorce on children and offer a model for including them in your parting ceremony.

In Chapter Seven, we offer a step-by-step outline to help you prepare and perform your parting ceremony.

In Chapter Eight, we explore the promise and pitfalls of transforming your marriage into a friendship.

In Chapter Nine, people who have witnessed a ceremony talk about what it meant to them.

In Chapter Ten, the people who told their stories tell what has happened since and where are they now in their lives.

In Chapter Eleven, we offer examples of parting rituals and ceremonies from a variety of traditions.

In the Appendix, we offer information about books and contacts you may find helpful as you plan for a healing divorce.

Between each chapter is a personal story or two by a couple or an individual who created and performed a ceremony or ritual to bring consciousness to their parting and healing to their divorce. In these stories you will find borne out what research suggests: the critical factor isn't the parting itself, but *how you go about it*. When trying to effect a positive transition in your relationship, the way you make the change is even more important than the change itself. To that end, we have also included recommendations for activities that will contribute to a conscious parting and a healing divorce.

Writing this book has been an inspiring process. It has also been part of our healing. We have learned more about ourselves even as we learned from the experience of so many others who successfully struggled to find a better way to end their relationships. We now know that there are churches and synagogues where you can find spiritual guidance for this process. Given such examples and support, it's all the more possible to create your parting in any way you choose. As Alan Cohen (1999) said in *Happily Even After*, although pain is a given "suffering is optional." Grieving loss is to be expected, but who's to say that you must separate in anger or guilt, or that you can't go on to enjoy a friendship that lasts a lifetime?

Ritual is one of the most creative ways to transition from being married or living together to being single — and perhaps being friends. It can harness the tension and pain rolling through your life and transform them into the positive emotional energy you need to gain new awareness, promote healing and initiate the delicate process of growth. Rage, conflict and revenge need not damage your heart and the hearts of your children or compromise your future relationships. The more conscious you can make your parting, the more life affirming the end of your relationship will be for you, for your family and for the world.

Carolyn's Story

This story was written by Carolyn Elizabeth Dyche, copyright © 1999, and appears here by her permission.

I return to the gazebo at South Park
to experience
the last sunset of my twelve-year marriage.

It's a different season.
I remember the golden shades of fall.
Now it is summer, and everything is green.

Bryan and I began our journey here
as husband and wife.
Now we have Elizabeth and Lindsay,
many memories
joys, sorrows, and distance
between us.

Tears stream down my round cheek
as I search for a way to say good-bye
to the father of my children.

Such grief, sadness and loss
and loving commitment
to each other
and to our offspring.

I consider ours a successful marriage —
we served each other well,
we created beauty together,
and this is our time of parting.

This is the end of the hopes and dreams
we shared for our lives together.

I pray as I weep.
My heart is broken open
and in this place

I see more clearly ...

For many years
I have been defended with my husband.
I blamed him for my pain:
I have made many mistakes
learned many lessons.

In fear
I cause the ones
I love most
heartache.

I've unconsciously
created pain and separation
when my longing is to share
love and intimacy.

I pray to find a way
to honor the love
we have been graced to share.

I stay at the gazebo until the sun sinks into the earth.
I am comforted by the darkness of this womb;
I can feel the gestation of new life.
I am aware that in order for this birth to take place,
part of me must die.

God help me
with this task
of bittersweet
surrender.
Thy will be done,
Thy will be done.

I return home
with life's energy
pulsing through my body.
I feel movement
which carries me
onward.

I am open to
my own heart
to love
to loss.

I accept grief
as a consequence of loving.

I am inspired to create a ritual
to honor Bryan
and our marriage.

I want to give my best
to the very end.

I fax Bryan an invitation
to meet me at the gazebo
before court proceedings
to celebrate our marriage.

He replies favorably.
We will meet in twelve hours.

I pray to stay present to the myriad of feelings that
rise to the surface of my awareness —
Grief, relief, joy, sorrow, love, fear...

At other times
this mix of feelings might have been conflicting
and now I experience them
as wholeness.

14

I release tears of gratitude
for ALL —
grace and grit.

I open a box of photos collected over our years together.
We were so young when we were married at 22,
a couple of romantic idealists.

I lay out hundreds of images
in a circle around me
and listen as they speak.

We have loved each other
to our capacity
and the struggle has
taken a toll on our souls.

Now lines of separation
divide
and are revealed on our faces.

I take a large piece of paper
and begin to create
a collage of these images.

Each photo represents a story
forever held in my heart of hearts.
The images come together like a jigsaw puzzle,
snapshots from OUR life —
engagement, weddings, honeymoon,
lover, student, parent —
each image has its place.

I make a color copy of the collage for Bryan
and decide to make color copies
as a keepsake for our children,
and to send to close friends and family.

I write a note with each collage,
sharing the joys and sorrows of this transition.
Then I create a booklet of appreciations
to honor my partner.
Over the past several years
I have said mostly negative things to him,
pointing out my disappointments,
failing to be grateful
for all he brought to my life.

My intention is to love and accept him
and all that he graciously gave me
for so many years.

I want to give him a token,
something to remind him
of the places of love and tenderness
we shared.

I remember how fully present he was at the birth of our children.
I thank him for rubbing my belly as he talked to our unborn child,
for telling me the more I grew, the more there was to love.

I thank him for catching our son
when he decided he was ready to pop his head out
before the midwife arrived.

I thank him for defending me like a gallant knight,
for standing by me through my darkest fears.

After the booklet is complete,
I begin to gather items for the altar
I am called to create.
I remove our "Happily Ever After" wedding photo from our bedroom wall
and place it in the Rubbermaid tub with the other symbols of our life I will carry to the gazebo.

16

I select readings from Marianne Williamson's book, Illuminata,
choose two candles, one for the old way
and one to illuminate our new paths.

I want to give Bryan a gift of beauty,
a symbol
for his new life,
for his new home.

I drive to a 24 hr grocery store
and purchase a peace lily plant
which has two blossoms in full bloom.
I return home and replant it with loving attention,
water it with my tears
as I mindfully press the soil around the roots.

Finally, I go to sleep for the night.

A few hours later
I wake up
and dress for this important day.

I wear an ivory linen dress
and on my left wrist
the gold and pearl rope bracelet
my grandmother
willed to me,
and on the other
I wear the topaz bracelet
her sister gave to me
when I was a child.

I arrive early to set up the altar
and to pray in silence.

I walk around the gazebo,
burning sage to cleanse

and purify,
offering thanks for the opportunities
relationship brings.
Bryan and I are
more healed and more whole
than we have ever been.
We were called to each other
and now we are called to let go,
to end our union.

My husband arrives fashionably late,
wearing the silk Italian tie
I gave him for our first nuptials.
I am touched by his thoughtful attire
and forgive his timing.
We look like we could be getting married again,
and yet, this is our divorce —
an ending
and a new beginning.

In silence we connect
and communicate
the love held
captive in our hearts.

We join our hands
and our eyes
kneeling at the altar
united in love
and pain.
We weep.

I begin to pray out loud.
I ask for the presence of God to be
with us
as I recite prayers
of gratitude and surrender.

I give him the collage
and watch the images open his heart
as they did mine the night before.
I can feel his love, grief and vulnerability.
I give him his little book of appreciation;
he seems to take in my offering.

Bryan takes my hand
and offers me a gift.
My husband shares gratitude
for my presence in his life.
He asks for forgiveness for
failing to live up to his hopes
for himself, and for us.
He honors me for being the mother
of his daughter and son
and acknowledges he is glad we will
always have a connection
through our children.

With court proceedings impending,
it's time to remove our wedding rings.
We choose this conscious, loving divorce.
With care we remove our rings
and return them
to the burgundy velvet boxes
we received from the Goldmaker
twelve years ago.

We each pose for a photo at the altar
to mark this momentous occasion.
We want to share this experience with our children
someday,
to tell them stories
of the love and good will
their parents shared.

Bryan assists in
clearing the altar.
We return these objects to the
Rubbermaid carrier
and lock them in my car.

We share a tender
and bittersweet walk
across the parking lot
to the courthouse.
We walk
hand in hand
toward the rest of our lives
apart.

We feel lighter,
relieved
anticipating
our unknown
future.

Love flows through our open hearts.

As we approach
the door to the court house
our eyes meet.

We take in a deep breath.
As we exhale in unison
we release our clasp.

Together we cross a threshold not to be forgotten.

We let go of each other
and are held
in the embrace of the Beloved.
In gratitude....

2

Parting Through Divorce

Conscious Parting

The more consciously you part, the more healing your divorce can be. By conscious we mean "aware." Consciousness is like shining light into darkness. Knowledge really *is* power. What you know about the process of parting through divorce will prepare you for the feelings that inevitably arise. The more you know about yourself—your background, your relationship, your motives—the more capable you will find yourself when coping with those feelings, and the more open you will be about your own responsibilities for the break-up. Remember, it always takes two. Also, the more aware you are about the power of ritual and how it can facilitate the transition from marriage to being single, the more you will understand how it can bring healing to your divorce.

Living In "Crazy Time"

Divorce is almost always sad and painful.

It's also often utterly chaotic when you get caught up in what Abigail Trafford (1992) described in her book *Crazy Time: Surviving Divorce and Building a New Life.* Your marriage comes apart and you go a little crazy. Soon, inner turmoil is reflected in your world as you racket back and forth between relief, euphoria, rage and depression. In this state you may desperately seek a new love to assuage the pain or withdraw, refusing the invitations of well-meaning friends and letting your machine answer the phone. Maybe you even think about suicide — oh, my god, where did that thought come from? You get scared and, like an airplane pilot diving out of control, you wonder, will I pull out in time? Do I even care?

The chaos of emotion after a break-up is a normal reaction. We emphasize this just in case you are fantasizing that somewhere out there, someone more intelligent or more together is handling the loss of a loved one with calm and equanimity. Whether or not someone actually dies, any parting is a kind of death. Grief, anger, sadness, fear, abandonment — all the feelings associated with death can also come with divorce. In fact, many people who have experienced both the loss of a loved one through death and the loss of a partner through divorce say that, in some ways, divorce is more difficult. While death is seldom welcome and often (from a human point of view) ill-timed, we know and (more or less) expect it as the end of life. Its permanence is reinforced by rituals such as funerals and memorial services that help us let go and move on.

Such is seldom the case with separation and divorce. For most people, either one comes as a shock. Death isn't usually a choice. Almost always, however, one person chooses to leave a relationship. Parting may have been "sweet sorrow" for young Romeo, but when your partner announces that she wants a divorce, all you may feel is bitter rage. Along with the gamut of emotions associated with loss, you feel the added sting of rejection and betrayal. Indeed, you may find yourself reaching for metaphors about storms to try to describe how out of control you feel. In the "crazy time" of divorce it is normal to feel profound ambivalence ("I'm out of here" — "How can I possibly leave?!"), 180 degree mood swings (happy—sad, rage—relief), and an overwhelming sense of uncertainty and disorganization (How will I live? Where did I put my keys?). It may seem nearly impossible to relate to others without venting anger, bursting into tears or both.

Complicating all of this is the inescapable fact that we humans don't much like change, especially when it is sprung upon us. Oh, we pay lip service to the inevitable cycles of life and tell ourselves we enjoy surprises. Maybe we do, on our birthdays. But surprises that announce fundamental change in our lives ("I'm sorry; it's terminal." "I'm leaving; I want a divorce.") usually evoke helplessness, fear and rage. Often, our impulse is to fight, flee or hide.

22

There are ways to work with your emotions to minimize the disruptive chaos provoked by such a transition. These might sound like platitudes, tempting you to dismiss them as such. We urge you not to. We have found profound wisdom contained in these familiar ideas.

The first way is acceptance. Accept your feelings. This is not easy, especially if the divorce wasn't your idea. Although your life is going to feel out of control for awhile, things will get better.

Probably the first and most difficult thing to accept is that you can't control your partner's feelings. Sad as they are, the words of a country western lament ring true: You can't make someone love you if they don't, and she (or he) can't make her heart feel something it won't. Certainly, reconciliation is possible, and if that's what you want, we encourage you to try. Try anything — we did: therapy, pastoral counseling, marriage counseling, whatever works for you. But if it doesn't work, you may have to accept that your partner still feels the time has come to say good-bye — even if she or he continues to love you. Or, if you are the one to leave, you may have to accept that your partner feels angry, betrayed and abandoned, even though that was never your intention.

The second way is reflection. Set aside some private quiet time. Do you meditate? Pray? Good; now's the time. But even if you don't meditate, and the last time you prayed was as a child, it will still be helpful to set aside thirty minutes a day to listen to your body and your heart. Even if at first the only voice you hear is an angry one that blames your partner — or yourself — for what has happened, keep at it. If you have patience and listen, you'll begin to hear other voices, too: grief, remorse, forgiveness and even love.

The third way is mindfulness. Pay attention. It's easier if you slow things down. Again, reflection and meditation can help. Observe your feelings and find a way to express them that doesn't create more chaos. Do you keep a journal? You may want to write down your feelings, especially when, in the midst of "crazy time," they are so unpredictable, ungovernorable. In addition, you may wish to talk with a professional helper, spiritual adviser or trusted friend.

The fourth way is patience. Remember, although change may happen suddenly, adjustment to change takes time.

The fifth way is courage. The question isn't *if* you're afraid in the face of divorce — most everyone is — but how do you choose to work with your fear? You can fight, you can flee, you can hide. Or, you can face it, asking for help when you need it, using this opportunity to learn more about yourself and to grow.

Acceptance, reflection, mindfulness, patience, courage.... Remember the Serenity Prayer? It's a favorite of ours and it's not just for recovering alcoholics:

> God, grant me the serenity to accept the things I cannot change, the courage to change the things I can, and the wisdom to know the difference.

Yes, some things you have to accept — and some things you can change, especially yourself. You have the power to deal with your unexpected and shattering experience in creative ways that can transform hurt into healing and rage into forgiveness. Chief among these are ritual and ceremony.

Recommendations

1. Set aside some private time to be quiet and reflect on your experience and your feelings.
2. Keep a journal.
3. Ask, am I living in "crazy time?" How can you tell? Give some examples. Be specific.
4. Meditate or pray, or both. It's OK to pray for a specific outcome (for example, help my partner come to her senses). We also suggest that you pray for the highest good of all involved, however that may turn out in the end.

The Leaver And The Left

Despite the occasional story about a mutual parting of the ways, our experience and the testimony of millions of others bear out that there is almost always one who initiates the divorce and one who resists, and reacts. As Ahrons (1994) describes the process in *The Good Divorce*, usually the leaver begins to feel small, nagging dissatisfactions, dissatisfactions that seem so amorphous and trivial they're too embarrassing to mention, or perhaps even to admit to oneself. These feelings grow, flare and retreat, sometimes simmering for years, sometimes becoming almost unbearable in just a few months. Then comes the announcement: I'm leaving; I want a divorce.

How you perceive the ending of your relationship depends a lot on whether you are the one who is leaving or the one who has been left. According to several experts on divorce, in a substantial majority of marriages (although not in ours), it is the wife who makes the decision to leave. For that reason, we describe the leaver's process from her point of view, informed by Phil's experience as a leaver. We'll describe the one who has been left from a husband's point of view, informed by Barbara's experience.

We'll also describe some differences between the leaver and the left so you can consider the situation from your partner's point of view. That's right, your partner's point of view. No, we're not crazy, and if you're convinced that this exercise is a waste of time because your mate is such a terrible person, fine. However, we invite you to consider the possibility that the more you understand about what he or she is going through, the more empathetic you'll be. And the more empathetic you are, the more likely you will respond to your partner with thought and consideration rather than reacting reflexively out of a chaos of emotion — although sometimes one or both of you may do that, too ... and it's OK. Ahrons (1994) noted that the degree of stress in a separation — and whether or not the stress blows up into a crisis — depends in large part on how angry and vengeful ex-spouses feel. Because you are reading this book, you probably wish to decrease stress on everyone involved — especially your children. Understanding and empathizing can help lessen angry, vengeful feelings. Empathizing doesn't mean you agree with your ex-spouse or overlook what has been done. But when you are hurt and furious, you are inclined to lash out and demonize your partner. At these times, remember that this is a man or woman struggling just like you, a man or woman you have loved and may love still.

If you are being left, your leaver may not be as cool, calm and collected as she appears. Most likely she feels guilty about her doubts and dissatisfactions with the marriage, ambivalent about her pending decision and scared about the consequences. This is doubly so if children are involved. It's important to understand that her apparent equanimity, at least compared to your shock, outrage and despair, is not evidence of lack of feeling. It's just that she has already been struggling with her emotions for awhile. Because she has contemplated divorce, she's been grieving this loss in anticipation and has already started a process of detachment.

If your relationship has been blessed with good communication, her doubts and dissatisfactions were known to you and the announcement, when it came, was probably not entirely unexpected. In the unlikely event that your leaver kept her dissatisfactions secret, it is important to remember that her deception was probably not malicious. Rather, it might have been a misguided effort to protect your feelings or to avoid a crisis. Or, she may simply have feared she would be perceived by you and the world as the "bad guy."

If you are the leaver, the announcement of your intention to leave always — always — will come as a shock to your partner, a shock that can feel overwhelming. No matter how often and how clearly you believe you have communicated your doubts and dissatisfactions about the relationship — even if your partner says he has heard them — at the moment of your announcement you will probably find him unprepared and unwilling to accept it.

It is also important to remember that once you have initiated the separation, the two of you are unequal in power. From his point of view, he has had no time to adapt to an overwhelming threat — literally, the loss of his life, the life he has known. He feels helpless and vulnerable. True, that vulnerability may be expressed as rage. But this is no time for impatience on your part ("I've told you over and over again how I feel." "Oh, pull yourself together and stop being melodramatic."). You simply need to accept the fact that you are ahead of your partner on the wave of grief and it will take him awhile to catch up.

In the meantime, it's to everyone's advantage if both of you can listen to what the other has to say. Don't talk; just listen. This is especially critical if you, the leaver, have kept your doubts and dissatisfactions secret before your announcement and your partner has not had a chance to express himself. Ahrons' (1994) research showed that "when leavers share their doubts with their partners, in the months or years prior to making the decision, it is more likely that the decision will eventually become more mutual" (p.90). If you haven't communicated clearly before, now is the time, especially if the two of you expect to negotiate a settlement or work out cooperative arrangements for child custody. And remember, if you want to continue as friends — well, friends *listen*. Of course, listening does not mean submitting to physical or psychological abuse. However, we urge you to resist the temptation to use common conflict as an excuse to disengage. Do your best not to flee. You don't have to agree. You don't have to change your mind. You don't even have to justify your decision (though you'll probably be tempted to do so). Really, you don't have to *do* anything — either of you. Just *be* there, listen to your partner's feelings and try not to react, even if sometimes those feelings come clothed in accusations and blame.

Easier said than done? Of course. Don't get discouraged. We didn't manage this as well as we're recommending it to you, and we still came through the experience as friends. For example, while it's true that one of us (Phil) had made his doubts and dissatisfactions known for some time, what he did not do was make it clear that he was actively considering separation and divorce. Though he thought he had been clear, later he realized that he had held back because he felt guilty and scared and feared hurting Barbara. Such withholding has consequences. As

27

Vaughn (1986) noted "Initiators who are unable to be painfully direct are usually painfully indirect" (p.194). As a couple, we also put a premium on avoiding expressions of anger in the name of good will. When the time of the announcement came, this proved a problem for both of us. Barbara had a difficult time expressing her hurt, grief and anger for fear that it would drive Phil further away, and Phil had a difficult time hearing Barbara's feelings because of his guilt.

If you have been left, are you able to empathize with the courage it took for your partner to finally say, "I am not going to do this anymore." Having made the decision, now she must face the disapproval of children, family and friends who want to know — *demand* to know — why?! They, too, are shocked, confused, hurt and angry. Although you get their sympathy — "How could she leave? You poor thing." — your partner must cope with suspicions, accusations and the constant temptation to justify her decision by casting you in a negative light. That's right, poor you — you who almost certainly are being encouraged by family and friends to throw yourself into the role of victim and demonize your partner in order to explain why she would abandon someone so wonderful.

In our experience, this is a critical point in the process of parting through divorce. Even though many states have no-fault divorce laws on the books, the Myth of the Bad Divorce still promotes the idea that one partner is the victim and one the victimizer. Entire industries have been built on this premise — adversarial law and country western music, for example. At a personal level, it's understandable that family and friends might search for an explanation, or someone to blame. If they can find a reason, it will relieve them of the anxiety of a painful paradox: most likely neither partner is to blame — and both are.

If you are the leaver, the situation is particularly tricky. The fact is, you *are* leaving the relationship. Sometimes there is something clearly wrong with the partner you've left. He may be physically abusive or abusing alcohol or other drugs. But in many relationships — certainly in ours — it simply comes to pass that for some reason your needs are not being met. Unfortunately, it's all too easy to slide from the generality that "I

28

have needs that are not being met in this relationship" to a more specific complaint that borders on blame, such as "my partner doesn't meet my needs." In retrospect, this is a mistake Phil feels he made.

If you are the one who's been left, at this stage in the process you may be tempted by denial. For instance, Barbara refused to believe there were any problems serious enough to warrant a solution as drastic as divorce. As Vaughn (1986) noted, "The initiator's signals may, indeed, be vague, intermittent and hard to detect. But the other side of the story is that the bad news may be so inconsistent with the self and the world [of the one who's being left] that it is heard but denied" (p.72). Ask yourself, have you used self-deception and denial to avoid recognizing your partner's dissatisfaction? Yes, your partner may have avoided or delayed telling you the bad news. But how open were you to receiving it? Is it possible that you warded off information in order to maintain the status quo in the relationship, postpone a difficult choice, or avoid a threatening situation?

As the one who's been left, you may find yourself tempted to continue this denial even after your partner has announced her decision. You may rationalize the difficulties in your relationship: "All marriages have trouble;" "After awhile, all couples lose their interest in sex;" "Why now? It's been like this forever." Or, encouraged by friends whose good intentions may mask anxiety about the fragility of their own relationships, you may insist that whatever is wrong is your partner's problem and has nothing to do with you.

There is another temptation for the one who has been left: "the blame game" — not just blaming the leaver but also yourself. Your self-esteem probably has taken a blow, and you may assume more responsibility for the end of the relationship than you deserve. In retrospect, this is a trap into which Barbara feels she fell. More commonly, however, you're probably tempted to blame the leaver, even if you yourself might have entertained some thoughts about ending the relationship. This can be a comfortable role to play, but it's easy to slip from victimization into self-righteous martyrdom. That is, if family and friends can identify something wrong with the leaver ("she's

29

lost her mind"; "mid-life crisis"; "she's got a secret lover"), then it "makes sense" of what otherwise can be too terrifying to contemplate: the possibility that you can be a good husband or wife and in the end still find yourself in the midst of a divorce.

We managed to negotiate this stage of the process with reasonable success. We understood the risks of denial and the temptations to blame and did our best to avoid both. But we definitely could have done more, as we've discovered doing research for this book. Recently, we came across a couple of exercises that we wish we had known about at the time. Both are deceptively simple. We recommend you use them when trying to assess your own responsibility for the end of your marriage.

Of course, these suggestions are in no way intended to diminish your feelings or to rationalize hurtful and destructive behavior by your partner. Sometimes, it's necessary to set firm boundaries. But instead of starting with blame, these exercises are a helpful way to create some balance and come closer to your individual truths, painful as these truths might be.

The first exercise is from *The Conscious Heart* by Kathlyn and Gay Hendricks (1997). In the midst of your chaotic feelings, take some private time to be quiet and reflect on this question: What if you took 100% responsibility for the problems in your relationship and for its ending? What would that look like? Write down what you discover. Be specific.

The second exercise we've adapted from a little book by Bill Ferguson (1990), formerly an adversarial lawyer who changed his approach, as described in *How to Heal a Painful Relationship And If Necessary Part as Friends*. Bill believes:

> We are 100% the cause of everything around us and 100% at the effect, both at the same time. You react to the world around you, and at the same time, the world reacts to you.
>
> This is also true of relationships .... Both people are 100% responsible for whatever happens in their relationship. It's not 50/50, it's 100/100....
>
> It doesn't do much good to point at another's responsibility. Although you may have plenty to be

30

upset about, blaming doesn't change a thing. The other person is responsible, but so what? When you point at someone else's responsibility, you give away all your power. You make that person the cause and put yourself totally at his or her mercy. You lose your effectiveness and put yourself at his or her effect ....

As soon as you can see that you are the cause of a situation, it begins to clear up. You are able to take the actions necessary to have the matter resolved. Resistance falls away....

When you can acknowledge to yourself and to the world that you single-handedly, without any help whatsoever, destroyed your relationship, both you and your relationship are on the way to some major healing. As long as you insist that you are not responsible, you stay stuck. (pp. 61-62)

Bill also shows how you may have been responsible, which we frame here as a series of questions. We suggest you do your best to answer them honestly and specifically.

- Did you make sure that your partner had the experience of being loved by you? How?
- Did you accept and appreciate your partner just the way he or she is? How did you show it?
- Did you resist your partner? How?
- Did you encourage your partner to withdraw from you? How?
- Did you push your partner away? How?

Recommendations

1. Understand and accept that the leaver and the left perceive the same situation differently. How is this true in your case? Be specific. Write it down.
2. Try not to blame your partner. To help you with this, do the exercises that involve taking 100% responsibility. Be specific. Write down your answers.

31

3. Empathize with your partner. Do your best to see the situation from his or her point of view. What is your partner's point of view? Be specific. Write it down.

4. If you are the leaver, understand that you are ahead of your partner on the wave of grief and it will take a while for him (or her) to catch up. Be patient. Resist the impulse to justify your decision. Listen. Listen some more.

5. If you are the one who's been left, understand that your partner's comparative equanimity is not a sign that she doesn't care. All it means is that she has had an opportunity to do some grieving before you. Express how you feel. Resist the temptation to be a victim. Listen. Listen some more.

Third-Party Complications

Probably nothing is more difficult for a couple to deal with than the knowledge that one partner has fallen in love with someone else. This happened with us. As you may imagine, we feel some ambivalence about sharing such intimate details. Our reluctance stems less from embarrassment than from a fear that you will judge our experience and dismiss what we have to offer about conscious parting and a healing divorce — in effect, throw the baby out with the bathwater. On the other hand, it may prove encouraging for you to know that our experience wasn't perfect — far from it. That's why, in the end, we decided to be open, honest, transparent and undefended with you about our life and our parting, one just as fraught with complicated relationships and powerful cross-currents of emotion as most. Perhaps you will come to appreciate that even when tolerance and cooperation seem impossible, there is always room for empathy and good will, and an opportunity to work together for the highest good of everyone involved.

The involvement of a third party can escalate the craziness of separation and divorce. Vaughn (1986) notes in *Uncoupling* that for divorce initiators, having other lovers can offer self-

32

validation without requiring commitment or the need to develop an intimate connection. Sometimes, though, having several lovers narrows to one, and because this new, intense relationship offers an alternative intimate relationship, it can precipitate a transition (see Nancy's Story). As Trafford (1992) cogently described,

> A central passage in the divorce experience is falling in love. In the midst of pain and doubt — you're not sure how it happens — just when you least expect it, you fall desperately in love. It's the classic *coup de foudre* — bolt of lightning — romance, and you are swept away. It's like being a teen-ager again. Just touching each other, looking at each other; you feel you've known each other forever. You stay up late talking and talking, and then you make love as you've never known it could be....
>
> You've been dead so long in marriage, it's time to be alive again, to be born again. Falling in love is your emotional midwife.
>
> Therapists call this phase in the divorce process the search for the romantic solution. It usually happens early in the separation period — within the first six months. Sometimes the *coup de foudre* takes place just before the actual separation, when you're foundering on the rocks of a broken marriage, and evolves into the grand passion in the early phase of your single life. (pp. 206-207)

Needless to say, these descriptive explanations are cold comfort if you're the one who feels betrayed. Suddenly, you're plagued by unwelcome obsessions: Who is she? What's the attraction? Is he better in bed?

If you're the one who's leaving, and it's your affair that has precipitated a marital crisis, the betrayal felt by your partner can shatter trust, evoke jealousy and escalate conflict, making a crazy time even crazier. As Ahrons (1994) observed, affairs, while painful, are not as destructive as lies. As each lie is revealed, the partner who feels betrayed begins to question the entire history of the relationship until soon everything — the

33

marriage, the roles both partners played — all of it seems like nothing but deception. Even if involvement with a third party comes after the decision to leave has been made (as with us, although there remains some disagreement about this), it inevitably complicates a situation that is already emotionally complex.

This is what happened when, soon after the decision to separate, one of us (Phil) unexpectedly fell in love with a mutual friend we'll call Chris. The power of this experience was compounded by the fact that Chris lived in another part of the country and was also in the process of parting from her husband. What began as an unanticipated attraction (we three had worked together in a small group for almost three years without any Eros) rapidly became a passion difficult to control and, although sexual boundaries were maintained, it was clearly an affair of the heart.

While there were no overt secrets between us about this affair, for a time we practiced a certain self-deception concerning both the degree of Phil's emotional involvement and the effect it might have on the process of parting. Phil did this because he felt guilty. Barbara did it because she did not want to acknowledge the power of the connection and intimacy between two people she loved, an intimacy that despite their best efforts had remained unrealized in her relationship with Phil. However, as we discovered, no matter how honest a couple may be about such a situation, it still has a powerful impact on the process of parting. As Vaughn (1986) pointed out, the leaving partner has begun a new life in which a separate world is created from which her partner is usually excluded. This further weakens the already frayed bonds of the marriage. It was Barbara's complaint that Phil's increasing emotional involvement with Chris drew him away from the marriage, diminishing any possibility of reconciliation. In addition, it confused the situation, making it impossible to tell whether he was leaving for the reasons he had stated or simply because he had fallen in love and desired to consummate a new relationship.

For his part, Phil agreed that the timing was awful. His attraction to Chris made sorting out his feelings more difficult and his motives suspect, even to himself. However, precisely because it was unexpected, because it was so powerful and met the very longing for emotional intimacy left unsatisfied in the marriage, Phil considered the love he felt for Chris a gift. He believed it had come as a consequence of his decision to follow his longing for connection and, although he remained committed to carry out the parting with consciousness, he would not — felt he could not, if he was honest with himself — deny his feelings.

It is, however, usually possible to control one's behavior. Difficult, but possible. At various times during the several months between the stated intention to part and the parting ceremony, for example, the three of us agreed on certain boundaries to preserve the integrity of the process. These boundaries included, for Phil, no sexuality with Chris (who set the same boundary for herself) until after the parting was complete, either through divorce or some ceremony that would symbolize the end of the marriage. Phil and Chris also committed to several periods of no contact when that seemed supportive.

Recommendations

1. If you can, avoid an intimate emotional or sexual relationship with another during the process of parting.
2. If you can't, seek assistance from those prepared to help you work with your feelings and maintain your personal integrity — a dispassionate third party such as a minister, rabbi or a therapist may be more helpful than friends.

No Man's Land And Shadows

In any life transition there's a psychological no man's land between the way things were and the way things will be. This state of being may feel just as dangerous as the terrain between the borders of two suspicious countries. In no life transition is this more dramatically true than divorce. Even if you're separated and don't feel married anymore, you're still not legally divorced and don't feel single, either. What's worse, in the midst of this transition you often find yourself regressing to coping behaviors that you haven't used for years. In his book, *Transitions: Making Sense of Life's Changes*, William Bridges (1980) made the point that in the absence of formal rites of passage in our culture, how one has dealt with transitions earlier in life, particularly the segue from adolescence to adulthood, might indicate behavior during later life transitions. If early transitions had involved moving to a new place, as was the case with Phil, is it any wonder that for him separation and divorce involved not only selling a house but also moving to another city?

Life transitions also tend to re-evoke unfinished business from the past. Human development theories suggest that each phase of life has a task that must be completed in order to move on. The truth is, most of us never complete all of each task, so we're usually carrying unfinished business from one phase to the next. When stressed by a life transition, especially a severe one like divorce, unresolved developmental issues are going to re-emerge. In one of Bridges' (1980) workshops a woman reported, "I feel like I'm sixteen again. The divorce took away the main identity I'd had for six years, and I find myself now trying out different ways of being, different roles, almost different personalities, the way I did when I was a teenager" (p.35).

A less discussed observation about unanticipated reactions under stress of divorce has to do with what noted analytic psychologist Carl Jung called shadows. We all have parts of ourselves we don't like or fear. Usually, these are "negative" traits of personality or behaviors that, when we were children, proved unacceptable to our parents or to the culture we lived in

36

— rage, jealousy, deceit, greed, lust and impulses toward violence or revenge. Some of these we may be aware of. They may cause problems only now and again — losing one's temper is a good example. When we're conscious of them we can work to bring them under control. But the parts of ourselves we aren't aware of are more dangerous, especially during the stress of parting. Psychologists say that we often "disown" these traits, repressing them into the unconscious beyond our awareness. Unfortunately, it's the shadows we're least aware of that can cause the greatest havoc.

How do you tell if a shadow is at work? Pride in some personal virtue or trait may be one clue, and also the vehemence with which you reject the opposite trait in others, or in yourself. Adamant language is often a signal: I *never* lie, I *always* tell the truth. Of course, you find lying distasteful — most people do — but the extreme energy that drives your rejection of deceit suggests that lurking within your unconscious is some deceptive impulse of your own. If you can accept that previously disowned part of yourself — you, too, are tempted to lie — you will have gone a long way toward bringing the shadow into consciousness and rendering it harmless. If you cannot accept that part of yourself, you will tend to project it onto others — seeing dishonesty in everyone else — and often act it out, beginning to exhibit the very characteristics you so abhor.

Friends can be wonderful mirrors for reflecting shadows back to you. If asked, a friend might say, "Yes, you really are an honest person — except when you think someone's being deceptive, and then you can get amazingly judgmental. Sometimes you even begin to exaggerate the other person's dishonesty, which makes you look dishonest yourself."

Here's a personal (and embarrassing) example from our experience. Phil has always prided himself on his honesty and has been intolerant of lying and liars. During the process of parting, he and Barbara agreed that the parting ceremony would represent the symbolic end of the marriage. After the parting ceremony, both would be free to live their lives as if no longer married. What Phil did not say was that he planned to consummate the sexual relationship with Chris the day after the

37

ceremony. At the time, he had many rationalizations for the timing. Chris lived in a different part of the country and it would be some time before he could see her again. Despite great mutual desire, they had held the sexual boundaries and "deserved" this opportunity. He also had several "good" reasons for not telling Barbara. It would hurt her unnecessarily. He didn't want to feel as if he was asking her permission. Because it would occur after the ceremony, it was really none of her business.

Now, years later, the shadows seem pretty obvious. At the time, however, they were mostly unconscious — and, it got worse. Chris asked several times if Phil was sure about the timing. He told her he was. Not only that, when an opportunity presented itself to tell Barbara the truth about his plans after the ceremony, Phil kept silent and lied by omission. Even though he recognized his lie and could have come clean, he chose not to do so for fear that he would lose his anticipated time with Chris. In the emotional stress of the situation, fear and anger (the shadows of love) and deceit (the shadow of honesty) had for the moment completely taken over. When a few days later Barbara found out that Phil and Chris had been sexual shortly after the ceremony, her pain and anger at their insensitivity were compounded by a sense of betrayal because of the deceit. There's a saying among Jungians: the brighter the light, the deeper the shadow. An act of consciousness and light — the parting ceremony — had cast shadows that were, in contrast, dark, painful and destructive. Despite the love and care we had shown for each other during the process of parting, this experience shattered trust and evoked Barbara's shadows, too — envy, jealousy and rage.

Recommendations

1. Are you living in no man's land? Reflect on how you've handled life transitions in the past. What are the similarities and differences with how you're handling the life transition of divorce? Be specific. Write your observations in your journal.
2. What are your shadows? Ask yourself, about what in myself am I especially proud? Ask, what is it in others

38

that I really hate? What do I deny in myself? Be specific. Ask your friends. Ask them to be specific. Listen, even if it's painful — and it probably will be. Write these observations in your journal.

Making Haste Slowly

In many partings through divorce, one or both partners seem to be in a great hurry to just get it over with. Such an impulse is understandable. Once the decision has been made, there is a natural tendency to want to relieve the pain and anger of parting by rushing ahead.

But this can have unfortunate consequences for all involved, especially your children. In a crisis, it's important to collect yourself and not act precipitously. While it's perfectly understandable to want your partner out of your life as soon as possible, sometimes restraint is the more skillful and constructive option. It takes time to adapt to change, to process what's happening and to plan ahead for physical separation. Easing through the transition will help minimize the sense of crisis in your family. Slowing things down also allows time to listen. If rage is too savage to permit discussion, this mutual tactic lets you cool off before one of you just stalks out. If you need to, seek professional assistance. Just a few sessions with a therapist, a pastor or a mediator will help. Even talking to a member of your family, who will listen without encouraging anger, negativity or victimization, can be extremely productive. To slow down the process so it doesn't career out of control takes patience and restraint, as well as a willingness to sacrifice the temporary satisfactions of unbridled rage for the long-term benefits of compromise and cooperation. Trust us when we tell you that when you look back — and you will — you'll be glad you resisted the impulse to just get out and stayed with the parting process long enough to work out a more conscious and healing end to your relationship.

We know all of this is easier said than done; it's difficult to stay in a crucible of fury and pain. If you feel you can't stand it

39

for another minute, certainly, take some time out. But we urge you not to flee. Remember, research and the personal experience of others confirm that *how* you end your relationship will have important spiritual, psychological and economic consequences for you, your partner and, especially, for your children.

Again, we speak from experience. Our decision to part was made in early August, and we chose to give ourselves plenty of time to see if that's what we really wanted to do. During this time we agreed we would continue to live together and still take an already scheduled vacation. We also decided to work intensively with other people who could help us. We (and Chris) sought advice, counsel and assistance from our spiritual group, and the two of us consulted friends, therapists, channels and even astrologers as we struggled to come to terms with a decision that would affect the rest of our lives. However, because we did not want the process to drag out indefinitely, we also set a time limit: we would make a final decision by our wedding anniversary in early November.

Despite our good intentions, however, we now know that we overlooked some insights that would have made a difference in how we handled our parting. If you're the one who's been left you may identify with the bleak situation Vaughn (1986) described in *Uncoupling*: "The power imbalance between initiator and partner is made vivid by the initiator's readiness to withdraw, potentially changing the partner's life regardless of personal wishes about how that life might proceed" (p.110). If you're the one who is leaving, remember that you have created a situation in which you are the one who holds the power and makes the decisions. Your complaints about the relationship set up the conditions for your partner's attempts to change. Although both of you may agree to work on saving the relationship, it's the one who's being left who assumes the greater burden.

As Barbara painfully experienced, this is an all but impossible dilemma. Hoping Phil would change his mind, like many other partners in such situations, she felt desperate. She believed that failure to make changes to meet Phil's needs would result in losing the relationship. But the harder she tried, the

40

greater the imbalance of power became. She complained of her lack of control and, in the end, simply had to let go of any attempt to change Phil, herself or the relationship and simply trust in the process.

On the other hand, if you're the leaver, you may find yourself with an unexpected burden, too: increased ambivalence about your decision. But isn't your anxiety only fear of change? This is most likely a partial truth. When you see your partner trying his best to make things work, even if you are convinced that parting is the best solution, you may find yourself responding with love and compassion — and find yourself fearing your response. You've been so certain. Why all of a sudden do you doubt yourself? Is a divorce really necessary? Is it the right thing to do? If it is, why are you plagued by all these questions? Why are you wondering what your spouse is really like? Will he change? And if he does, is that what you want? Just because things have improved or you have a pleasant time together, does that mean you should get back together? As Trafford (1992) puts it:

> If you are to face the reality of divorce, you have to confront your own ambivalence over it. This is a crucial moment in the divorce process. If you reject the anxiety of ambivalence by escaping into a new relationship or retreating into an emotional box of pure anger or despair, you die a little inside....
>
> Allowing yourself to feel torn on the rack of ambivalence is a sign you're coming alive, that you're working through painful emotions triggered by the loss of an important relationship. (p.129)

In a general way, we believe these reflections about powerlessness and ambivalence accurately describe us during the period of time we slowed everything down and struggled with the issues of parting through divorce, together and with various helpers.

Barbara remembers:

41

I felt simultaneously desperate and enraged that every action I took was being judged and evaluated. Everything I said or did felt like it carried enormous risk. In the end, I knew I just had to accept because there was nothing else I could do. These were issues we had struggled with for years which not going to be resolved overnight, if they could be resolved at all. I knew Phil was suffering, too, that he was trying to be honest with himself and with me. At the time, I guess I convinced myself that it was possible to make an informed and balanced final decision even in the midst of all that stress. But now, looking back, I'd say that despite his good intentions he had already left the relationship; that his feelings for Chris had already compromised whatever chance we might have had to work things out; that his heart was already with her. Maybe there was even a part of me that knew this at the time. And still, there were times when all I could do was to fall on my knees and beg him, "Please, please, please don't leave me."

Phil remembers:

I felt such love for Barb, and compassion, and guilt for what I was putting her through. There was so much good in the relationship that I did not want to lose. And yet, I felt a powerful calling to leave. I was aware that my feelings for Chris were part of this, but I also clearly remembered the moment of my decision — the time, the place, the answered prayer — a decision that had come in response to a desire to follow my longing. This was before any feelings for Chris had appeared. Were they already there unconsciously? It's certainly possible, I suppose. But I'm reluctant to reduce a difficult and complex decision — as Barb says, we'd been struggling with certain issues for years — into a tabloid headline: he left her for another woman.

I felt an agony of ambivalence about ending the marriage — years later I still feel it. At the same time, I don't want to minimize how my feelings for Chris buffered me against some of the pain of loss. I knew this was happening at the time. But did it result in my leaving a relationship I otherwise might have stayed in? I don't think so. Still, I agree — I agreed then — that under the circumstances it's impossible to know for sure. I felt like the best I could do was hold a tension of opposites — my love for Barb and my conviction that I had to leave; my love for Chris and my commitment to give the relationship with Barb every opportunity. I had to be willing to live with the pain of the paradox.

As we discovered, if you are the one who is being left, the challenge is to remain true to yourself even when faced with your loss. To do otherwise is to compromise your sense of self, which already may be fragile because of your feelings of rejection. You could be tempted to give up other activities and friends to concentrate on "fixing things." Although there is certainly value in acknowledging mutual problems and doing what you can to work with your partner, giving over your life to "save" the relationship can actually make the situation worse. You may begin to resent your partner and, if the relationship finally ends, you could also feel as if you've sacrificed yourself — your Self — for nothing. This is a potential source of more anger and despair.

If you are the leaver, however, your challenge is to resist closing your heart in anger or detachment for fear that, if you show other feelings, your partner — or you, yourself — may take that as a change of heart. As Trafford (1992) suggested, if you do not allow yourself to feel the fullness of your ambivalence and loss, you may well die a little — or a lot — by shutting down. You may also miss an opportunity to confront your decision to leave, not in silence or secrecy but now in a crucible of pain you can share with your partner.

Yes, it's hard to stay open-hearted in Hell. We don't pretend to have done it perfectly. But instead of anger, which separates,

43

if you can find even brief moments when the two of you can share your grief, you will discover a healing paradox: even in the midst of parting, you will feel more loving and together. Such an experience could be the foundation of a reconciliation. But even if in the end you separate or divorce, this sharing makes it easier for you both to let go, forgive and move on.

Recommendations

1. Make an effort to slow down the process of parting. Give yourself time — days are good, weeks or months much better — to mull over what's involved in the process and how long you think it might take. If possible, discuss this with your partner. If that proves too contentious, talk to someone you trust who will give you honest feedback.
2. Avoid precipitous actions, even if you feel provoked.
3. If you are the leaver, do your best to embrace rather than deny your ambivalence. Also, to redress the imbalance of power (to be as responsible for change as your partner) try taking 100% responsibility for the difficulties in your relationship.
4. If you are the one who's been left, don't deny the problems you face, but also take care not to give up your Self just to preserve the relationship. To avoid falling into the role of victim, try taking 100% responsibility for what's happening. If you're having difficulty with all of this, seek spiritual counseling or professional help.

Going Public

There are always two partings, one private between the partners and one public, which involves children, other family, a network of friends and, if you get to court, even strangers — lawyers and judges. The quality of your public parting depends largely on what is happening between you and your partner. If both partners are furious and vengeful, this will confirm the

Myth of the Bad Divorce with blaming and name calling. She's crazy! He's insane! Anger might be a universal reaction but "that doesn't mean you should feel free to express your anger without restraint. Anger takes a terrible toll. If you throw more fuel on the inner fires, they'll flare higher and higher and you'll be stuck with the damage. When we focus on rage, we stifle our ability to get on with life" (Ahrons 1994, p.81). How you make a public declaration will to some extent depend on whether you're the leaver or the left. However, unbridled rage and vindictiveness can make this part of the process much more difficult for both partners, inflicting wounds and causing separations that last for years. It can also force children, family and friends to choose sides.

It doesn't have to be this way. Although self awareness and knowledge can't take away the pain or the anger, they can help you understand the dynamics of the process of going public and prepare you to deal with your own feelings and the feelings of others.

The reactions to your announcement of parting will, to some degree, be dictated by people's ignorance about your situation and their insecurities about their own relationships. This is true whether you are the leaver or the left. In every relationship, there are secrets no one else knows, especially when the union is troubled. Most of us collude with our partners to turn our best face to the world of family and friends. That is why, when you go public, you may be surprised by other people's surprise: *But what happened? You're the perfect couple!* Often, even intimate friends are taken aback: *Are things really that bad? Can't you work it out? You've invested so much. Think about the children.* Your decision will often cause other couples to reassess their own relationships and question if it's worthwhile to go on. Such questioning is disturbing and can cause friends to either distance themselves or push for a reconciliation. If you do reconcile, this will reassure them that things weren't really that bad — and aren't so bad in their own relationship. Or, they may project their fears onto you or your partner in the form of judgements. Anger and vindictiveness between you and your partner will feed such

45

judgements and often make them more harsh and intractable, increasing the emotional distance between you and others.

The partners in a divorce might contribute to this distancing in other ways as well. If you yield to the temptation to cast your partner in a negative light, you could start a chain reaction that is difficult, if not impossible, to stop. By blaming your partner to justify your position, you might force your family and friends to make the painful choice of agreeing with just "one side of the story." Be aware that even if they've been "your friends," it's by no means certain that they will choose you. Often, in an acrimonious divorce, shared friends feel so conflicted that they will simply withdraw from both partners. Also, research suggests that a wife is more likely than her husband to allow her social relationships to lapse and is more tentative about expressing her need for support. "In a 1979 study of fifty divorced adults, nearly half of the men and women reported growing more distant from their close friends after separation; the people getting divorced seemed to be as responsible for the estrangement as their friends" (Trafford 1992, p. 171).

There's another problem with attacking your partner. If you change your mind and want to go back, it's more difficult. Reconciliation may be the furthest thing from your mind when you're angry. What about after you cool off? If you've spent weeks telling others what a jerk she or he is, not only will you have to overcome your ambivalence about your partner, you'll also have to swallow your pride (never easy) and offer an apology.

As much as we could, we wanted to help family and friends avoid "choosing sides." This can be as important as what you say. In her description of Matthew and Anne Surrey's amicable divorce, Mary Shideler (1971) observed:

> First, together Matt and Anne told their closest friends of their intention. Together, they received the brunt of the initial surprise and regret, answered any questions, and gave any explanations asked for. What-ever the procedure accomplished for them, it saved their friends from considerable embarrassment which can

follow when [only] one party to a divorce confides individually in someone who has been close to both parties. (p.554)

Like the Surrey's, we decided that we would agree, when we could, about what to tell other people. When we could not agree, each of us committed to express honestly his or her own disagreement, *as well as include each other's point of view*. We would share intimate details only if we were convinced that the listener was prepared to discuss the situation with thoughtfulness and consideration. Because we had a lot to deal with emotionally, we also recognized a need to be discerning and protective of ourselves and of each other. We were not prepared to satisfy anyone's prurient curiosity. And, we would not betray each other. We agreed with what Stephen and Ondrea Levine (1995) wrote in *Embracing the Beloved*:

Perhaps most important for our little mind not to get lost in the paranoia that accompanies abandonment, anger and self-image issues is a clear stipulation not to betray the other's secrets. Indeed, the first precept to such a commitment to conscious separation may be to keep silent all confidences. To hold sacred those moments when the heart revealed itself, so as not to condition mistrust or abuse the confidentiality of "pillow talk." (pp. 294-295)

Obviously, we're not talking about the kind of secret keeping a perpetrator of abuse coerces from a victim. Think for a moment about your own life. Have you said or done things you are ashamed of? About what do you feel vulnerable? Perhaps you were sexually or physically abused as a child. Perhaps you had an abortion. Maybe you lied or were in some other way dishonest. Maybe you have sexual fantasies or private desires.

Although the list of possible secrets is infinite, you can know if a particular secret is one your partner would prefer be held sacred. Imagine lying in bed after making love. During that gentle time when your partner felt most willing to share tender

47

confidences, can you see this vulnerability? Feel how his trust touches your heart. Now imagine exposing what your partner has shared to the world. In your mind's eye, does she cringe? If you break this confidence, would he feel wounded? Betrayed? If so, keep the secret.

Again, we cannot say that we did all of this perfectly. On the whole, however, it worked well enough for us to recommend it. As we had anticipated, people not privy to our private life were shocked and immediately began to take sides. But our intention to speak well of each other and to remain friends, as well as our honesty about our feelings and our disagreements, turned most people's dismay into bewilderment. This wasn't the way divorcees were supposed to act. Some people insisted that our relative equanimity proved we had never really loved each other, had fallen into denial or were not telling the truth. There had to be other, darker reasons. Some of those who had heard about Chris did, indeed, conclude that Phil had left Barbara for another woman, and a younger one at that. Many more people, however, heard our story with sadness and admired our intention to use ritual as a means to conscious parting and a healing divorce.

The reaction of Phil's family was typical. He spoke in person to his mother and three sisters, and to his brother on the phone. His mother expressed sorrow about the parting and remarked, "I wish that your father and I could have handled things in such a kind way; what a difference it would have made in everyone's lives." One sister wanted the whole story. While she reacted with more empathy for Barbara, she, too, expressed admiration for our willingness to take the risk of change. A second sister, who had been through a difficult divorce, immediately asked, "Is there someone else?" When Phil said he would be glad to share the details of his life if she was prepared to take the time to listen, she chose not to and remarked, "I love you as my brother but as a man, I hate what you're doing." A third sister also asked if there was someone else and listened to Phil's explanation skeptically. In the end, however, she simply expressed the hope that, if we did manage to part as friends, Barbara would continue to be a part of the family. Phil's brother also wanted the whole story, listened, and expressed sorrow for our loss and admiration for what we were trying to accomplish.

Recommendations

1. Though anger is natural, do your best to be discerning about expressing it. Find a professional helper or a trusted friend to whom you can vent your anger. Write your angry feelings in your journal. Never disparage or vilify your partner in front of your children.
2. When the time comes to share what's happening, agree on a truthful explanation to tell others. Acknowledge differences of opinion and include an honest representation of your partner's point of view. Try to announce the separation or divorce in person and be prepared to talk about it and answer questions.
3. Do your best not to blame your partner to justify your decision to leave or your victimization.
4. Reach out to family and friends. This will help maintain your network of social relationships and reassure people — especially if you tell them about your plans for conscious parting and a parting ceremony — that they don't have to take sides.
5. Never betray the secrets of your partner's heart.

Ending With An Open Heart

Now that you have explored the process of parting, you may wonder: All right, fine, but what's the point of doing some ritual? Especially if my partner won't participate?

In Chapter Four, we will explain more about the purpose and power of ritual. For now, let's just say it's a way to keep your heart open and transform the relationship between you and your ex-partner. Research after divorce reveals that whatever the quality of the marital relationship, almost everyone wished they were on better terms with their ex. As Ahrons (1994) reported in

The Good Divorce, divorced couples expressed sentiments such as these:

> "I really miss hearing about his old friends and the people he works with;" "I wish she would tell me more about her life;" and "I wish there was less bitterness between us." When we asked them to describe an ideal divorced parenting relationship, even the fieriest of foes mentioned the importance of open and frequent communication. (p.7)

People ending their relationships no longer want to live out the Myth of the Bad Divorce. Like you, they sense the profound truth in what Stephen and Ondrea Levine (1995) say in *Embracing the Beloved*:

> It is said that the longest journey begins with the first step, but it also is ended with the last. That last step is as important as the first. It is the first move of the next journey. How we end one relationship affects how we will begin another. It is a teaching in continuum. Just as a divorce contract can be as crucial as a marriage agreement, a divorce ceremony is as important as a wedding. Each is a ritual of transition. A subtle mourning, a considerable expectation. Each has the power to heal or enslave. But a divorce ceremony is not a wedding ceremony in reverse. It is another whole moment of birth. Another opportunity for lightenment. A triangulated divorce [between beloved, beloved and the Beloved] offers the anger and confusion into the great "don't know" vastness of the sacred, and feels the ground return beneath its feet. It is a balancing of heaven and earth. It is the next moment of the life you so long for. (p. 297)

Whether you are the leaver or the one who's been left, ask yourself: do you yearn for a way to end your relationship that will honor you and your partner and all you have shared? Do you hope that both of you will go forth from this experience more whole than you have ever been? It's your choice. You can travel the old way, full of pain, conflict, bitterness and estrangement — a way you will travel mostly alone, and with a closed heart. Or you can find a new way, perhaps equally painful but one you can travel with an open heart, sharing your memories and grief and doing your best to help each other forgive and let go. Remember the well-known poem by Robert Frost in which he reflects that taking the road "less traveled" has "made all the difference?" In this world where so many still believe the Myth of the Bad Divorce, choosing to end your relationship with ritual and ceremony can make all the difference to the hearts and souls of everyone involved, to the quality of the life you long to lead and to the healing of your children and the world.

Recommendations

1. Explore with your partner the healing potential of using ritual to help end your relationship. If your partner is willing, read and discuss the stories and suggestions in this book.
2. If your partner isn't emotionally prepared to discuss creating a ritual, or is unwilling to even consider the idea, talk it over with a professional helper, a member of the clergy or a trusted friend.
3. Write your thoughts and feelings about creating and performing a ritual or ceremony in your journal. What do you imagine it would it be like to create and perform such a ceremony with your partner? What do you imagine it would be like to do this without your partner?

Scott's Story

M. and I were married on May 22, 1993. Destiny, the stars lining up, God's will being done, finally becoming an adult, proof to the people who said I would never amount to anything — that's how it felt. I think that the way people are brought together is more than just chaos.

It all started with theater in Birmingham, where I grew up. I was exposed to theater when I was 13. It truly changed my life. I had been an incredibly introverted person and overnight became this wild extrovert. I used to throw these parties in high school. They started as cast parties but then turned huge: a quarter of the school would come by, live bands, cops paid off. I learned how to really go all out. Incredible parties. Lots of fun. And that's when I first met M.. She was dating a childhood friend of mine. I don't remember it that well but she always did, vividly.

Then, several years later, in my senior year in college, this same friend banged on my door; he needed a last-minute double date. And, when I went out on the double date, who was there? M.! Now, my friend didn't dance. I'd learned to dance in theater so I asked her. I was just trying to be a gentleman. She really wanted to dance, and he wouldn't let her. But she never forgot that I'd asked.

Three years later an ex-girlfriend of mine asked me to go to a theater show. A family friend was in town and was supposed to meet us after the show. He needed a date so we could be a foursome. So who did he call up? His ex-girlfriend — M.

Three months later, I was doing a play in my church and M. was assisting with the costumes. I was Methodist, she was Baptist, non-attending. Well, at that point she wanted to start a relationship. She went out and bought an old distressed wedding dress from Goodwill and brought it to rehearsal as if it were a costume. And, of course, it caught my attention; I jumped off the stage and did a fake proposal to her. And that first night after rehearsal, we stood in the church parking lot until 4 a.m. just talking.

52

During our long conversation she said several times, "This is karma; three times over six years and you just keep coming back into my life."

But I didn't want to date her. I thought she was a lot of fun, but I was just halfway through a one-year moratorium from dating. I'd just got out of a two-year relationship and didn't know if I wanted to get in another one — I was 23 and so-o-o-o serious. But I didn't really need to date. I'd done so many wild things in college. I didn't need the excitement or the sex. I said to M., "You know, ma'am, when I date again — it's not like it has to be the one or anything; I just want to date as a mature adult." There I was, in my early 20s, on my own, growing up — I really didn't want to date. But we'd talk and we became very good friends. We were inseparable for about four weeks before I finally gave in and agreed that it was time for us to start dating. Actually, she pinned me up against a wall. It was really exciting to be pursued by somebody who wanted me so much. I found myself believing what she had so passionately shared: we were supposed to be together, two misfit toys that God had been trying to bring together for a while for some very important purpose. From the start, we spoke about how as individuals we felt chosen for something out of the ordinary. We both agreed we were not Presidential material or anything like traditional role models; we were special in ways we had not figured out quite yet. In time, the "I(s)" became "we(s)." We completed each other's sentences. We talked about how our marriage was going to be different. Better than that of any of our parents. Better than friends who were married. We grew confident that our relationship was so strong we could actually make our dreams come true. Our several meetings couldn't have just been coincidence; this was destiny.

Fifteen months later we got engaged — in New York City. This was the first time for her to ever be on an airplane, the first time ever to be in the Big Apple, the first time ever to see a Broadway show (Phantom of the Opera). I proposed in an odd little burger dive off Washington Square called Ed Debevik's.

When the waiter, dressed in trashy drag, asked us what we were doing there, we said, "By starting at Ed's, there's no where for our relationship to go but up."

It was a wonderful wedding. Simple ... a couple of hundred people. The night before we'd had a wonderful non-traditional party we called the Wedding Ball and Chain with a lot of theater friends who'd probably go up in flames if they walked inside the door of a church. The service itself was very important to us. We'd done twelve sessions of pre-marital counseling with the pastor, Dorothy, and her husband, George, and in the end chose to have almost a high Methodist wedding. Although everything was casual we did communion; it felt very important to us to share in breaking the bread. We paid for it ourselves. At the reception, we had Girl Scout cookies, gummy worms.

In the early days, it was wonderful, very playful. We both slept with stuffed animals; she had a teddy bear and I had a sock monkey — Quincy and Spank. We were grown adults doing what kids do. A very playful relationship. Very creative. We bought a house and gutted it down to nothing and rebuilt everything.

So that's how it began. Legally, we were married for five years, five months and eight days. We had the same small problems that most people encounter and worked through them. However, after a while M. stopped investing in even the most basic activities of our marriage.

Earning an M.F.A. in Costume Design was her number one priority. So it was just a matter of time before she no longer valued our relationship. I knew things were very wrong when she didn't call when she was on a tour in Europe for two months. When she returned I saw her all of sixteen hours, two of them in counseling sessions I had scheduled out of desperation. It looked like there was no saving the marriage at that point. She was heading off to Utah to work in a theater and requested that I not contact her. She said she just needed to get her head straight and she'd let me know when she got back. So I celebrated our fifth anniversary alone. It felt really bad because I knew it was probably the last one. A few weeks later, I got a letter saying, "I've thought about it; go ahead; call an attorney; I'll see you in Knoxville."

When I realized that the marriage was over, I also realized that I needed to find some kind of closure. I just couldn't let the relationship break and leave the pieces scattered around. I couldn't carry around this open wound. I knew too many divorced people who were sour, bitter, broken. I had a lot of years ahead of me and, even though the fun I'd anticipated with M. was gone, I still needed to enter the next stage of my life without baggage. If I were going to be in another relationship, I didn't want to get hurt again, and I didn't want to hurt other people, either. I didn't want to end up another bad example of a divorced person.

In the South, people speak down about divorce, but divorced individuals are embraced, kind of in secret. I didn't want to end up being quietly embraced in back rooms while in public I'd be "the divorced guy," ostracized when just the day before I'd been welcomed into church and social groups. Five different friends said, "Please, we feel for you, we'll pray for you, and when you're through this and you have someone else in your life, call." Or, they made excuses: "My wife and I are about to have a child," or "We just moved," or "We really feel for you but we just can't have you in our lives right now." No room for divorced people.

It's strange. Going in, I got pre-marital counseling, along with a piece of paper that said I was a married man; no longer a single guy. Going out, I got another piece of paper and therapy — a lot more expensive.

When we both invested in our marriage, we had a relationship that was very beautiful. We were able to bring out something spiritual together. Our relationship was a kind of trinity; we had this covenant between God and ourselves. And here I am now, divorced. We had a beautiful wedding. Lots of people came to bear witness. But where's the public witnessing of sorrow? M. and I, we no longer have a future. We no longer have a present. I have to accept that.

The hard thing for me was giving up the past. In her last letter, she complained, "We never communicated — never!" That hurt. But it also was not true. I would not let the past get taken away, or trampled. I needed to have for myself the

55

acknowledgement that the past we'd shared was something special.

Alison, a friend who'd been divorced about two years, came up to Knoxville from Birmingham with her little sister to join me on a hike in the Smokeys. We were hiking and talking about God and kind of laughing about our relationships and out of the blue this comes into my mind and out of my mouth: What if Jesus had divorced? What would he do?

When I went to therapy I found myself saying, "Oh, woe is me, it's official now; it's really going to end."

And my therapist asked, "Well, do you have in mind any closure, spiritually? Have you prayed? Gone to see a minister?"

"There are no prayers out there that make me feel comfortable saying good-bye to my marriage."

"I know somebody who held some kind of service once, in California," she offered.

And I said, "Really?" It turned out this woman's husband had left and run off and she'd had a bonfire burning. "That's cool." I thought, hey, I'm kind of a hip guy, I could do something like that bonfire.

But then, I started thinking about the conversation I'd had with Alison; what would Jesus do? How were we going to say good-bye to Scott and M.'s marriage? And when I talked to Alison, she said, "Hey, if you do some ceremony, I'd love to be a part of it."

I called Lee Borden, an old theater friend and mentor for the past sixteen years, and he said, "Oh, yeah, I've heard of people doing something like that. I'll bet there's a service out there." But Lee couldn't find anything. I called Dorothy, the minister who married us, and she started researching, but couldn't find anything either. So I started writing a service myself.

As it turned out, the ceremony happened on our engagement day and just a few days after our legal divorce. I didn't plan it to be that close; the divorce was supposed to have been final a month earlier but got delayed.

I sent invitations to about thirty very close friends. Twenty-one wonderful people actually attended.

The service addressed the past, the present and the future. It was done in the very same church we were married in, only in the chapel instead of the sanctuary, which was more intimate, quieter. It was necessary but very tough. How do I get this thing done without tearing myself to pieces? But there had to be some way to transition to the next part of my life. Oh, I can wax poetic for hours about the miracle that brought us together. Everybody can talk about that in their own relationship. But then, when it falls apart, it feels like this terrible tragedy, this death, a murder, really, spiritually. And the social stigma keeps it ugly. I think ceremony helps erase the stigma and brings closure.

Lee and I talked about all this; early drafts of the service went back and forth. I knew there had to be praying and I knew I had to break bread, as we did in the wedding service. In the wedding, we'd lit the unity candle — together you light one candle from two — except we didn't blow out our separate candles. Not that I wanted to run the wedding tape backwards, but that was kind of what happened. We weren't a unity anymore. So as part of a prayer of thanks, Alison and I lit two separate candles from the unity candle, and then I extinguished it. Our lives were continuing, M.'s and mine, but the marriage was gone. I think of that as the center of the service, bringing closure to the past.

Even though my father did not understand my need for the service, he supported me wholly and even read the prayer of Thanksgiving. Lee read scripture and shared a few stories about our relationship and marriage. Dorothy gave a beautiful short sermon about brokenness as the way we come to Christ. She shared how her marriage and divorce had affected her spiritual journey and suggested that the service could help others beyond those in the throes of divorce — people still married, single people yet to be married . . . anyone hurt and broken for any reason. I have heard this word, brokenness, many times since the service and am always reminded of Dorothy's words of wisdom. Then, after the sermon, she offered communion.

Alison served two roles. First, she was a supportive, spiritual friend. We prayed together and played together. Early on, when I felt like I was dropping like a stone, she took the time to drive up from Birmingham to listen to me whine. For hours. In a very sad state. She helped me transition. I'm not a touchy-feely person, but I was with M.. Now I had nobody to touch, nobody to hug, and although Alison and I didn't hug or touch, she helped me be intimate verbally; I could just cry and she was all right with it.

Second, she edited what I wrote from a feminine perspective. She helped organize the Giving Thanks prayer into a logical flow and suggested the different names of God. She would also pull me back down out of the clouds so that the service would be useful for other people, and not just personalized for me. I wanted to make sure everyone could understand it. She helped me universalize it. Also, Alison was there because she needed it for herself. Not that she was necessarily going to get up and say, this is for me. Some days she'd acknowledge it, some days not. It was a way for her to ride on the service energy, to help resolve some issues and bring closure to her own marriage and divorce.

Years ago, B.B. King said that he never wrote a single song in his life — they were all revealed. Now, I don't know if I'd go that far — to say that this service had words inspired by God — but I do know that it provided an opportunity to heal. I didn't ask to write this. I didn't want to do this. But I felt I had to ... still do — to help myself and to help others with spiritual healing. I think it's so important.

I did dress up the service. I didn't want it to be too formal but it needed to have some structure. The burning fount had been used by one of the Unity Churches in Birmingham. They let me borrow it.

The illustration I chose to put on the program is symbolic, a small shoot growing out of a tree stump — new life growing out of something that's been cut off.

It was also important for me to have an explanation about the service in the program. A lot of people, mostly married friends, had said, "Why are you doing this? It's sacrilegious. The Pope would never stand for anything like this." They'd told me it was wrong, that it just shouldn't be done. Or they said, "We've always known you're weird, Scott, but this one takes the cake." Even one friend of mine who's been divorced twice thought it was the most terrible thing.

I kept telling them, "No, we're not going to run the wedding videos backwards, or have some stomp M. thing or anything like that."

The ceremony went remarkably fast and was attended by an eclectic collection of dear friends — five gay friends, three friends who had been divorced, one engaged couple, several married couples and several parents of divorced children. It was healing for everyone involved. My grandmother, who has beginning Alzheimer's, at first said, "This is crazy." But after the ceremony she commented, "This was beautiful. It's going to be all right; you've worked so hard. I know because you care so much, you'll be so much better someday because of this." Another woman, whose daughter had been divorced a few years before, came up afterwards and said that in a way, my service was also for her. It had helped bring closure in her heart for her own daughter's marriage and had helped to wash away a lot of the pain and hatred toward her ex-son-in-law.

That day, there was a blues festival scheduled, and some of us intended to go after the ceremony. I'd planned to have a small, informal reception at the festival; a friend ran a food booth. But the promoters ran away with the money and the festival got cancelled. Instead, I went out to dinner with a friend. It was a rainy day anyway.

Later, I found information about services done back in the '70s and saw that there had been a service for two people. I thought, gee, I could have done this with M.. But then I thought, no, that would never have worked; she wouldn't even have come into the room. Sometimes I think if I were on fire, she'd have a hard time spitting on me.

And that's real sad. It was a beautiful relationship and I'd love it to be a friendship but her attitude has been, "Well, it was a mistake to begin with; we were just two kids who never should have gotten together. We messed each other up. We should've had a nice little quickie and been done with it." She's trying to tell me now that it never was destiny, that we were foolish and infatuated and that it really wasn't that significant. That's how she's trying to justify what happened. But I'll have no part of that. I know that we were two good people brought together for very special reasons. And that our marriage was not a mistake or a temporary stepping stone in life. We were not too young or too foolish. Our marriage was more than just a romantic fling by idealistic kids who got out of control. I believe God wished us to be together.

I gave M. a copy of the service, and I tried to speak with her about it. She was polite but her attitude seemed to be that somehow I was self-righteous and depended too much on religion. And was being too loud about it. She used such phrases as "judge not lest you be judged." She said that maybe the ceremony was the right thing for me, but to her it smacked of the religious right.

I miss M. more than words can describe. Sometimes, I wonder if I did the service too quickly. Because a lot of days I wake up with this sinking feeling and realize, oh, I'm divorced. It still comes back to haunt me. I talk to people who are happily re-married, and even they still remember that first relationship long after it ended. Still, I accept that our marriage is over. I know God blessed me with a very special person, a person who lost some of her faith; He makes remarkable yet imperfect creations. No matter how "right" our relationships might feel, they are like plants: without good soil, water, weeding, pruning, nourishment, sunlight and, yes, communication, they will die. Sometimes, even when all the good things are provided, they still die.

I'm a romantic but I'm also a realist. I went into marriage knowing it wasn't going to be a lifelong honeymoon. I know this is why the wedding vows say in good times and bad times, in sickness and in health, for richer or for poorer.

Fifty percent of the time things are not going to be wonderful. It's how God made things — night/day, good/evil, up/down. Accepting these contrasts and working with them is what separates good marriages that last from those that fall apart. Going against this natural order is like trying to beat the law of gravity.

I look forward to getting together with M. someday, to know that she's had some closure, too. Right now, that's not possible. She's just not at that stage in her life. That's sad. I know she's not mine to care about anymore — of course, she never was really mine — but now she's no longer a spouse, friend, lover or soul-mate. But I know we're still connected. I've had days when I know exactly what she's doing, and vice versa — Twilight Zone — which makes it all the more important to bring closure. It's not fair to any new relationships we might have. Someday.

Writing this hasn't eased the pain of the loss for me. But I remember Dorothy's sermon. She said that when broken bones heal, at the place where they fuse together they are stronger than they were before. I know I will heal just like those bones. I will be happier and healthier than I am now — when, where and with whom, I don't know. Until then, I will do my best to just be the person God needs, others need and I need, too. There's nothing I can do except just let it be.

Rev. Dorothy Scott Reflects

In the United Methodist Church we have our standard rituals as well as something that's known as a Book of Worship, which we've had in some form or other forever.

But this service was Scott's baby. Scott was the one who wanted to do it; he felt the strong need for it. I felt that my role was as a pastor and a friend who cared. It was a wonderful throw-back to some real positive memories for me because when we started a contemporary worship at my previous church, he had been on the early design team. He's fun to design worship with.

Scott did a really great job of welcoming everybody at various points in the service. He didn't make you feel like you

61

needed to be divorced or single or young or old. He said, "You're here because somehow you have a connection with me and you were kind enough to show up. Knowing me may be the only reason you're here, or there may be some other reason, and that's OK." I thought that was really good, too, because it's important to give people permission to be in worship for whatever reason they might need it. We all feel the need to come at different times for different reasons.

One of the things that struck me very early on in the whole process of going through my own divorce is that the church's structure, the very structure that I am a part of, has many, many ways of not speaking to the divorce situation. And so this service and what it meant was important to me. It spoke to the whole concept of new life; that new life is not in divorce or marriage or any other specific event in life, but in God, and in trusting in God.

Ritual, Religion and Divorce

People who use ritual to create a conscious parting intuitively grasp that this is as much a sacred event as a wedding or a funeral. Some perform a spiritual ceremony, taking care to sacralize the experience with cleansing, music and decoration, prayer and blessings. Others choose to create ritual within a particular religious tradition. You might think, as we did when we began this book, that no churches include divorce rituals as part of their liturgy, but you would be wrong. However, if you plan a religious ceremony, you will probably need to deal with differing theological traditions and points of view that can confuse your intentions and complicate your plans. In this chapter, we offer the reflections of ministers and rabbis who, like Rev. Scott, have struggled with these issues.

The Christian Tradition

If you are a Christian, one of the greatest trials of divorce can be the fear that you are breaking a sacred vow: "til death do us part." All Christian churches discourage divorce, and some still forbid it. Although some churches are more accepting when divorce occurs, and even sponsor divorce recovery programs, stigma and social ostracism associated with being a divorced person can still occur in a Christian community. Sadly, Scott found this to be as true in 1997 as Nancy did in 1974 (see Nancy's Story). Divorce evokes a disturbing ambivalence in many Christians, even when they support the idea that sometimes it is best for all concerned to end a marriage. They may be kind and supportive to those suffering the pain of loss, but for many Christians divorce represents a spiritual as well as a relationship failure.

This ambivalence is best illustrated by comments made to Phil by a prominent Protestant minister whose workshops, books and tapes are well known and widely used in divorce recovery programs. For him, a divorce ritual would be sanctioning sin. "The way I read the Bible, divorce is a tear in the fabric of God's intention. 'What God has joined together let no man put asunder.' It's a sin." This is the theological crux of the matter and perhaps explains why Nancy and Scott — and perhaps you, too — sometimes feel uncomfortable as a divorced person in a Christian church.

Is divorce a sin? Is a ritual for divorce an endorsement of sin? Ultimately, this is a question you will have to answer for yourself. But here are some reflections from clergy of different Christian denominations that we believe you will find relevant and helpful.

The Catholic church is theologically opposed to divorce. Nevertheless, James J. Young (April, 1985), a Paulist priest, wrote about the dilemmas of divorce among Catholics in an article titled "Ministering to Divorced Catholics."

> The divorce crisis is a spiritual crisis for all, even for people who have not considered themselves particularly religious. It is spiritual in that one's spirit, one's deepest identity, is tormented by questions and fears that won't go away. . .
>
> Many of us grew up believing that it was the words of Jesus in Scripture which left us Roman Catholics so little flexibility in dealing with divorce and remarriage. Modern Catholic Scripture studies have filled in much of the religious background and social context of Jesus' teaching and helped us appreciate the Lord not only as a demanding prophetic teacher about the permanence of marriage but also as a compassionate, healing servant toward the flawed and failed.
>
> He took a strong stand on permanence in marriage, but he also stood at Jacob's well with the woman who had been divorced five times and tenderly revealed himself to her. The Scripture scholars point out that in the New Testament itself we find Jesus insisting that his followers, when they marry, should commit themselves

to each other until death, but we also find St. Paul and St. Matthew adapting that teaching to troubled human circumstances and permitting divorce and remarriage in certain circumstances.

Theologians today insist that we must be nuanced and careful in applying the norms of Scripture and Church teachings to the couple we know down the block, judgements about the decisions others make about their failed marriages, and resist labeling anyone as an "adulterer" or "sinner." (p.3)

John Selby Spong (1990) is an Anglican Bishop who reflected on divorce and sin in his book *Living in Sin*.

The necessary stance for the church today, it seems to me, is to take both marriage and divorce quite seriously. The church should recognize and state quite openly that divorce is not an unforgivable sin, nor is it always tragic; indeed, in some instances divorce is and can be positive and good. After having done all it can to fulfill its vow to support the marriage, the church also needs to undergird divorcing persons when they make that decision. Passive, benign rejection is neither helpful nor compassionate....

Approximately half of all the marriages performed in my Episcopal jurisdiction are of divorced persons. It is time we stated positively that divorcing people are not always evil, not always sinful, not always to be condemned. Sometimes divorce is the way to an abundant new life for one or both of the formally linked partners. (p.63)

Other authors have combined theological considerations about divorce with the development of ritual to help bring closure and healing. In a remarkable book, *Rituals for a New Day: An Invitation*, a chapter by a United Methodist minister, Jeanne Audrey Powers (1976), took care to discuss the nature and meaning of marriage and divorce.

For Jesus and Paul, marital faithfulness was a metaphor for the relationship between God and God's people; it was the most powerful human symbol available for communicating an understanding of the Old Testament concept of covenant. John Snow, professor of pastoral theology at Episcopal Divinity School, reminds us, however, of the character of marriage in New Testament times. It was essentially "a convenient social and legal arrangement . . . that put sexuality to the uses of faithfulness rather than letting it become an agent of social disintegration. The Christian family was a safe and trustworthy place for children." The New Testament family was not characterized as nuclear families are today; rather, it was seen as integrally related to the small community of Christians in the early church. In First Timothy, Paul shows that its principles were faithfulness in the marriage itself, openness and hospitality in the family to those in need, and loyalty to the Christian community. [Because of] a short life expectancy within a subsistence economy and a concern for practical property arrangements in the uniting of the social structures of two families, sex was totally indivisible from procreation, and there was no emphasis on marriage as we would know it today as a mutually fulfilling relationship.

[In *Christianity and Crisis* (1974)], Dr. Snow suggests that the church's call for covenant and faithfulness in marriage must also be declared in our times, but in a way which is appropriate for our changed circumstances. Faithfulness must continue to carry with it a commitment, but we need to affirm that this commitment is to a person rather than to the institution of marriage. At a time when one out of three marriages performed this year [1975] will end in divorce, what does continuing faithfulness mean *after* the marriage bond has been severed? Might it not mean the mutual

66

concern for the general welfare of the other and serious effort at the raising of children on a mutual basis?

[Dr. Snow says], "If the Church held its members accountable in divorce and remarriage for this kind of personal faithfulness ... it would also be working toward reconciliation in relationships that have tended to be permanently shattered by old attitudes towards divorce ... and most important, it would maintain the centrality of faithfulness and forgiveness as Christian values that reflect directly God's relationship with God's children ... The form and shape of Christian marriage and family are not prescribed by the New Testament, but the values of faithfulness, forgiveness, hospitality and love as benevolent helpfulness and concern most certainly are." (pp. 76-78)

Phil spoke to Rev. Powers about her work with alternative ritual and with Rev. Hoyt Hickman, who also contributed to *Rituals for a New Day*. Both are retired and still share strong feelings about the efficacy of ritual as part of a healing divorce. Although *Rituals for a New Day* is now out of print, Rev. Hickman pointed out that other rituals for healing and reconciliation, often used for divorce, can be found in the United Methodist *Book of Worship*. Rev. Powers was good enough to share letters she received in response to her chapter on divorce rituals. While a few were critical, most speak to the intense yearning of many Christians to bring healing to the end of their relationships. Here are some excerpts.

A former church attendee: "Lucky for me, I learned of your work. Though I am not divorced, I had turned away from the church because I have seen it act hypocritically with my divorced friends."

A Christian contemplating divorce: "We have worked a long time on our relationship and know that this divorce is the right thing for us to do. But there is pain involved and a lot of that comes from the fact that we have many friends in common. It is important for us

67

to have a way to say some of the things that we both know and be released from a lot of the feelings that overtake us even though we know we have come to a good decision. I think a public declaration of the sort you are talking about would make it easier for all of us to deal with each other and for people to relate to us in a more honest way."

A Christian divorcee: "We care for each other and will miss sharing life's moments. And so we smile and cry as we live. We would very much like to read and perhaps recite the kind of ritual you speak of."

A Christian anticipating divorce: "I was married at 16, my husband was 18. Now, six years later, we know that our marriage is not going to work out for us. We have no bitterness towards each other as so many people seem to have in our situation. We would like to participate in a ritual that may help us to experience peace with ourselves and with others."

A Christian divorcee seeking peace and forgiveness: "I, too, am a victim of divorce, and live almost totally estranged from my ex-wife and child. We felt the spiritual aspect of our marriage was a strong one. I want to begin to take the initiative in establishing a rapport which ought to exist between two human beings (even though we are no longer married)."

Christian parents seeking healing: "I feel your work is an answer to my prayers as we feel the devastation of our son's divorce so deeply. There is so much hurt, pain, and confusion that we feel submerged in the futility of it all. Your idea of a Christian ritual is tremendous. Just bringing these feelings out in the open would be a healthy release. It's like someone opening a door and letting fresh air into a dark and gloomy room."

Rituals in the United Methodist Church to facilitate a healing divorce did not end in the 1970s, as Scott's service demonstrates. In a personal communication, Jim Robey, a minister in the South, reflected on divorce and religion. Here are examples of several brief rituals he has helped design and perform.

I worked with three people to formalize their ritual of divorce. All three shared one thing in common: they came from a very conservative religious tradition and felt like they had committed the unpardonable sin of divorce. I spent several months counseling with them, helping them to see divorce not as the ultimate sin, but just one of many sins that we commit, which God forgives. He wants people to have full lives. Jesus came so that we might have life in all of its abundance and sometimes that means we have to leave things behind.

Each person I worked with took a general format and customized it in his or her own way. One woman found several scriptures in the Psalms and the Gospels that had been very meaningful to her. There were just the two of us in the church. I read those scriptures for her and then, at the altar, she said words of confession for her part in the ending of her marriage. I then shared words of pardon and forgiveness, and we concluded with one of the Psalms that she had selected. The ceremony itself took about five minutes, but it was preceded by two months of counseling.

Another person I worked with was a man. I had counseled with him about his feelings of guilt. During the ritual, he knelt at the altar and made his confession to God. I shared some words of scripture for forgiveness. It was very simple and very effective.

The third individual did her ritual a bit differently. She involved her parents and her children, then 19 and 16. This was kind of a family ritual. It occurred in the chapel of the church in front of the altar. I talked a bit about the beginning and the ending [of the marriage], read some scripture, and then proclaimed God's forgiveness and his grace for the new beginning that she was making for herself and her family. I also affirmed that she had the love and support of her family, and God,

69

and of her church. She was then free to live without the emotional baggage of divorce.

Other denominations have also created rituals for divorce. Rituals used by the United Church of Christ and the Unitarians, for example, are specifically designed to help couples end their marriages or partnerships. Rituals for healing can be found in the United Methodist and Presbyterian books of worship and are commonly used for divorce. Episcopalian, and even Catholic liturgy, has been adapted for rituals of divorce (see Margaret's Story). Other ministers and priests have told us that even if a denomination doesn't offer a specific ritual for divorce, such rituals and ceremonies are often created and performed at the congregational level.

In her book *Single in the Church*, Dr. Kay Collier Slone (1992) describes two such rituals (see the Appendix) and offers some reflections on the role of the church in dealing with the divorce and subsequent singleness of its members.

Whether the death is of marriage, spouse, dreams or life expectations, there is a necessary letting go and hearing God's call for this particular season of life ... Singles speak to themselves in their own aloneness: "What does my life mean if I am to live it alone? If I am no longer a husband or wife? ... Does God really mean for me to live by myself for the rest of my life? Why?"

"Why does it feel so empty? Why am I so scared? Why won't the hunger go away?"

"Can I be happy without a mate?"

The journey from these questions to self-affirmation in life as a single person uniquely created by God is not an easy one. There is sadness, fear, anger and loneliness.

And there is the incredible grace of opportunity to move from loneliness into solitude and, in that solitude, to encounter the mysterious and all-encompassing relationship with God, which fills the emptiness, feeds the hunger, heals the fear, as no earthly relationship can.

70

There's the incredible grace of opportunity to know
life more truly whole than ever imagined, to live the
experience of transfiguration and transcendence.

It is to this journey that I believe the church is called
to minister. (pp. 79-80)

The Jewish Tradition

Phil spoke with several rabbis about the Jewish practice of
divorce, an ancient tradition enshrined in religious law that pre-
dates Christianity by thousands of years. In the Orthodox
tradition, a *get pitturin,* or simply *get,* which means "bill of
divorce," is given and received today much as it has been for
centuries. As described by Isaac Klein (1979) in *The Guide to
Jewish Religious Practice*, the actual process of the divorce was
ritualized according to religious law:

> ...Thus do I set you free, release thee, and put thee
> aside, in order that thou may have permission and the
> authority over thyself to go and marry any man thou may
> desire. No person may hinder thee from this day onward,
> and thou are permitted to every man. This shall be for
> thee from me a bill of dismissal, a letter of release, and a
> document of freedom, in accordance with the laws of
> Moses and Israel. (p. 122)

The *get* had to be written by the husband and delivered
personally by him to his wife. The writing materials had to
belong to the husband. The husband had to strictly adhere to the
formula of the *get* and any deviation would render it invalid.
Once the *get* was received by the wife she, in turn, gave it to the
rabbinical court. This court then presented her with a document
affirming that she had been divorced according to the law.
Divisions of money and property were also carefully regulated,
often depending on whom the court found at fault. With
sufficient proof, this could be the husband. While the Jewish

71

divorce ritual was clearly the product of a patriarchal culture, it was not without compassion and justice for women.

In Reform Judaism, significant changes have occurred concerning the practice of divorce. Rabbi Allen Maller (1979) of Temple Akiba in Culver City, California, expressed an alternative view of the *get* in "Is Divorce a Mitsvah?", a paper he wrote some years ago for people going through a divorce. Here are some passages that offer the gist of Rabbi Maller's thoughts.

> Most Jews would be surprised to learn that divorce is a Mitsvah. It is one of the 613 Misvot to be found in the Torah. Most Jews think of a Mitsvah as a good deed. [But] divorce is a painful experience, an affliction, sometimes a tragedy. It is a breakdown of something that was good. When a marriage fails, the people involved suffer. They are hurt and in pain. They often feel guilty because they feel they have hurt their children or their parents. They sometimes feel ashamed because they think others view them as failures. Even when they know in their hearts that this isn't true, the feeling may still persist. All of this is the natural result of love that has gone sour. But there is no reason for Jews involved in divorce to feel that they have acted wrongly or to judge themselves as sinners.
>
> Jews should take this for granted, but because we live in a Christian society we tend to be influenced by other ideas. There are millions of Christians, both Protestant and Catholic, who for years to come will feel conscience stricken that they have sinned by getting a divorce. Most of these people have been taught that marriage is "until death do you part" and that "what God has joined together, let no man put asunder."
>
> Judaism, on the other hand, teaches us that divorce is a Mitsvah. Everyone makes mistakes. Picking a marriage partner is a difficult process. Some people do it when they are too young. Others are right for each other when they marry but grow apart through the years. Sometimes the divorce decision is mutual, sometimes it

72

is one-sided. In any case, if you've really tried and a marriage doesn't work out, divorce and try again ... To be willing to love again is to revive hope, and to express faith in the future. To be willing to trust someone again is to also revitalize faith in one's self. This is exactly what God wants us to do ....

A divorce marks the end of an old way of life and the beginning of a new way. When a couple is married they are supposed to write a *ketubah* in which they establish their mutual responsibilities for, and commitments to, each other, and also express the goals of their relationship. When a Jewish marriage is ended a *get* is written. Both the marriage contract (*ketubah*) and the divorce decree (*get*) are primarily legal documents in the Orthodox tradition. But for Reform Jews, the *ketubah*, and especially the *get*, can be an expression of faith in the future, and in one's ability to meet the challenges of life and grow with them ... [because] divorce is a Mitsvah, why not write a *get*? Why not express your faith in where you can go?

How do you go about writing a *get* and what should you experience while writing it? The purpose of writing a *get* is to face a new situation realistically and to set realistic goals for one's self in the new situation ....

To write your *get*, start out by listing at least ten assets and ten liabilities in your personal situation. Then try to anticipate the greatest difficulties you will have to confront in the forthcoming year. Start planning what you will do to deal with these difficulties. Take responsibility for your own actions. Don't rely on others to make decisions for you. Spend several weeks revising your lists and then meet with your rabbi and discuss your self-evaluation. He will help you gain insight into your feelings about yourself and your future. The writing of a *get* should take at least one month because you will find that your mood will change rapidly during the divorce process. Don't hesitate to meet with your rabbi more than one time. When you have finished your inventory, you are ready to begin writing your *get*.

The orthodox *get* is a simple document which terminates a marriage. It states that it is a document of freedom, a letter of release, and that no person may hinder you from now on. It also states that you have authority over yourself. In writing your own *get* you must accept the authority to lead your own life. You must affirm that no other person will hinder you. State both your near term and long term goals. Expand on the areas where you will grow. Stress your assets and explore how you will develop them. When you have finished writing your *get,* feel free to read it frequently and to revise it whenever necessary. On the anniversary of your divorce, reread your *get* and observe how much you have already grown. Remember, while writing and reading your *get,* that it is a religious document. There is a source of strength available to you through your faith in God. Avail yourself of God's presence. Your *get* will help you grow and God will be with you in that growth.

Rabbi Earl Grollman, the author of many books on crisis and healing, told Phil that he decided to create a divorce ceremony after a woman he was counseling challenged him.

She said, "You spend a lot of time going to medical schools and talking to physicians about how to treat dying patients. You work with hospices, with parents whose child has died. But you don't help me."

"What would you like me to do?"

"You know, I'm going through a separation and divorce."

"I know, but what can I do?"

"Have you ever been to a divorce court before?"

I said, "Fortunately, I haven't."

She was an attorney and said she'd go with me. It was a cold and dehumanizing experience.

74

Afterwards, she said, "Would you have a funeral for us?"

I was taken aback because I still didn't fully understand. I said, "But you and your husband are living. What do you mean, a funeral?"

"Yes," she said, "we're living. But our marriage is dead."

Recognizing the need for a divorce ceremony, Rabbi Grollman (1978) designed one (see Chapter 11), published originally in his book *Living Through Your Divorce*. In a personal communication he described the concept underlying his contemporary ritual.

> The divorce ceremony in Judaism was not meaningful for me because it's the man who gives it to the woman. I think it's great that they were insightful enough to understand the importance of a ceremony, but it's the wrong ceremony. Over 40 years ago, I created one of the first divorce rituals because I realized that the children, especially, need some sense of understanding that their parents' marriage is over. When a person is born, we have ritual; we make mountains out of moments such as baptism or circumcision. When we go through puberty, we have *bar* and *bat mitzvah*s. When a person goes through marriage, it's called a sacrament or, in Hebrew, *kedoshin*. When a person dies, we hold a funeral. With death there is closure. You may love the person, you may hate the person, but there's the casket and there's the hole in the ground; it's over. But what do you do when there's a divorce?
>
> Each ceremony should be separate and distinct. Couples should understand that part of the therapy is for them to help create it. As a clergyman, I can assist by giving them an outline, some possibilities. But they must pick and choose. The more personal the ceremony becomes, the better. It's also very important that when they come together for the ceremony, you don't separate

75

one family from the other. The idea is to bring everyone closer together.

I've done over one hundred ceremonies through the years. Of course, it's not for everybody. As far as timing goes, it's never the first year. Many people want it right away, imagining that it's a quick fix. But the first year is too soon. Although there are exceptions, it's usually three years or more before a couple settles down emotionally and is ready to do it. Also, I'm not there to adjudicate. Only when a couple has come to a firm decision will I perform a ceremony. Always, I want to know the reasons why they want to do this. Usually, it's because of their children; so that the children will come to accept that they're really divorced. We know from the psychological literature — and my experience has borne this out — that children almost always fantasize that their parents will somehow remarry, even if they've remarried other people.

Here's my criterion: people come to me and say, "I'd like to do this." And I say, "How about your husband?" I remember one woman saying, "I'll never forgive that bastard as long as he lives." I've also said to people, "You're not ready for it." The capacity for forgiveness is vital — not forgiveness itself, but the capacity, the willingness to make an effort. I don't say, "Will you forgive?" I say, "Will you forgive the best way you know how?"

Also, I'm careful about the word closure. I think the correct word is "healing," especially if there are younger children. Closure implies it's over, done with — when there's a divorce, it's never over. There are always memories. But even if a ceremony can't offer closure, it can provide great healing.

Research also led us to two other rabbis who have done work with divorce rituals. Rabbi Eliot Stevens of the Central Conference of American Rabbis shared with us the Ritual of Release you will find in Chapter 11, developed to meet the need of member rabbis for a model divorce ritual. This ritual also includes a Document of Separation and Release designed to serve as a *get*. Rabbi James Bleiberg sent us a copy of a remarkable ritual he and his congregation created and performed when he left his Temple in North Carolina — a ritual that clearly demonstrates the healing potential of conscious parting in a broad spiritual context (see Jim's Story).

Recommendations

1. Do you believe that divorce is a sin? If so, take some time to counsel with your minister, priest or rabbi about your convictions and your feelings.
2. Do you feel called to create and perform a religious divorce ceremony? If so, does a specific ritual or liturgy already exist in your church or synagogue? If not, can a ritual of healing or reconciliation be adapted to meet your needs? Is your religious adviser willing to help you create and perform such a ceremony, perhaps using a model from this book?
3. If your minister, priest or rabbi is less than enthusiastic about helping to create and perform a ceremony, call upon clergy from a denomination that does perform such rituals. Share with him (or her) the stories, rituals and ceremonies in this book.

Margaret's Story

This story was written by G. Margaret Downs and published originally as "Closing the Wound: A Ritual after Divorce" in *Festivals*, Vol. 6, No. 4., date and publisher currently unknown. It is reprinted here as it originally appeared. (**Note**: If you know how to reach Ms. Downs or *Festivals*, please let us know.)

When I separated from my husband of almost 25 years in 1984, I thought that the end of my life had come. I was in a deep depression, sure that I would never feel hope or life or love again, and angry at my husband because I did not want the separation or subsequent divorce.

I already had a spiritual director, and she was one of the first people to whom I fled for help. Upon her suggestion, my husband and I sought counseling from a minister-psychologist. After several visits, together and separately, it became evident that the marriage was unsalvageable. His recommendation to remain separate did not go down easily, but my decision to continue to see him and gain some insights for my own new life was a life — and mind — saving one.

Over the next year and a half, many changes took place in my lifestyle, not only as a "separated" person, but also as a working woman on my own, no longer living in a family context. My counselor helped me to overcome the challenges to my personality of felt rejection and loneliness. And, with the help of my spiritual director, I began to believe strongly in the power and will of God for my life, and in God's forgiveness and encouragement to move on from this tragedy to a fulfilling life of ministry and prayer.

In a discussion with my spiritual director, we spoke about the need for closure on certain parts of our lives, parts that are painful but full of growth, parts that need to be put in perspective as containing events of import in our lives, yet passed through and ended. As time went on, she encouraged me to design for myself a ritual that would accomplish this for me.

In a class on the Roman Catholic Liturgy of the Hours, I found a prayerful and, for me, very meaningful way of daily prayer. The lay music ministry group that I had helped found was already modeling its communal prayer times on the Liturgy of the Hours, and as we all explored this form of prayer, song, psalm recitation and intercession from the earliest days of the Christian church, I became aware of its potential for adaptation to what I call a Ritual for Healing and Closure.

The Liturgy of the Hours, formerly the Office of the Breviary, was once considered the prayer of those ordained or in vows. Recent reforms in the Roman Catholic Church, however, have made clear that it is not and was never meant to be the exclusive prayer of the clergy and the monastic orders, but the prayer of the people. The General Instruction on the Liturgy of the Hours invites "groups of laity, whenever they meet ... to pray the Office of the Church and celebrate part of the Liturgy of the Hours whenever they come together, whether it be for prayer, apostolic work or any reason whatever."

As I reflected and prayed, I decided that I wanted to do something about my own process of passage, of healing and closure. It would be a passage from one lifestyle to another, from wife to single person, from parent to friend. It would be healing for the wounds of a 25-year marriage that had ended in infidelity and brokenness. It would be closure on that era and blessing for the next part of my life to come with its adventure and surprise.

For the site of the ritual, I chose a large chapel in a church office center with moveable furniture so that I could arrange the chairs in a circle. The lighting was subdued, with candles and flowers placed around the room.

As a primary symbol, I used a drawing of a spider web. On each arm or branch of the web was written the name of a person or a place, word or thing that had been or still was part of my life. The spider web was ripped almost in half, but not quite, so that part of it was still intact and the spider could begin again, spin some new webs and repair it in the same pattern as the first but with new time, strength and intent.

I adapted the shape of the Evening Prayer of the Liturgy of the Hours with songs based on the Psalms, Psalms prayed antiphonally, readings, prayers, intercession and the Lord's Prayer. I put together a worship aid and sent out invitations to those who had remained friends and been supportive over the two-year period since separation. I asked several people closest to me, my spiritual director, the friar who was chaplain to the parish divorced and separated group, a musician-singer friend from the music ministry group, and my best friend, to participate with me in reading, singing and carrying out the ritual.

That evening, as people began to arrive, I was aware of a feeling of presumption and fear — presumption that I would do such a thing for myself and fear that others would think I was on some sort of ego trip. But as I expressed this to my spiritual director, I knew that it was a time for me to pray with all my friends in thanksgiving for my wholeness and survival. My family came, some from 400 miles away, to be with me as I moved on with my life and dreams.

Even now, I still find it difficult to put into words the peace and affirmation that God, through my friends and family, by their presence and words of care and hope, blessed me with that night. As the web mends, and as the brokenness in my life heals with the prayer and care of those whom I love and who love me, I know that I needed this ritual of healing and closure so as to continue the process of passage, to affirm my own goodness and strength, and to acknowledge the presence of God in my life to permit me to forgive, to heal me, and to enable me to move on.

Jim's Story

This story by Rabbi Jim Bleiberg tells how he and members of his congregation created and performed a ritual to mark the occasion of their parting. The relationship between a rabbi (or a minister) and a congregation often feels like a marriage, especially when things aren't going well. In many ways, the difficult feelings between Rabbi Bleiberg and his congregation are similar to those that characterize divorce between husband and wife: hurt, misunderstanding, anger, a sense of betrayal, distrust and a temptation to lash out or withdraw. The intention of the ritual they created and performed (see Chapter 11) is similar to others in this book: to end a relationship with truth, love, care and forgiveness — or, as Rabbi Bleiberg put it, justice, truth and peace. We include it because of its thoughtfulness and beauty, and because the ritual evokes themes and employs symbols in ways that can be helpful as you prepare a parting ceremony of your own. It also demonstrates how a parting of any kind can be made conscious and healing.

I was the Rabbi of a congregation in Raleigh, North Carolina. After an initial "honeymoon" I started feeling discontent. My salary was the focus of my dissatisfaction but money wasn't the real problem. I was slowly becoming disenchanted with my work and the way that I did it. I wanted something to change but I wasn't sure how. By the end of my fifth year I decided to leave this position. I thought that the congregation was going to offer me an extension on my contract and that I was going to turn it down. For some reason, it was important for them to say that they wanted me before I could then say, no — this after twice telling them I would accept no more than a one year extension. In retrospect, it's easy to see that they felt rejected by my refusal to make a further commitment and didn't want to put themselves through the same painful process again.

81

After a Board meeting, the president called to say they had decided not to extend my contract. I was livid. He came over to my house to talk to me — in retrospect, a generous thing to do. But I didn't feel it was generous at the time. I was furious with him. I saw him as weak and deceptive. Of course, I'd been deceptive, too, in not telling them honestly that I felt it was time for me to leave.

It was hard to admit that my work as a Rabbi had not worked out. In my previous position as an associate Rabbi in Baltimore, it had been easy to imagine that any problems I had were because it wasn't the right congregation and I wasn't the boss. When I finally got to a congregation where I was the boss, I told myself, then everything would be OK.

The congregation in Raleigh was the kind of community that I'd thought I was really looking for. It wasn't too big but still had the financial resources to do what I wanted to do. The members seemed enthusiastic about my ideas and things I wanted to try. But it didn't work the way I had imagined. I felt I couldn't figure out a way to be a rabbi in this congregation in a way that I could live with. I'd decided to return to graduate school to get my doctorate in clinical psychology, but then they wanted our relationship to end.

All of this happened in November. But I wasn't actually leaving until the end of June. I was relieved that things were settled, but I still had to show up for work every day. In some ways, nothing had changed. So I resolved to change the way I related to my congregation. I wanted to be more open, more honest. In the newsletter I wrote:

"The Jewish tradition provides us with many rituals for death and dying but does not give us any for the separation of a rabbi from a congregation. I am in the process of creating a special ceremony for this purpose ... It is my hope that this ceremony will give the congregation and myself a unique forum to say a final good-bye and to honor the six years we spent together....

"If you would like to be involved in preparing or leading this ritual, or helping to organize the reception that will follow it,

please call me at the Temple. Your help would be very welcome."

Four people volunteered to help. One was a retired rabbi who had recently joined the congregation. The way in which they helped me was imagining how we could make the ritual parts of it work. They left me to come up with the words, but they were the ones who suggested the symbolic acts that would make clear what was going on.

I had already thought of the idea of using a quotation from a text in the Talmud as the basis for the service. Usually this text is translated: "The world endures on account of these three things: justice, truth and peace."

But, I asked myself, what is it that continues in the world? What is the source of that which remains in the world and doesn't disappear, no matter what happens? It was my sense that both the congregation and I needed to find out what would continue, even though something was ending. It was very clear by then that our relationship was going to end, but there were also some things that I was going to take away with me from this experience, and so were they. This text explained that those things rooted in justice, truth and peace endure. These three elements became the basis for the service.

We held the ritual in the social hall instead of the sanctuary, both to facilitate the process and so everyone would be more comfortable, less formal. The challenge was to convert the social hall, usually used for eating, into a sacred space. We did this by arranging about 150 chairs in concentric circles so that I wouldn't be up on the pedestal, so to speak, but seated with everyone else. By the way, this was the first time I had ever sat with my family during a service.

We started with music, a familiar song I had often used to begin a regular service: Ya-ba-bim-bam. This is a meditative song in which the melody is more important than the words. Because it was familiar, I hoped the song would help everyone buy into the idea that this strange ritual that no one had ever done before was actually a worship service.

After the song, I explained the background of the ritual and encouraged everyone to participate to the extent that they felt comfortable.

The first element of the ritual was called "Justice." I retold an old story, trying to make it as relevant as possible. In ancient Israel, a man clearing his land tosses stones onto public land. A wise man says to him, "Well, you're such a fool because you really don't own that property even though it feels like yours. What really belongs to you is the public domain and yet that is where you're foolishly throwing those rocks."

As I interpreted it, this story is about how we cast stumbling blocks into other people's way in the guise of making things better for ourselves. Often we're quick to get angry and blame others. We take our private struggles and enact them in the community. Certainly, I thought that I had done this and I think that other people in the community, especially the leaders of the congregation, had done this as well. It seemed important that parting be a time for all of us to own our own behavior. This ritual was about finding a way to help us all reclaim the stuff that we were responsible for as individuals, but that we had blamed on other people.

Everyone was seated in concentric circles — all the chairs were full. In the center of the circle were three small tables, each with a big, flat woven basket. In the baskets, the committee and I had placed smooth pebbles, like river rocks, pleasant to touch and hold. At the end of the reading about justice, members of the committee carried the baskets around the circles and gave everyone a chance to pick a stone, to keep as their own. Symbolically, this was taking back rocks cast by all of us into the public domain. The blessing, a traditional Jewish one that's usually used in an entirely different context, was said in English because I wanted it to be really accessible and I was afraid that the Hebrew would distance people from it. So we held onto our stones and together said a blessing to thank God for supporting us in doing what's right.

In the second part of the service, called "Truth," the text explains — and this is also from the Talmud — that some letters in the Hebrew alphabet stand on two legs but some stand on one;

for example, in English, F has one leg but N has two. The word for falsehood in Hebrew — shekar *— has only one leg on each of the letters. But the word for truth —* emet *— has three letters that have two legs. The rabbis were using that as a clever way to illustrate that truth rests on two legs; that truth is not a single thing — there are always two sides to the truth. In terms of the ritual, this was an opportunity for people to stand up on their two legs and speak their truth — what this particular moment meant to them or anything they wanted to say about the six years I'd been at the congregation. I didn't say anything. I felt like I'd said pretty much everything that I needed to say. It was their turn.*

It was really amazing. Of course, people had selected themselves to be there so they were already motivated. But still, there were 150 people present and many of them, one by one, spoke to the whole group. We listened for as long as people had things to say. For the most part, people talked about what they appreciated about what had happened between me and them. Or how sad they were at the way things had developed. Afterwards, other people approached me during the reception. The whole tone of this was very sweet and easygoing and relaxed. It wasn't tense at all. I know people might imagine that this truth telling would have been really charged, but it wasn't. Perhaps this was because we had talked about so many things already and the congregation had found a new Rabbi. So it was OK for me to go and for them to go, too. At the end of the truth section — when no one else had anything to say — we said a blessing thanking God for giving us insight and the opportunity to learn from each other.

Then there was a song. It had been written by the person who did music for the congregation and meant a lot to me, not only that he wrote and performed it, but that I could accept it. I had said that I wanted to be a different kind of rabbi. This was the kind of rabbi I wanted to be, someone who allowed more room for other people to express what they felt.

Then came the final section, called "Peace." Here the ritual was borrowed from a traditional Jewish practice at Rosh Shahana. It's not part of the synagogue service but a folk custom

85

that's often done at home. At the meal that opens the Jewish New Year, it's often customary to have apples and honey as a way of wishing everyone in the family a good year to come.

In the ritual we mixed the ideas of apples and honey with prayers for peace in sort of an unconventional way. While this ritual did represent an ending, sharing apples and honey marked this as a beginning. I was starting a very important and challenging change in my life, and they were beginning a new phase of congregational life, too.

In the center of the room were several large platters with sliced apples — a member of the committee had sprayed the apples with lemon juice so they wouldn't turn brown. In the center of each platter was a bowl of honey. After we'd read the prayers, the members of the committee walked around with the platters. Although everyone knew what to do because it's a Jewish custom, it took some time to get around to everyone. But people waited without impatience in what seemed a contemplative way. When everyone had been served, we said the blessing and then ate the apples and honey.

After the ritual but before the reception, the congregation gave farewell presents, not only to me but also to my family. This was a complete surprise. Part of my way of being a rabbi had been to be completely self-contained. I didn't need anything; I was the one who gave them things. Here, symbolically, I showed that I was a person who could receive things, too. As they gave us these presents, I felt cared for by the congregation in a way that I never had before — perhaps because now I had changed and was prepared to consciously receive.

4

Preparing the Ritual of Parting

Ritual And You — Yes, You!

As a culture, we have lost much understanding of how ritual helps us cope with the transitions in our lives. Also, many traditional rituals have been trivialized or sentimentalized — birth, coming of age, marriage and death. The symbolic power of most rituals has thus been diminished or lost. For some life transitions, indeed, there are no rituals — illness, injury, loss of a job, forced retirement and, these days, separation and divorce.

The Appendix lists excellent resources for understanding ritual. These have informed us of the process we and others have gone through and are well worth reading. Here, however, we focus less on theory and more on practice: how couples and individuals have planned, created and performed parting rituals or ceremonies specifically in the context of a separation or divorce, and how you can do this, too.

Nevertheless, before you begin creating your ritual of parting, please bear in mind several things. First, note the difference between ritual and the exercises sometimes described as ritual, prescribed in some books and articles about the ending of a relationship. Some of these can be helpful in clarifying and expressing your feelings and others in helping prepare psychologically for creating and performing a ritual (see the Appendix). In our experience, however, these resources are no substitute for a ritual that is fully embodied. We disagree with those authors who suggest that the process should remain private. Your journal is an excellent tool, and it's also important to take some action — physical action, symbolic action. There is a time for solitary prayer and meditation, and for exercises and vizualizations that help you come to terms within yourself. But once you have worked with and clarified your feelings, seize the opportunity to make manifest forgiveness and healing — for yourself, your children and the world.

87

Second, all ritual is "composed of metaphors, symbols and actions in a highly condensed dramatic form ... The power inherent in symbols is the ability to speak to the innermost depths of our individuality while binding us to the collective whole of the group" (Imber-Black 1988). This is what sets a ritual apart from our everyday lives and gives it the power to effect change.

Our hearts and mind come together through symbols to realize what is difficult or impossible to express in any other way. Symbols can be sensed — typically seen or heard, or both — and have the power to convey personal meaning as well as communicate that meaning to others. Take, for example, Margaret's use of a broken spider web as a symbol for her life, and the possibility of healing. Or Jim's use of river rocks as symbols of blame and self-responsibility. Later, you'll read about Matthew and Anne who baked a spice cake for their after-ceremony party and, cutting it, neatly separated the bride and groom dolls they had placed on top (see Matthew and Anne's Story). As Wall and Ferguson (1998) pointed out, "Symbols . . . can evoke critical feelings and emotions that attend personal change, and they do it with far greater speed and at a deeper level than is possible with language alone" (p.9). In your personal ritual, the most effective symbols will usually be those that connect you most specifically to your current circumstances.

Third, a personal ritual is akin to a work of art. In *Rites of Passage*, Wall and Ferguson (1998) suggest that you "think of yourself as an artist and of the steps to ritual as the framework on which you will build a sculpture. The framework gives form and strength to your efforts, but the creative process — the final shape, texture, color and meaning of the work — is up to you" (p.5). A ritual expresses your emotion, any emotion — pain, love, grief, anger — rising out of your unconscious in the form of inspiration. Inspiration means "the breath of the divine." If you are prepared to listen to the whisper of this breath what you do next can be a creative and hallowed act. Like any work of art, the power of a ritual will reflect the energy you put into it and the careful selection of each and every element you decide to include. As with a fine poem or a musical composition, nothing should be there by accident — including room for spontaneity.

With Or Without Your Partner?

How wonderful when estranged partners value conscious parting and surprise each other by agreeing to participate together in a divorce ritual. For that reason, we will discuss a ceremony as if it's being created and performed by a couple.

The fact remains, however, that more than half the rituals described in this book were undertaken by a single person, usually with the help and participation of friends and family. Most of these involved separation through divorce. But as Jim's and Jessie's stories demonstrate, even if there has been no "official" marriage, ritual can be helpful and healing. For example, we know several gay and lesbian persons who have used the stories in this book as inspiration, and the ceremonies as models for rituals of their own. The same can be true of common-law marriage partners. People long estranged might find that a ceremony offers closure and promotes forgiveness years after a parting (see Gene H's remembrance in Chapter 9). Seniors who did not have the opportunity to speak their hearts because of estrangement, or because a partner died unexpectedly, might find that a parting ceremony is a way to bring healing to the end of a relationship. Whatever your particular situation, we encourage you to adapt what we say here to your own needs.

But before you decide to do a ceremony on your own, know that a ceremony with your partner may not be as impossible as you think. When you're caught up in "crazy time," you might not even want to speak to your ex, much less plan and perform a ceremony. He or she may well feel the same about you. You may tell yourself: Fine; a ceremony of parting sounds like a good idea. But there is no way we could ever do something like that, not together, not now, not ever. Besides, even if I wanted to, he'd never participate.

Really? Never? Could you be caught up in the all-or-nothing, back-and-white extreme thinking promoted by the Myth of the Bad Divorce? Remember, feelings change. Also, it's possible that, like you, your partner may be feeling several contradictory emotions at the same time. Perhaps he, too, feels hurt and angry *and* wishes there was some way other than the ABCs of divorce for the two of you to end your relationship. If you can step out of the world of "either-or" (either I love him or I hate him) and into the world of "both-and" (I can be angry at her and still want to find a way to bring healing to the end of our relationship), you have taken the first step toward the possibility of a shared ceremony.

Just a step. Just a possibility. Take a deep breath. We're only talking here, and if you decide that you're not ready for this, that's fine. But what if ... ?

What if ... your intention is to bring healing to the end of your relationship for all concerned?

What if ... you give your ex the benefit of the doubt — OK, lots of benefit, little doubt — and assume that she, like you, might have mixed feelings; that though she's hurt and angry, she may also want to find a way to promote a healing divorce?

What if ... instead of angrily assuming that he won't participate, you take responsibility for raising the possibility and offer to get him a copy of this book?

What if ... he says, cautiously, "Maybe," and instead of getting upset at his lack of enthusiasm, you willingly accept this level of comfortable involvement? (See the stories by Carolyn, Marcy and Kurt.)

What if ... he says, "No way," and trashes the idea? Could you say, "I'm sorry you feel that way; I think it will be healing," and let him know you're going ahead and will welcome his participation if he changes his mind?

What if ... you go ahead with the ceremony, by yourself and with your children, family and friends, meanwhile keeping your ex well informed?

In the end, your ex may want nothing to do with this. Or, one or both of you may decide things are too challenging for you to create and perform a ceremony together. Only you know your particular circumstances, and whatever decision you make is all right. And — not but, *and* —we believe that even if you create

90

and perform a ceremony by yourself, your effort to include your ex will make the experience of healing and closure more complete.

Recommendations

1. Honestly assess if you desire to share a divorce ritual with your ex-partner.
2. Honestly assess if you are emotionally ready and able to share a divorce ritual with your ex-partner.
3. If you answer, "No", to one or both of these questions, proceed with your own plans to create and perform a ritual without your ex-partner. Remember, this does not mean you must perform the ceremony alone. Family and friends will support you. One of them might even stand in as a proxy for your ex (see Kurt's Story).
4. If you answer, "Yes", to both questions (or even just the first), share this book and discuss how the two of you can best work together to create a healing ritual for your family. Invite your partner to join you and accept his or her degree of involvement.
5. If your ex answers, "Maybe", share this book and proceed with your own plans, asking for a decision by a specific date.
6. If your ex answers, "No", proceed with your own plans while leaving the door open for your partner's change of mind.

Setting Your Intention

Before you begin to actually plan, it's important to know why you want to do a parting ritual or ceremony. With benefit of hindsight, we would say that our intention was to end our relationship with healing — truth, love, care and forgiveness — in a way that would help us transition from marriage to a friendship. At the time, however, we were less clear and precise. All we really knew was that we didn't want to fall into the usual

ABCs of divorce. We also wanted to honor what we had shared and, if possible, to find a way to remain friends.

If we had the opportunity to set our intention again, here are several questions we would ask and try to answer honestly. As you consider them, do your best to be specific. You might also find it helpful to write your answers in your journal.

- What is inspiring you to do a ritual to help end your relationship?
- In the context of your process of separation or divorce, how do you want the ritual to serve as a transition between your former life to a new life?
- Who will be involved in the ritual and how do you anticipate it will affect them? Benefit them?
- When you imagine yourself two years from now looking back, what do you hope this ritual will have accomplished? What feeling or mood will you have created? What healing will you have promoted?
- Given where you are in your process of separation or divorce, is the aim of the ritual you have in mind realistic? If not, is it possible to limit your objective for this ritual and do another ritual later?

Either together or individually, we suggest each of you next write out your intention to see if it's clear and if you agree. You might try completing the sentence: "My intention for this ceremony of parting is...."

If your intention still seems vague, or if you have disagreements that would interfere with the creation of the ceremony, you may want to spend more time clarifying. But the goal is not perfection. Given the tumult of emotions you're feeling, it may not be possible to get perfect clarity and agreement about what you're trying to accomplish. It's also possible that, as Colette and Lea describe in their stories, your intentions may change through time.

Also, another word here about the concept of closure. People often say, "I want to bring closure to the relationship." As Rabbi Grollman pointed out, this word has a connotation of finality that may raise false hopes and expectations. Although using ritual can be a symbolic and conscious way to separate one time of life from another, you can't bring closure to memories and feelings. After every ritual or ceremony you'll still remember your former relationship, your ex-partner and the life you shared. But a ceremony can help transform *how* you remember. It can help you anticipate and live into the future with understanding, compassion, empathy, equanimity, generosity and a forgiving heart.

Recommendations

1. With your partner or a friend (or by yourself), consider why you want to do a parting ceremony. Ask and answer the questions that will help focus and clarify your intention: What do you hope the ceremony will accomplish? Looking back two years from now, what do you hope the result with be — for you? your ex? your children, your family and friends?
2. Write your intention. Try completing the sentence: "My intention for this parting ceremony is ...." If the intention isn't clear, if it seems too large in scope, or if there's disagreement, give yourself more time for further consideration and discussion. Wait a few days, or weeks, or even longer. There's no hurry. Remember, how you do this is as important as what you do, and a lot more important than when you do it. Get quiet and try again. Keep trying — slowly. Be compassionate with yourself. It will come.

Right Timing

What's the "right" time for a parting ceremony? Anne Winther-Rasmussen (1998) did a review of the literature on divorce rituals for her master's thesis, "Divorce Ritual: Your Personal Guide to a Healthy Closure to Your Marriage." She concluded that there is no strong evidence that a divorce ritual benefits from being performed on some specific date. Some writers she reviewed insisted that a period of preparation is required, preferably with professional help, before a couple or an individual is ready to create and perform a divorce ceremony. Others suggested that a couple should deal with "all essential issues" before contemplating a ceremony. Another was convinced that any ritual should occur in three phases, corresponding to stages of the process of separation and divorce. And yet another recommended a "disengagement" period prior to any divorce ritual, similar to the "engagement" period prior to a marriage.

We mention these different viewpoints just to give you an idea of the range of opinion on this subject. As far as we can tell, however, all opinions were written by therapists who had not themselves actually created or performed a ceremony. Please don't misunderstand. We have the greatest respect for therapists — Barbara is a therapist herself. Yet, a review of these articles reveals them to be long on theory and short on practice. Although we incorporate such theory, we base our discussion of timing more on the actual experience of people who have created, performed or facilitated such rituals. This includes Ms. Winther-Rasmussen (see Anne's Story) and several ministers and rabbis.

Many experienced people stress "emotional readiness" as the most important criterion for planning and performing a ritual. When are you emotionally ready? Well, no matter how much you may want to do a parting ceremony, if you're living mostly in "crazy time" with its extreme emotions, particularly anger, perhaps it's best to wait until things calm down. This is especially true if you want to include your partner and your children. But even if you prepare and perform the ceremony for yourself, by yourself, you will still want to give yourself the gifts of time and compassion. Hence, what you create will arise from reflection and deep feeling rather than any passions of the moment. Remember, make haste slowly; there's no hurry.

You may find it helpful to ask yourself questions. Can you face your feelings of loss? Can you move beyond blame and guilt, taking some responsibility for your part in the end of the relationship? Are you able to put yourself in your partner's place and experience the parting, even if just for a moment, from another point of view? This is empathy, and with it will flow other signs of readiness including an ability to step back now and again to see, as Wall and Ferguson (1998) put it, "through the eyes of forgiveness and conciliation."

We believe you are ready to undertake a parting ceremony in service of a healing divorce when you have achieved a perspective that allows you, at least sometimes, to appreciate the good as well as the bad in your former relationship. When you begin to anticipate that better times lie ahead, you're ready. Also, remember that your feelings will change continually, so there's no need for perfection. If you wait until your feelings are completely stable, you'll die before you ever get around to a ceremony and the healing that can flow from it — including the equanimity you seek.

The timing of a ceremony may also depend on the symbolic intent you wish it to serve. Keep in mind that the goal is to bring healing to the end of your relationship and help you make the transition to a new way of life. To these ends, we suggest three possibilities for the timing of a parting ritual. Each has its advantages and disadvantages.

A ceremony of parting can be used

- Prior to a legal divorce. In this sense, it's like a divorce without the lawyers and the paperwork. Even if you're a Christian, it can work more like a Jewish *get*.
- At the time of a legal divorce. In this sense, it's roughly analogous to a funeral just after a death.
- As a transition after a divorce, to symbolize the change from being married to being single. In this sense, it's like a memorial service held some time after a death and funeral.

Let's consider each of these options.

95

Ritual Prior To A Legal Divorce

This was the timing we chose. We wanted our parting ceremony to represent an emotional and spiritual divorce that would supersede (in actuality, by two years) the impersonal, formalized courtroom ritual involved in a legal divorce. In some ways, Colette's initial dance ritual was similar in intent and effect, as was the ceremony that Lea and David performed and the ritual Jim created with his congregation.

Advantages

- Using a parting ritual in this way allows the partners to focus on what they believe are the most important aspects of parting — spirit, feelings and people — rather than waiting on the cold and often adversarial legal process.
- The ritual process provides a container for many powerful and difficult feelings that often, in the usual circumstances of divorce and separation, go destructively out of control.

  If you agree on the need to part, the very process of planning a parting ritual offers an opportunity to create something important and healing for all parties that renders the legal proceedings all but moot. But even if you merely recognize the parting as inevitable and wish to make your actions as conscious as possible, planning for the ritual can still be a healing experience. Part of this planning might be consultation with a mediator about practical issues of money and custody, as well as sessions with a spiritual adviser about how to integrate a ceremony into both of your lives. This may not be easy, coming as it does near the "crazy time" of separation. It wasn't for us. On the other hand, this choice of timing can compel couples to struggle with issues that many do their best to ignore or avoid, fearing it will just cause conflict or pain. If you and your partner can work with your polarized and fluctuating feelings, planning in a cooperative way can lead to a ritual that creates harmony and promotes healing.

Disadvantages

- Sooner is harder. Using the parting ceremony in this way can be difficult because of "crazy time" feelings of hurt, anger and ambivalence.
- Using the parting ceremony as an emotional divorce can discourage the full experience and expression of some powerful feelings.

As we discussed and planned our parting ceremony, we experienced a lot of grief. The tenor of that grief was somewhat different for each of us — one of us was leaving and the other one felt left. Still, we grieved and wept together, and even raged. By the day of the parting ceremony, we were convinced we had felt all the feelings that mattered and were both clear and ready to go on.

We were wrong.

We failed to consider that our heartfelt desire to transition from marriage to friendship had caused us to suppress some feelings of fear, jealousy and anger. These feelings suddenly erupted the day after the parting ceremony. Even with a clear agreement that the parting ceremony symbolizes the end of the marriage, emotionally it may not work out that way. Despite your best intentions — or, perhaps, because of them — you may carry a lot more emotional baggage than you realize. In your eagerness to remain friends, don't let emotions denied become unconscious shadows that can erupt and cause havoc. In our case, this meant that we ended up having a lot more to forgive.

Ritual At The Time Of A Legal Divorce

Some people have used ritual at the time of their legal divorce. The most dramatic of these was Carolyn's, in which her husband was invited to participate on the morning of the final court proceedings. But Scott's ceremony took place only a few days after his divorce, and Anne as well as Matthew and Anne actually planned their rituals for the day of their legal divorce. Anne Winther-Rassmussen personally believes that if there's been enough work done in the separation period, it is more powerful and effective to do the divorce ritual on the legal divorce date. This means that one or, preferably, both partners have taken the time to work with their feelings to a point where they are emotionally ready.

Advantages

- A parting ceremony can bring heart and soul to what is usually a cold, routine, dehumanizing courtroom ritual. Taking place at or near the time of the legal divorce, if the partners can agree and cooperate, it offers healing that won't be found in court.
- Because some time usually elapses between the partners' separation and their actual divorce, this gives everyone an opportunity to cool off, gain some perspective and work out practical issues before the ceremony.

  The delay between the decision to part and the legal divorce allows both partners to work through "crazy time" feelings and develop some empathy for each other. This contributes positively to the planning and performance of a ceremony and to its potential for healing. Once a legal agreement is in place, a ceremony tends to soften any hard feelings involved by reminding both partners (and others, especially children) that there was more to the relationship than disagreements and fighting.

Disadvantages

- The separation and divorce may be too contentious for partners to contemplate a ceremony, much less plan anything together.
- Even if the separation has been amicable, the actual divorce may reignite difficult feelings, making it harder for the partners to cooperate.

   It's unreasonable to expect that difficult feelings will magically disappear. It would be unhealthy if they did. Nevertheless, as David observes in his story, the parting ritual is not a time to vent anger or jealousy. If it isn't possible to mutually focus on shared remembering in the context of truth, love, care and forgiveness, one partner (or both, individually) might better plan and carry out a ritual alone or with a few family and friends.

- One partner may simply refuse to participate.

   In a situation like this, as Colette and Kurt note, focus on your own inner process, trusting that such a ritual, if offered from an open heart, ultimately will have a healing effect on you, your partner and your children.

Ritual Following A Legal Divorce

Many people, we found, waited until some time after the legal divorce to plan and carry out a ritual of conscious parting.

Advantage

- Waiting awhile to do a ritual offers partners the opportunity to work through many difficult feelings and increases the likelihood that they will bring perspective, empathy and forgiveness to the creation of a ceremony.

   Time heals. As the intensity of feeling diminishes, the entire process is less burdened with anger, jealousy and guilt. Cooperation between you and your partner is more likely, as well as creative and rewarding. Time can also be a friend if you are creating and performing the ritual by yourself. For example, Margaret took a year and a half to work through her feelings of anger and betrayal and bring more perspective to a painful part of her life.

Disadvantages

- You may be reluctant to stir up difficult feelings again.

  It is well known that even if legalities follow a long separation, the actual divorce stirs up unresolved feelings — and there will always be unresolved feelings. Partners can actually wait too long for their ritual, even when it offers the promise of further healing and closure (see Gene H.'s remembrance in Chapter 9).
- Partners may be involved in other relationships or otherwise unavailable.

  People go on with their lives. Partners may have moved, or be with a new partner who is resistant to the idea of any further involvement with the ex, even if it's intended to bring healing.

Hindsight is always twenty-twenty. However, looking back on our own experience, and reflecting on the experience of others, we probably chose the most difficult of the first three options. Sooner is harder and more painful. On the other hand, too long a delay may diminish feeling (or contribute to repression) and seem to render a ceremony irrelevant. We emphasize "seem"; no parting ceremony or ritual is ever irrelevant or too late. But we believe if we had to do it again, we would take more time to plan and perform our ceremony at the time of our legal divorce.

No matter which option you choose, success will depend on your ability to work with feelings — work *with* them, not set

100

them aside. Denial and suppression of feeling will hinder healing and hamper planning for a parting ritual. This is true whether you act with your partner or by yourself. Even the intention to do a ritual can have a positive effect and make the process of parting easier. Why? Because setting a sincere intent encourages one to confront difficult feelings and take responsibility in the service of healing and growth. As part of this process, you may benefit from counseling with professional or spiritual helpers, or participating in any one of a number of excellent divorce recovery programs.

A Second Ritual

There is one more model for how to use a parting ceremony as a transition that we think may prove the most realistic and effective for many people.

No matter when you decide to do your ritual, consider a second ceremony sometime later. In the end, we did this. So did Lea and Colette. As David and Colette note in their stories, the process of grieving and letting go isn't linear. As you come "full spiral" through the experience, circumstances and feelings change. The same ceremony that was appropriate and effective at one time can feel incomplete later.

Think of this process as a vision quest, if you will. A person who is uninitiated leaves all that is familiar, wanders for a time seeking a vision of what his life could be and then returns to live that new reality. On the one year anniversary of this creative experience, the quester revisits the same place and reflects on the changes in her being and her life. Perhaps, if she feels called to do so, she performs a second ceremony to mark that memorable transition.

The parallels with separation and divorce are obvious and striking. Every divorced person reflects later on how tumultuous and confusing the early stages of the process were, and how unsettled and out of control they felt. The emotional turmoil and polarization of the situation was as if they were undergoing a trial in an unfamiliar wilderness. Later, they often regretted what they said or did — or did not say or do. They may have bungled

101

an early attempt at conscious parting and a healing divorce. It's never too late. A second ceremony offers another chance for reflection, amends and forgiveness.

Jean Houston (1998) observes:

> The lovely thing about ritual is that it's an open door and is always there. In many situations people do fail, maybe in more than not. But they come back until they get the vision. They stay with it until something happens. The point is not failure; it's sticking to it — that is what ritual is all about. . . . (p.25)

Recommendations

1. Honestly assess your emotional readiness to prepare and perform a parting ceremony, either with your partner or by yourself. If you don't know if you're ready, ask your friends or consult with a professional helper or a spiritual adviser.
2. Ask yourself what symbolic purpose such a ceremony might serve?
3. Is it possible to work cooperatively with your partner, performing the ceremony without rancor or vindictiveness in a way that will help heal the hearts of everyone involved? The quality of the experience is far more important than how quickly you do it — emphasize how you work with the process rather than what you ultimately create.
4. If your partner is unavailable or unwilling, choose the timing that feels best for you and for your children.
5. Consider parting as a vision quest. Give yourself permission to say things later that you cannot or forget to say now.

Practical Matters

As with a wedding or a funeral, there are always choices to be made that will affect the ceremonial process.

Where? Sacred Space

An appropriate setting for your parting ceremony will contribute to the ritual's healing power. Some people believe the event should be on neutral ground; not, for example, in the home you once shared or in a place associated with other relationships. We agree, although you'll find successful exceptions in the stories of Marcy and Lea and David. But whether you are doing your ceremony with your partner or alone, we think that the most important consideration has to do with the creation of a sacred space that will help you manifest your intention. That is, through your intention and action, any space can become a hallowed container for your ceremony. It can be a church, the beach, a park, a friend's home — it really doesn't matter as long as the setting speaks to you symbolically. Do what you can to consecrate it through acts such as prayer, blessing, ritual cleansing (as with sage) and perhaps decoration.

Carolyn, you may remember, invited her husband to join her in the park gazebo where they had been married. She made this space sacred by prayer, cleansing and creating an altar.

Scott chose a chapel in the church where he and his wife had been married.

Jessie burned her fire on a ceremonial plateau.

Lea and David used a room where they had spent intimate, sacred time, and they lit candles and burned sage.

Nancy went to her home church.

Margaret chose a familiar chapel.

Anne picked a place in nature that had special meaning and sacralized the space with drums, chanting and fire.

Kurt and Matthew and Anne used the home of a friend, and Marcy used her own home, all made sacred by symbolic objects and the presence of a minister or rabbi.

Colette chose a space made sacred by hours of dance as a form of meditation and prayer, and by the energies of like-minded women.

Jim and his congregation used a part of the temple they had long shared.

We chose to perform our ceremony in a place that held sacred symbolic meaning for us both, a meditation hall at a retreat center where we had participated together as part of a spiritual group. The hall itself had been imbued with the spirit of peace through countless hours of prayer and meditation, and the grounds outside were lush with grass and the smell of flowers and oranges. We decorated the space with one simple arrangement of flowers (brought by a friend) and two candles, and we arranged the space to serve the needs of our ceremony. Having made this choice, we felt supported by what became, for us, a consecrated sacred space.

Recommendations

1. Whether alone or with your partner, choose carefully where you will do your ceremony, with special attention to its emotional and symbolic importance and how you will be able to sacralize the space.
2. If you have no place with emotional or symbolic meaning, choose a place that is neutral and supportive. Sacralize the space.

When? Sacred Time

As far as season, day or time of day is concerned, it really doesn't matter when you perform your ceremony, as long as the time you set aside is exclusive, free of distraction and sufficient to do the inner and outer work that will fulfill your intention. Given the "crazy time" emotions and changes that accompany separation and divorce, setting aside exclusive time isn't always easy. This could prove a factor in the timing of your ceremony.

But no matter when you decide to do the ceremony, creating sacred time is important and will serve you in the end.

When you plan the time and date of your ceremony, try to avoid all conflicts. Of course, emergencies might arise, but don't fool yourself into thinking (or let someone else convince you) that something is an emergency when it is not. What would it have taken for you to postpone your wedding? Your parting ceremony is just as important.

From our experience, it is also important to set aside time for planning the ceremony. Planning will inevitably evoke a lot of emotion, and the more time you can allow yourself to work with these difficult feelings the better.

Carolyn used the quiet of the sunset hours alone at her gazebo in the park to feel her feelings, center herself and clarify her intention. She stayed up all night, when her children were in bed and she could be certain no one would interrupt her creative process. The next day, she scheduled the ceremony before the awakening of the workday world so she could be reasonably certain of privacy.

Scott spent weeks working on his ceremony with the help of friends and a minister and conducted a sacred service at a special time. So did Margaret, Nancy, Jim, Kurt, Marcy and Matthew and Anne.

Jessie also set aside a special, uninterrupted time for her fire ritual.

Lea and David set aside an evening for their ceremony.

Colette chose a time when she would be with other women who could bear witness to her ritual of dance.

We devoted quite a bit of time to planning over the course of more than a month. The time we shared together allowed us to review and reminisce about the best of our relationship, and to begin to grieve our loss. We also set aside exclusive time to perform the ceremony — two evening hours during a weekend meeting of our spiritual group.

Recommendations

1. Set aside and protect a sacred time when you will be uninterrupted and free from distractions to perform your ceremony.
2. To the extent practical, also set aside and protect time to prepare your ceremony.

Witnesses

A ceremony of parting that includes family and friends will help other people avoid feeling like they must take sides in a separation or divorce. This encourages them to remain friends with both partners. More important, including witnesses will help facilitate your transition from one stage of life to another. As Wall and Ferguson (1998) point out:

> ...people [who do such a ritual] feel more committed to walking new paths in their lives when they share their intention with others. Making a divorce ritual communal, no matter how unusual to you now, is important, even if, in the end, you share it only with one person. What's more, the impact of that sharing isn't a one-way street. Witnessing this kind of event helps others acknowledge divorce as a part of life. And with that acknowledgement can come new perspectives for them, including an increased willingness and ability to relate openly and honestly to a couple after they split. (p.98)

Almost all of the parting ceremonies we've come across, even when done alone, have included at least one witness. Although a few were performed in the context of a spiritual group, such as a congregation, most were small affairs attended by only family and a few close friends.

Scott sent formal invitations to family and friends, as did Margaret, Anne and Matthew and Anne. Colette shared her

106

ceremony with members of her sacred dance circle and Nancy and Jim with the members of their home congregations. Jessie worked with a friend. Marcy's children were present at her ceremony, along with a rabbi. Only Lea and David and Carolyn chose to perform parting ceremonies privately, but Carolyn later included witnesses by sending copies of her remembrance collage to relatives and friends.

At first, we thought that our parting ceremony would be just between us. As we worked with our feelings, however, and thought about the meaning of such a ceremony, we decided that it was as important to have witnesses for this important life transition as it had been to have witnesses for our wedding and our ten-year renewal of vows.

Inviting witnesses might not be easy. It wasn't for us. Nobody likes to expose what is often judged as failure by the world, and we were no exception. Our ambivalence showed up as indecisiveness and delay in inviting family and friends. Unfortunately, by conducting the ceremony as quickly as we did, and in a remote location, we limited the opportunity for many people to attend. This we now regret. Because people we cared about would not be there, we made a videotape of the ceremony so that they could share the experience. If we had it to do over again, however, we would wait longer and include more people important to us.

Recommendations

1. Share your ceremony with at least one other person who can serve as a holy witness, hold the memory with you and help make the process more real.
2. Invite family and friends. But remember, this is a sacred occasion, not a social event.

Including The Children

We believe it is important for you to include your children in the process of conscious parting, and perhaps in the ritual itself. We discuss the details of their involvement in Chapter 6.

Music

In many parting ceremonies music plays an important role. Carolyn told us later that she used music played at her wedding. Scott's service included music selected for its spiritual content. So did Margaret's. The ritual Jim performed with his congregation included a song written especially for the occasion. Lea and David selected music that had been part of their relationship. Colette used an Indian lament with special meaning to express feelings of sorrow and loss. Kurt used songs that symbolized the changes in his marriage from his wedding to the moment of parting.

Music was an important part of the ceremonies celebrating our wedding and renewal of vows, so we wanted it to be part of our parting ceremony, too. It seemed like a good idea to choose songs from different times of our life together and include them in a videotape tribute to the relationship. For example, Elton John's "Your Song" had captured a certain feeling when we were first together and, years later, Journey's "I Want to Know What Love Is" had come to express our mutual frustration and desire to find a new way to relate. In the end, however, we used a piece of music for the tribute that we'd used for our wedding and renewal of vows, Bach's "Jesus, Joy of Man's Desiring." For the ceremony itself, we decided on two songs offered by a friend that we felt expressed our feelings of sadness, grief and hope about parting: "We Will Find a Way" from the soundtrack of the movie *Corrina, Corrina* and "You're a Part of Me, I'm a Part of You" from the soundtrack of the movie *Thelma and Louise*.

Recommendation

If you decide to use music, make selections that speak to you personally because they have played a part in your life together, express how you feel or symbolize something important to you.

Clothing

What you wear may seem unimportant, but your choice of clothing for the ritual will have an effect on how you feel and on the tone of the ceremony. Several people have told us that if you don't spend some time thinking about it, you may regret your choices later.

Carolyn selected a white linen dress which, she told us, symbolized for her a new life. The jewelery she chose symbolized the support of the women of her family.

Anne wore the dress she had worn when she proposed to her husband.

Lea and David wore clothes that they had worn during their time together.

Colette wore her Indian wedding dress.

We spent a surprising amount of energy trying to decide what to wear, mostly because we couldn't agree. At first, we considered wearing what we'd worn for both our wedding and our ten-year renewal of vows, but one of us didn't care for the symbolism of wearing the same clothes for parting as for a wedding. We then explored the possibility of combining wedding and other clothes, but that proved impractical. Then, after further reflection, one of us decided against any symbolic connection between our wedding and parting. We finally agreed to disagree, planning that each of us would wear what we felt was most appropriate. In the end, we both wore simple, casually elegant clothing that felt beautiful in a subdued way.

Recommendation

Choose clothing that feels suitable and comfortable. If it has a symbolic meaning for you, even better.

Lea and David's Story

Lea

I met David after he put an ad in the paper stating that he was looking for "an open hearted woman to teach me Tantra." A year before, I had ended a long marriage and after a year of grieving finally felt ready to put myself back into the world. David was not looking for a relationship and, at that point, neither was I. I offered to be David's "Firewoman" as I had considerable experience with Tantra and was excited about getting to teach it. Despite the fact that I am more than 20 years older that he is, we found a great deal of compatibility, and the sexuality and spiritual connection was intense. After several months practicing Tantra, the relationship transitioned from one of student-teacher into lovers and Tantric partners. By that time, I was thoroughly in love with him. He continued to say that for him this was a transition and learning relationship; although he loved and cared for me, he did not consider me a candidate for a permanent life partner. After six months, although he did not want to end the relationship, David was ready to date again and try out with other women what he had learned with me. In spite of all evidence to the contrary, part of me was fantasizing that the relationship would be more than it was. As much as I had wanted a full relationship with David, I had to accept that it wasn't going to be. I knew that because an enormous amount of my energy was tied up with him, little was left to attract the full and complete relationship that I wanted in my life. We agreed to end the relationship so we could both move on with our lives. To bring closure to what we'd shared, we decided to do what we called a Celebration Ceremony to honor what we had brought to each other.

We met on a Sunday evening. First, we smudged each other with sage, asking that our intention be pure and clear. We entered the healing room (a special room in my home), lit candles and asked blessings from the Divine for what we were

111

about to do. We sat facing each other on a futon. We each centered ourselves and then extended our energy fields to include the other. We meditated using a favorite piece of music. We performed a blessing; each of us placed a hand on the other's heart and asked that we be present and speak the truth of our hearts. For the next two hours we reviewed our entire relationship, starting with the ad in the paper. We each talked about all the little things that we remembered — the funny times, the griefs, the joys, the surprises, the fears, the moments of insight and inspiration. We said all the things that we'd been afraid to say, asked all the questions we'd been afraid to ask and told each other what we'd learned in the relationship. David had learned a new confidence in himself as a man and as a sexual being. I had learned that I could open my heart and love again. We then sat facing each other, hands on each other's heart, gave thanks and offered a prayer. We asked that we take the love between us and what we had learned into the world to share with others, and that our work together be dedicated to the healing of the world and the healing of the relationships between men and women. After the ceremony, I felt very clear and proud that we had concluded the relationship with such consciousness and clarity.

Two months later David got married. Even though we'd ended the relationship, this came as a shock; I felt an enormous amount of grief and found myself missing him terribly. I decided that I needed to do an additional ceremony for myself, to let go more completely. For this ceremony, I wrote a letter to David, one I knew I would not send, thanking him for his presence in my life and letting him go. I wrote out a poem that meant something special because it expressed my feelings of grief and my hope for change, to give myself courage in this place of emptiness and waiting.

With the help of some local balloon specialists, I put the letter, the poem and David's picture into a helium balloon — a green balloon, the color of the heart chakra. It had been my intention to use only one balloon, but to provide enough lift, I attached two other balloons — a green one for the heart chakra and a silver one on which a cartoon figure said, "You'll be

112

missed." I cut a picture of David and myself in half, attaching each piece to one of the green balloon strings.

I took the balloons to the beach along with a silver chain — which symbolized my continued attachment to David and longing for what might have been — and a stone I'd found that was the color of his eyes. Out on a rocky point, with the waves crashing all around, I said a prayer for my release and cut the balloons loose, watching them rise into the sky until they disappeared. This symbolized letting go of all my wishes that things with David could be different, as well as an acceptance that what had happened was for my highest good. I used balloons instead of burying the letter, poem and pictures in the ground, which had been my other impulse, because I liked the idea that the balloons would come down in some unknown and unexpected place — like life. I then cut the silver chain in half and tossed the two pieces and the precious stone into the sea, asking that I release all the attachment and longing for things to be other than they were. I asked for a blessing on each of us and for the grace to let go of him completely, and that only the learnings and blessings of the relationship remain. And again, I gave thanks for knowing that I could open my heart and love again.

While I still feel some grief, I also feel an immense gratitude for my time with David. This second ceremony made a real difference in my ability to go forward with trust that I will find what I am looking for in this life.

David

I met Lea through a personals ad I put in the paper. Before I met Lea, I'd always wanted to study Tantra but couldn't find a partner. I just decided, well, I'll put out exactly what I want and see what the Universe brings me, and when Lea called with a long list of qualifications I thought, "Wow, I really hit the jackpot!"

We met and decided that it was OK to practice Tantra with each other. And so we did — for a while. And then, as much as I was only looking for a teacher-student relationship, it became a lot more than that. And the relationship felt very good and it felt very appropriate and wonderful. I feel like I grew a lot from everything that we learned and did together. And even though for me it wasn't a romantic relationship, I could definitely feel that my experience with Lea — all the loving and healing we shared — had prepared me to go back out into the world and be someone's romantic partner in a much stronger way. Which doesn't mean it was necessarily easy. There was a lot to miss.

And so we did our Closing Ceremony. Lea actually brought up the idea of doing the ceremony. But even before she did, I was thinking of it, too — that we should ceremonially honor the change. I prefer to look back and really honor what's gone on — where we've come from and where we are. That feels a lot cleaner to me than just letting things end. You have to honor the feelings and if you don't, I think that instead of feeling the sadness of parting, you can feel hurt and abandoned. Doing a ceremony, I think, helps prevent that, because you are honoring not just what the two of you were together, but who you each are now.

In terms of the timing of the ceremony, Lea had a very strong sense that I was about to be in a full blown relationship with a person I had met. It seemed important to do a ceremonial ending before it got all blurred — to try to do it as energetically cleanly as possible and not confuse our lives. I think it is really easy for me to fool myself — I want this and that — to think, well, I can have them both.

It was important that we did the ceremony within a couple of days after the decision to end the particular form of our relationship. Sun Tzu said, "The first one to the battlefield usually wins." If you make the decision first, that is probably better than just letting something happen to you. And in this case, and I think in relationships generally, it is important to go where your heart is — with what you know to be true — and then to officially recognize it, ceremonially if possible, for both people's clarity, for everybody's well-being. It doesn't mean that it won't be really hard. But the relationship deserves it.

The ceremony was private — just Lea and me. We didn't have a common community that we interacted with together. So it didn't need to be public. It felt good that it was just her and me. It took place in her healing room, a sacred space in her home. It felt important to go back to the place where we had begun — to recognize the full circle of the beginning and ending. Although it didn't just come full circle. It came up and around. It didn't close back in on itself. It came full spiral.

I didn't really plan for the ceremony because when I try to plan things, I feel like it comes out scripted. I feel like I am not at my best then. It was important for me to be able to tell my story. I love storytelling. That works for me. But I had no idea what I was going to say. Everything that needed to come out, came out. I guess you could say it was spontaneous within a framework. I was pretty clear within myself. When we did the ritual, I saw it as the changing of one state to another. For me it was, "Now, here is my friend Lea." Not, "I'll never see her again and it is good-bye forever." Every time I thought about it, I always imagined that we'd still know each other, still have some sort of relationship. That's what I was thinking. It's also what I wanted when I was thinking of an ending ritual. Not an end. Just a change. It's just a change of one way of relating to another. The deeper love doesn't end.

We meditated first and got centered in ourselves and connected energetically. That was very important for me because I know sometimes if I am not really centered, I'm not really sure what I want to say or even what I feel.

115

I remember that we sat for a while face to face, cross-legged, palms out and holding hands. We did some breathing together. And we stated some intentions. That was also a habit of ours, to state an intention. That helps because I can have trouble talking and revealing what I really want to say because I'm afraid that what I have to say may be hurtful. So stating an intention was helpful: "My intention is to be clear and honest." We shared our appreciation, too — the things we appreciated about each other and what we'd learned and the growth that we'd both gone through.

Then we began the storytelling. We changed positions. I was lying down on my back — I think we were both lying down head to head with feet in opposite directions with our heads next to each other. I found that to be really comforting. Because I couldn't see Lea — it was dark, except for the candles — I felt like I didn't have to screen anything out. I couldn't see her reaction so I could just say anything. And I knew she could hear me because her ear was right next to my mouth. And it was comfortable lying down.

I told the story of my experience and then she told the story of her experience, right from the ad in the paper. That was really good. I liked telling the story from both of our perspectives. And it was done in such a way that both our truths were recognized. I could speak what was true for me even though our stories may have contradicted each other in certain places. I said, "This is what I wanted, this is what I did, this is what happened, this is the journey I went on with you and then here we are today." And then she told me her story — all the highs and lows and all the joys. And then, of course, whatever begins, ends. And there we were. And we shared our feelings about ending and we talked about the future, what we each wanted for ourselves. I wanted to take what we had learned and who I had grown to be and bring that to a more romantic partnership that could possibly lead to marriage. And ironically, it did. I felt like everything we had gone through had prepared me for the next stage of my life.

It was a very profound experience being with Lea. I had no fear. We told our stories, talked about our hopes for the future and then sat up and did our ritual blessing and just sat in the silence with each other for a little while.

Immediately afterwards, there was some sadness because the ceremony had really honored the process we'd gone through and the great experiences we'd had together, experiences that weren't going to be happening anymore. It made the transition really conscious. It made me aware that my path was calling me in a new direction and that I was honoring that calling. Over time, I think the effect of having done the ceremony has been the same. But I don't carry the sadness as much now. I have so many great memories of things that we did and the great experiences we shared. There is still a little sadness at the loss of that, but I am sure that I couldn't have what I have now if I hadn't had those experiences with Lea. When you do a ritual, you are committing to a course of action. Once you state that intention publicly, or even privately with another person, there is no turning back. The ritual helped me process that sadness and speeded the transition.

I've had some other thoughts since about the ritual....

A closing ritual is not a place to bring out your gripes or get in a last jab. It is a place to honor what you brought to each other and what you learned. No matter what happened, I think it is important to honor relationships without blaming the other person for anything and being willing to take responsibility for what happened. You were a part of it. You called it to you in some way. You have to be willing to say, I was attracted to you. It didn't last or it changed and I'm sorry for that — or I'm not sorry for that. You have to take responsibility for yourself and not blame or belittle the other person. The ritual space is not a place to take out your anger on someone or to try to cut them down. No matter how the relationship came about, I think it is important to honor that there was a larger reason for your coming together — even if you can't see it at that point. And to acknowledge that there were good times during the relationship and reasons why it lasted as long as it did.

117

Also, I think it's important to make a ritual personal. A lot of people don't have a sense of what to do for a ceremony. We do have certain ceremonies — weddings and funerals, for example — but other than that, most people don't have much experience with ceremonies. Especially how to create one. Find out what is important to you, what you want to convey, and think about how that might work for you. I'd say even write it down over and over again — so you can clarify and modify your general ideas. And if something particularly works for you — like for me, storytelling; I like to tell stories— it is important to include that.

Before doing a ceremony, I think it is really important for each person to go into his or her own sacred space and get as clear as possible about what they are feeling and what is actually happening. Without this, I can see how someone could come to the ritual and say things as a means of trying to hold on to what is ending — maybe even as a last ditch effort to get their partner not to leave and to try to save the relationship. "This is such a great thing. Why are we doing this?" Before the ceremony, you have to get clear that this is a closing ceremony, an ending. Feelings are going to come up about that. Some people are going to be sad. Some people are going to be frustrated and angry. Some are going to be fearful. Others may be happy. Some may even be indifferent. That's why it is important to come to the sacred space of the ritual as clearly and cleanly as possible. You are literally going there for a death. Something has died. And that's OK, because something is being born, too. If you can be clean and clear enough, you can take all those experiences you shared and use them for your growth, rather than seeing the relationship as a failure or using its ending to justify your own fears — you know, "all men are like that; you can't trust women."

Be as clear and responsible as you can about your motivations. Are you blaming your partner? Are you still holding on? Then take all the good things — the things you learned and how you grew — and honor them and be grateful.

Who knows, maybe you did something differently in this relationship than you did in other past relationships and it worked out better — or worse. But at least you tried. Tell yourself, "I grew in this relationship. I learned how to fight fair in this relationship. I learned how to express my wants and my desires in this relationship. I learned to risk telling the truth of my feelings in this relationship. I learned how to speak up for what I need in this relationship." But first, do your own work in your own sacred space and be clear before you get to the mutual sacred space of the ritual. Honor yourself as the full and complete human being that you are and bring that fullness to the ritual — not only for your partner's sake but also for your own sake — so you can be there with clarity and integrity and move on.

Be comfortable. I really like the idea of lying down head to head, both on your backs, so your heads are next to each other. Because, for me, that takes away a lot of fear of how the other person might respond. And you know that they can hear you because they are right there.

Let each other speak without interruption. There should be an understanding that each person is speaking his or her truth — their own story. The stories may be completely different, but that doesn't matter. That's not the point. The point is to honor what went on and to consciously bring the relationship to an end so you don't need to carry it around for the rest of your life.

For me, ceremonial endings are a way of marking time and events and transitions in my life. The whole ritual space for me — particularly because I like storytelling — is a time and a place to say, "This is where I've come from and this is where I am now." Or, if you're married, "This is where we've come from, this is where we are now." Life gets so busy that you can forget each other, not intentionally but just because that's the way life is. I think it's really important to honor where you've been together. I imagine doing rituals in my marriage every so often. My wife and I have talked about renewing our vows every five years. But outside of that, I'd like to sit down with her from time to time and tell the story of us from the last time we talked about this until now. To see what we've gone through and to look back on this time and laugh. I think ritual will always be important in my relationships now, even if it's just to recognize how they evolve.

119

In the end, for me ritual is about sacrifice. It's about being willing to give up something to come into a new place — even give up that one thing that you think that you can't live without. Having the courage to part even with that and doing so consciously, using ritual for an ending, helps you grow and honor who you've been, who you are now and who you are becoming. You can see the sacrifice as going through Hell or you can see it as surrendering. You have to give up something that you really don't want to give up and let the angels take away what is no longer for your highest good, to make room for what is coming next.

5

Performing the Ritual of Parting

Before You Begin

Now that you have completed your preparations, it's time to consider how you'll actually perform your ritual. This includes the content of the ritual itself — what you want to say and do, what symbols and symbolic acts you choose to manifest your intention(s) — as well as how you want to present this to the world. Remember, ritual is an art that rewards forethought yet also invites spontaneity.

All of the stories in this book describe the emotional context of a parting ceremony. We believe that these stories, as well as the ceremonies in Chapter 11, will prove helpful to you as inspiration and guidance. However, at this point we suggest that you put them aside. For now, it's important that you allow the creation of your ceremony to flow from within you — your heart, your mind, your soul.

As you read what follows, we suggest that you imagine yourself actually performing a ritual. To set the emotional scene, it may help to remember what it felt like just before your wedding. Certainly, many of the feelings will be different. That was the beginning of your marriage and now you are about to perform a ceremony that will mark the end. Then, there was the joy of anticipation. Now, anticipation is probably tempered by sorrow and, perhaps, relief. But in a larger sense, both ceremonies are a portal from one way of life to another. Each marks both an ending and a beginning. It may surprise you to discover that some of your feelings are similar.

Are you nervous? We were. We were also busy right to the last moment. Unlike a wedding, there was no one else to handle details (where to place the flowers) and last minute glitches (does the video camera have a good angle?). While several friends and retreat center staff did their best to help, we would ask for assistance sooner if we had it to do again, so that we could better concentrate on the emotional and spiritual essence of the experience.

As we made our final preparations, we felt a mixture of sadness and excitement. We took a couple of private minutes together, grieving our parting and also feeling pride and joy that we had successfully worked together to create a ceremony honoring the best we had shared. Before the ceremony, we held hands, sat for a few minutes in silence and prayed that our parting would be for our highest good. Then we took our places in two chairs set slightly apart in the circle and waited for people to gather.

Recommendations

1. Do your best to take care of all the logistical details beforehand so that you can concentrate on the emotional and spiritual significance of the ceremony before it begins. If your ritual is elaborate, with many witnesses, ask a trusted friend to handle the details.
2. Take time to be in silence before the ritual with your partner or by yourself. Breathe. Center.
3. Consider praying that the ritual and the parting be for the highest good of all concerned.

Speaking Your Intention, Invoking Sacred Energies

When preparing for your ritual, you did your best to come to a clear understanding of your intention: what inspired you to do a ritual; how you wanted the ritual to serve as a transition from your old life to a new one; who you wanted to be involved and why; and how a ritual would promote healing. As you actually begin your ceremony, it is important to speak these intentions. Doing this calls upon powers greater than yourselves and helps move you from the ordinary world into sacred space. As Beck and Metrick (1990) suggest in *The Art of Ritual*, "Though these energies may be called from within, as when connecting with the God of your heart, or your sense of spirit, they are transpersonal

122

rather than personal." Almost all examples of parting ceremonies we've come across make some gesture toward stating an intention and calling upon sacred energies, either by the ritual participants or by someone else.

Carolyn and her husband began their ceremony with silence and a prayer.

Scott's service, and Matthew and Anne's, began with a call to worship from the minister.

David and Lea meditated and centered themselves before they began.

Margaret's service began with an explanation and a call to silence. Kurt's, Jim's and Marcy's began in similar ways.

Anne's ceremony was preceded by a long walk up a mountain to the beat of drums.

Nancy's ceremony was preceded by part of a church service.

Colette passed by a "spiritual gatekeeper" to enter a sacred space created by other women.

For our ceremony, one of the leaders in our spiritual community spoke about our parting and its meaning in the context of community. We then began our ceremony with music and an attunement. All the members of our community held hands in prayerful silence until the first song ended. Following that, we each said a few words about how it came to be that we were there, and what we intended to do.

Recommendations

1. Call upon sacred energies to be with you in the ritual.
2. State your intention(s) for the parting ritual. If you have different intentions, acknowledge these.

Open, Honest, Transparent And Undefended

When you read our parting ceremony (see Chapter 11), you will see that we also set another intention: to be open, honest, transparent and undefended about who we were, what we had decided to do, and why. Conscious parting and a healing divorce ritual seem to call this forth.

In the context of their parting ceremony, Carolyn's husband felt called for the first time to take responsibility for his part of their break-up.

Lea and David made the intention to be honest during their ritual an explicit expectation.

Jessie wrote down and spoke the truths of her heart.

Kurt took some time in his ceremony to honestly express his anger and his pain.

Jim's ritual invited members of his congregation to express not only their positive feelings but also anything that had troubled them.

We set the intention to be open, honest, transparent and undefended because we believe that this is the most creative way to live. Sharing vulnerability and trust promotes love, unity and healing. We realize that living an open, honest, transparent and undefended life is an ideal most of us seldom realize. Vulnerability and trust are often two early casualties of divorce. However, we believe it is worth the attempt, and the risk. In our marriage, and in planning the parting ceremony, we did our (imperfect) best to tell each other the truths of our hearts, even when that was difficult and painful. We believe that sharing those truths during the ceremony and, later, through the video with friends and family, promoted love, unity and healing for them, too.

This is also why we chose to acknowledge Chris' involvement and the confusion it had brought to our process of parting. Her involvement was part of the truth of our experience, individually and together. Although we did not intend it to be the focus of our ceremony, to deny or ignore it seemed to us a capitulation to fear — mostly fear of others' judgements — as well as a prideful desire to pretend that ours was a "perfect" and "perfectly conscious" parting that would live up to some idealized image.

In a section of the ceremony, which we called "How This Parting Came To Be," we each described the personal process by which we had come to the decision to part with as much

124

openness and honesty as we could. This was not a tell-all or a confession. It was an explanation with discernment; we offered only those details that seemed relevant. We shared this process because we believe that parting, like marriage, is more than a personal act. Parting, whether separation or divorce, always involves a community of people — children, family, friends, and sometimes even strangers. Because of this, we felt an obligation to bear witness to our decision to part in the same way that we had borne witness to our decision years before to marry and, ten years later, to renew our vows.

Looking back, we're both aware that we weren't as clear as we thought we were at the time. Also, if we had it to do over again, we would have said and done some things differently. To some extent, this was the result of haste; trying to plan the ceremony before we'd had a chance to work with the full depth of our grief, jealousy and anger. On the other hand, we are writing here with the benefit of hindsight, which is notoriously twenty-twenty. Self-disclosure at any time is never easy, especially when it involves confessing failures, mistakes, shortcomings, regrets, confusion, grief and doubt — all emotions that are evoked by parting. We did the best we could. Given more time to reflect, could we have done better? Probably, and it still would have been painful and imperfect. No matter how painful it may have been in the moment, however, we still found that truth expressed in love was ultimately healing. That was our intention and that is what we tried our best to do when performing the ritual; to tell the truth of our hearts in the service of love.

But what if your partner wants nothing to do with being open, honest, transparent and undefended? That is certainly more difficult. It's scary to risk self-disclosure when it's not reciprocated. How many marriages have wrecked on the rocks of such distrust? Still, we encourage you to make the effort, for the good of your own heart and soul (this we guarantee) and also because if one partner is willing to take the risk, often the other partner may find the courage to do so, too. Naturally, this does not include circumstances when the revelations of your heart are met with ridicule or used to wound you. If that proves to be your

125

situation — and don't just assume that it is; how will you know if you don't try? — then it may be necessary to do as Colette, Jessie, Anne and Kurt did and work with this part of the ceremony in private or with family and friends.

Recommendations

1. Take the risk of being open, honest, transparent and undefended with yourself about the reasons for your parting. If you haven't done so already, use the exercises noted in Chapter 2 to take 100% of the responsibility for the break-up of your relationship. Write what you discover in your journal.
2. Take the first step. Offer to share your feelings and your own sense of responsibility with your partner *without* the expectation that he will reciprocate.
3. If you don't feel safe sharing with your partner, or if she is unwilling, find someone you trust. It's more important that you share than with whom.
4. When you perform your ceremony, if you decide to speak your truths, be as clear as you can and include what responsibility you believe you bear for the parting. Remember, it's your choice what to say in the ceremony. Honesty is important but so is discernment.

A Tribute To The Relationship

If you stop to think about it, there is probably more good than bad in your relationship, more that was loving than hurtful, more that was creative than destructive. Unfortunately, in a separation or divorce, most people tend to forget all that and focus on the negatives, because those are driving them crazy (and, they may believe, have driven them away). As we discussed in Chapter 2, focusing on the negatives during "crazy time" may help justify your decision to separate or divorce. But anger also enables you to deny your ambivalence or difficult

126

feelings of loss and grief. A tribute to the relationship you have shared can be a healing antidote to such negativity and denial.

Remember the photo collage and the handmade Book of Appreciations Carolyn made for her husband?

Lea and David spent several hours telling stories and remembering.

At their rabbi's request, Marcy and her husband wrote and then said several positive things about their marriage.

Another tribute included the invitations for reminiscence by others built into Kurt's and Jim's rituals.

When we decided that a tribute might be an important part of our parting ceremony, we thought at first we would each simply remember what we had loved, enjoyed and shared through the years, and then share these memories with each other. However, as our plans became more ambitious, we decided that some sort of photo tribute would more fully capture what feelings we were trying to express — love, appreciation and gratitude for the life we had lived together.

Like many people, we had taken lots of pictures and left most of them in boxes, promising ourselves that sooner or later they'd find their way into albums. We were not quite sure what kind of photo tribute to create, but we knew that the pictures we would need were in those boxes. That is where we began, sorting pictures — thousands of pictures. That is also when we began to understand the emotional relevance of what we were doing.

Every picture evoked a memory. Every memory evoked a story. Every story evoked a realization that our story as a married couple — all that we had shared — was coming to an end. The realization of that loss evoked new waves pain and grief. As we sorted, we wept, sometimes laughing through our tears. While we occasionally wondered if we were crazy to invite so much pain and grief, in the end we decided that what we were doing would ultimately be healing. Nobody ever died of too many tears. Many people, however, have made themselves sick unto death by choking down their feelings behind a stiff upper lip.

At first we thought we would make a photo album as a tribute to our marriage, just for us. Then we, like Carolyn, thought we would create some sort of collage. But there were too

127

many pictures we wanted to include. Finally, we decided to create a slide show. In the end, however, we realized that what we really desired was something beautiful as well as informative, so those who could not attend the ceremony could participate emotionally, too. That's when we came up with the idea of a video.

These days there are lots of small, independent companies that specialize in creating videos for special occasions (check your yellow pages). Usually, they shoot during the event and then edit the tape into final form. We hired a company called Video Memories to record the ceremony itself, but we also wanted something more unusual. Out of the 100 or so photographs we finally selected, we asked them to make a short film using a variety of techniques common in documentaries — pans, fades, dissolves — to suggest movement and add vitality. We could have made it any length but decided on ten minutes because of the cost, and because it would be just one part of the ritual. We made suggestions for refinements of the finished video until we felt it expressed the tribute we wanted to make to our relationship. We then had it set to music — Bach's "Jesus, Joy of Man's Desiring," the piece we had played at our wedding and when we renewed our vows.

There is no way to capture in words the power and effect of this video tribute. Even now, we cannot watch it without crying tears of joy and of sadness. One friend, who did not attend the ceremony but saw the video later, remarked that in a different context, the short film could have been in celebration of a 25th wedding anniversary instead of a joyful eulogy in a parting ceremony.

When working on the tribute to our relationship, we discovered something we hadn't anticipated: focusing on the positives of our relationship made us re-examine once again what we were doing. Given all that was good in our relationship, how was it that one of us had decided the time had come to part? At first, this gave us pause. But then we realized that what had happened was really another benefit of the process of conscious parting. By reviewing what was wonderful in our relationship, the tribute raised some doubt. And why not? If you're going to end a relationship, isn't it important to have a balanced view before you leave?

Recommendations

1. Take some quiet time alone to remember and write in your journal all the good and wonderful things about your relationship. If you get stuck, here's where some of the exercises recommended by other authors may prove helpful (see the Appendix). This will probably evoke a lot of sadness. That's all right; grieving is an important part of the process. The tears are cleansing.
2. From these memories, create a personal tribute to your relationship. This could be something you read, or a collage, or a video. However you choose to express your tribute, do your best to be specific. "You were a good father" is not a meaningful as "I'll always remember how you helped the kids with their homework and how you were willing to coach Jessica's soccer team even though you'd never played before."
3. Include the tribute as part of your ritual and share it with each other and with family and friends.

Letting Go Of The Past: Sharing Gratitude

As we created the video tribute, the process of sorting through old photographs and remembering good times reminded us again of how much we had to be grateful for in our marriage. Sometimes we valued the same thing — for example, the conception and birth of our son, Geoffrey, as well as the grief we shared at his early death. More often we were grateful for some of those little things that are personal in a marriage, things your partner may not even know you appreciate or has forgotten that you do.

Like many of the people who share their stories here, we wanted to set aside time to express our gratitude. Recall, for example, Carolyn's handmade Book of Appreciations and her husband's acknowledgement of her as the mother of their children. Think of Scott's Thoughts of Celebration and his silent Prayer of Thanks. Remember Lea and David's stories. Jim's ritual offered an opportunity for people to express their feelings of appreciation and to say what they would miss. Marcy and her husband expressed appreciation for what they had shared and Matthew and Anne and Kurt did something similar.

As we worked with this part of the ceremony, we realized that remembering and expressing gratitude for each other was another way of letting go of what we had shared. This felt important. Again, we found that the more specific we were, the more we felt — gratitude as well as grief — and the more it seemed we honored each other and the relationship we had shared. Letting go doesn't mean forgetting. Years later you may still feel grief, and certain memories may still have the power to move you to tears. That's all right. You still have to let go so that you can move on, nurture yourself and your children, and continue to grow.

Recommendations

1. Take some quiet time alone to reflect about what you're grateful for in your relationship. Write these reflections in your journal. Be specific; the power of the experience (and the memory) is contained in the sensory detail. The more detail you recall, the more you will feel — gratitude as well as grief.
2. If possible, share your reflections with your partner. If not, share them with a trusted friend or adviser.
3. Find a way to express gratitude and appreciation during your ceremony. This could be done with words, or it could be accomplished with some mutually understood private, symbolic act.

Releasing The Future

In a divorce — in a parting of any kind — it is not just the past we have to let go of, it's the future, too. All those dreams and plans we made — what becomes of them? Do they disappear? Wither away from neglect? Die with the relationship? This was the saddest and most difficult part of the ceremony for us. Even though letting go of the past was painful, we were left with our memories. But when we let go of the future, for a time all that remained was the Void. While we believe it is true that the Void ultimately can be a creative emptiness from which new life may be born, that is often cold comfort when you're walking through the icy Hell of separation and divorce.

As you let go of the past, so, too, you have to let go of your shared dreams for the future. Before you go on, feel the sorrow of lost opportunity. Grieve that although you may still do some of the things you had planned, it will no longer be together.

So important did it seem to us to let go of the future that we created a special ceremony within our ritual. Privately, we each wrote down all the things we would miss about each other and the relationship. Again, we were specific. During the ceremony, we shared what we had written with each other. Then, together, we burned the papers. By this act, we symbolized the release of our plans and dreams for our life together and our intention to transform the energy of what we would miss into energy to be used in the separate lives that lay ahead for both of us.

Others have used different symbolic acts to express letting go. Scott and Jessie also performed a burning. Anne buried a wedding necklace. Lea floated her dreams away with balloons and tossed a chain into the sea. Colette cast something precious into water.

Other acts of release might include tearing something (like a photograph) and scattering the pieces to the wind, or shredding, cutting, crumbling — any of these may serve you.

131

Recommendations

1. Take some quiet time alone to reflect on things you will miss about your partner, as well as plans and dreams that will never be realized together. Write these in your journal. Be specific.
2. If possible, share these with your partner. If not, share them with a trusted friend or adviser.
3. Read these to each other during your ritual.
4. Release your hopes and dreams in some symbolic way.

Forgiveness

Remember the movie *The Unforgiven*? A young kid who feels guilty because he's just killed a man justifies himself to Clint Eastwood: "He had it coming." And Clint replies in the way Clint has made famous: "We've all got it coming, kid."

In marriage and divorce — in life — we all have a lot to forgive and for which to be forgiven. Almost all of the parting ceremonies we have found include some words or acts of forgiveness.

As Rabbi Grollman observed, forgiving someone else is difficult, especially when you're caught up in tumultuous emotions such as jealousy and rage. As D. Patrick Miller (1995) said in one of our favorite books, *A Little Book of Forgiveness,*

> It might seem a lot easier to forgive someone if only he or she would show signs of changing. The paradox is that we are unlikely to see signs of change in others until we have forgiven them. This is true for two reasons: First, resentment is blinding. It limits our perception of what is real (or changing) in the present and shuts down our capacity to envision a happier future.
>
> Second, a subtle but crucial function of forgiveness is that it tacitly gives others permission to change. We are not nearly so separate from each other as we generally experience ourselves to be. We think that we

grow and change only within ourselves, but we also grow and change partly within others, and they within us. Some people may find very little space within themselves to change, and need others to let them into a psychic territory of forgiveness, where they can feel free to try a new way of being. (p.13)

Clearly, creating and performing a parting ceremony to help you end your relationship consciously is trying a new way of being. The ceremony offers an opportunity for forgiveness, and your forgiveness can offer your partner an opportunity to change.

Often, accepting forgiveness for the pain you have caused, and forgiving yourself, is even harder than forgiving your partner. Still, we all know from experience that anger — towards yourself as well as another — closes the heart and can end up turning it into stone. Without forgiveness, there is no way to let go of past hurts and resentments and no way to develop a new and healing relationship between divorcing partners that can soothe their wounded hearts and offer solace to each other and to their vulnerable children.

Letting go of resentment is one key to forgiveness. As Bill Ferguson (1990) reminds us:

Resentments are not the result of what happened; they are the result of how we handled what happened.

When we resent someone, we say very forcefully, that person is the cause, the problem and the fault. Not us!

To release a resentment you need to release your partner from all responsibility ....

Forgiveness is a choice, an act of commitment and declaration. "I'm angry, I'm hurt, but I forgive him." Forgiveness is an act of releasing.

You can forgive and still be angry. Anger is separate from resentment; resentment keeps the anger in place. Once you forgive, the anger quickly dissipates.

So forgive! Forgive just because you say so. (pp. 53-54)

133

The only change we'd make to Ferguson's excellent advice is to say, instead, "I'm angry, I'm hurt *and* I forgive him." Whatever follows the conjunction *but* negates the foregoing. It expresses a state of "either-or" rather than "both-and." What we believe Ferguson is saying here — and we agree — is that anger, hurt and forgiveness can co-exist. "You can forgive *and* still be angry." So when you mutter to yourself about your partner, using inclusive language will help guide your thoughts and feelings: "I'm angry, I'm hurt, *and* I forgive him."

Still not convinced? Perhaps you believe what you are doing is imperfect or hypocritical because you don't yet feel completely forgiving. Maybe it feels incomplete because you keep getting mad and have to work to forgive all over again. That's all right.

Forgiveness is often difficult — sometimes even too difficult. Take your time. We think Rabbi Grollman is right when he emphasizes the *intention* to forgive. In our experience, what's most important is that you be willing to forgive, and to keep on trying. We are great believers in the advice "fake it 'til you make it." A willingness to forgive can start the process, much as smiling even when you don't feel like it — especially when you don't feel like it — has the power to lighten your mood.

Even if you don't feel completely forgiving, acts of forgiveness as part of your parting ceremony can serve as a powerful statement of love and intention. It can also model behavior for everyone involved, especially (but by no means exclusively) for your children. But there's one caveat: when you offer your forgiveness it will be neither kind nor helpful to spell out in detail all the sins and transgressions included in the forgiveness. Your partner probably knows how you feel and already may feel a lot of shame and regret. Setting out to embarrass the other person would simply continue a destructive cycle of rage and recrimination, and that is the antithesis of forgiveness.

Remember, it is as important to accept forgiveness as it is to offer forgiveness. When you offer forgiveness you are giving a gift. But when you accept forgiveness you also give a gift — the equally valuable gift of receiving.

Recommendations

1. Take some quiet time alone and remember what your partner did that was hurtful or made you angry, or both. Write these things down. Be specific. Consider what you would like to forgive. Ask yourself, am I ready to forgive for this? If not, ask yourself, am I ready to *try* to forgive? If your honest answer is yes, you may be ready for a parting ceremony. If it's no, you may want to consider waiting longer to work with your anger and resentments.
2. Take some quiet time alone and remember what you did that was hurtful or made your partner angry. Write these things down. Be specific. Consider what you would like to be forgiven for. Ask yourself, am I ready to accept forgiveness? If your honest answer is yes, you may be ready for a parting ceremony. If it's no, consider waiting for a time to work with your resentments and your pride.
3. If possible, share with your partner what you've remembered. Do this without blame or invoking guilt. All you need to do is tell your truth, in private, and invite your partner to do the same. If this is not possible, share your truths with a trusted friend, a professional helper or a spiritual adviser.
4. Include statements of forgiveness in your parting ceremony. Perhaps you can also find a symbolic way to let go of resentment (see Kurt's story).

What About The Rings?

The wedding ring symbolizes enduring love. As we were planning our parting ceremony, we wanted to keep the rings that had been such an important symbol of our marriage and yet transform their meaning to support our new lives as separate

135

people. After some discussion, we finally decided that reversing the way rings are given in a wedding ceremony would have the most symbolic power. We each kept the other's ring for safekeeping and later, after the ceremony, placed the ring and a picture of our partner on our respective altars.

Carolyn and her husband also exchanged rings and returned them to their original boxes, which Carolyn then kept. Kurt saved his ring for his daughter. Matthew and Ann reconsecrated their rings to each other's freedom. Colette removed her ring during her ceremony and later left it in a sacred place.

Recommendations

1. Take some quiet time alone to consider what meaning your wedding ring has had in your life together. Is it just a piece of jewelry, or does it still have emotional and symbolic resonance for you?
2. If you want to keep your ring, consider if there is a way you could do this that would support your mutual (or individual) healing.
3. If you do not want to keep your ring, how might you symbolically let it go? Or, how might the ring be transformed to better serve you? (For example, melted down to create a new piece of jewelery from the precious metal.)

Vows and Commitments: An Intention For The Future

If you intend to end your relationship with truth, love, care and forgiveness, the close of the ceremony is a good place to restate that intention. One way to do this is to offer a vow.

Vows are the heart of a wedding ceremony. As we've seen, for many people breaking those vows is one of the hardest things about divorce. We believe that vows can also have an important place in a parting ceremony. They did in ours. We wished to release each other from our wedding vows, to create and express new vows for the future, as a commitment to our mutual love and support. As the ceremony came to a close, we each removed our ring and handed it to the other. As we each received the other's ring we said:

"I release you as my husband (wife) and will love you as my friend. I receive your ring and will hold it in my keeping as a symbol of my love and support for you on your soul's journey."

We then each made a new vow for ourselves, saying, "I commit to my heart, and with all my heart I will follow my soul's longing wherever it may lead and know that there is nothing to fear . . . even when I am afraid."

If we had it to do over again, there was another vow implicit in our ceremony that we would make explicit: a mutual promise to always hold in trust the intimate secrets of the other's heart.

Recommendations

1. Take some quiet time alone to consider what meaning your wedding vows have had in your life together. Write down what you discover.
2. If possible, share what you have written with your partner. Discuss some way to release each other from your vows. Consider making new vows as a commitment to love and support each other as you go your separate ways. If you cannot share or discuss this with your partner, do so with a trusted friend, a professional helper or a spiritual adviser.
3. In the ceremony, make a vow to hold in trust the intimate secrets of your partner's heart. For us, such secrets include anything that your partner has asked you to hold in confidence, or that you know was shared with you from a place of vulnerability. (This does not include a perpetrators' secrets of abuse or criminal activity.)

Leaving Sacred Space

One thing we forgot when we were planning our ritual was how to end it — how to make the transition out of the ritual process and return from sacred time and space back into the everyday world.

In Scott's service, the minister's benediction served as the transition from sacred space to the everyday world. Variations of this were also true of Margaret's, Nancy's, Marcy's, Kurt's and Matthew and Anne's ceremonies.

In Carolyn's ceremony, packing the altar away served much the same function.

Walking down a mountain symbolized leaving sacred space for Anne and Jessie.

Once we had said our vows, we knew there would be a final song, but when it began to play we felt uncomfortable just sitting there waiting for it to end. But after we had all shared a powerful emotional experience, it did not seem right to just walk out, either. What happened was quite spontaneous. As the song played, we each began to move around one half of the circle hugging people. The touch felt comforting for us and, so it seemed, for most of the members of the community, although a few were obviously disapproving or judgmental. We reached the end of our respective halves of the circles just as the song ended, and it was easy then to leave and share some private time.

If we had it to do again, however, we would think through this important transition and plan it more carefully.

Recommendations

1. As part of your ceremony, decide how you will make the transition out of the ritual process and move from sacred time and space back into the ordinary world.
2. Consider spending a few private moments after the ceremony to share last thoughts, feelings and an embrace.

After The Ceremony: The "Neutral Zone"

You may wake up the morning after your parting ceremony and say to yourself, today is the first day of the rest of my life. You may feel energized. You may also feel bewildered. Now what? What will you do with your day? Your week? Your life? You may feel suddenly empty.

William Bridges (1980) in *Transitions* called this "the neutral zone."

> In other times and places the person in transition left the village and went out into an unfamiliar stretch of forest or desert. There the person would remain for a time, removed from all the old connections, bereft of the old identities, and stripped of the old reality. This was a time 'between dreams' in which all the old chaos from the beginnings welled up and obliterated all forms. It was a place without a name — an empty space in the world and in the lifetime within which a new sense of self could gestate. (p.112)

For many of us, the emptiness of the "neutral zone" is so unusual, unexpected and anxiety provoking that what we want most is for it to end. Even if we're not sure what our new life will be, or where we're going, we just want to get on with it. We encourage you to do just the opposite — to stay in the emptiness for as long as you can. Try to tolerate the anxiety. Don't fill it immediately with a relationship or work or food or drugs or other distractions. You're being called. In a way, you have no choice. Even if you try to fill it with distractions, it will still be there, waiting for you. The sooner you pay attention, the better. On the other hand, as the old saying has it, you can't push a river. It's a paradox. There's nothing to be done — except to do nothing for a time. The key here is surrender. You have to stop fighting and allow the emptiness and the flow. Gradually, you'll discover new currents and possibilities.

We now know how important this time can be and strongly urge you not to make Phil's mistake of filling it immediately

139

with another relationship. In fact, don't fill it with anything. Leave the time empty. If possible, don't go right back to work, whether that be a job or raising children. If you need to, ask for help so that you can get away. True, many people may be puzzled by your request; after all, it's over now, isn't it? The truth is, yes — and no. If you are the one who's been left, you need time to grieve, rage and begin to heal. If you're the one who left, with empty time and space you may feel again the doubt, ambivalence and fear you felt before. Yes, and some of the "crazy time" swings of emotion and mood, too. Bridges (1980) quotes Tolstoy from a work called *A Confession*:

> I felt that something had broken within me on which my life had always rested, that I had nothing left to hold on to, and that morally my life had stopped ... I could give no reasonable meaning to any actions of my life. And I was surprised that I had not understood this from the very beginning. My state of mind was as if some wicked and stupid jest was being played upon me by someone ... [I asked myself,] what will be the outcome of what I do today? Of what shall I do tomorrow? What will be the outcome of all my life? Why should I live? Why should I do anything? (p.118)

There are three reasons why the emptiness between your old life and your new life is so important. First, your parting ceremony is symbolic of an end and a beginning. A relationship is dying and a new future is being born. A part of this process of death and rebirth involves a descent into chaos. Chaos may feel like a swirling, painful mess but it's also an indispensable source of creation at the time of every new beginning.

Second, a process of disintegration and reintegration is going on which can be a source of renewal in your life. Your old life — your marriage, your relationships, your hopes and dreams — all have disintegrated. Nothing has yet formed to take their place. You may think it has — a new relationship, a geographic move, another job. But that's just filling the emptiness with old ways of being in order to salve your anxiety. Unfortunately, it also prevents your new Self and life from manifesting.

Third, the "neutral zone" offers you a unique perspective on the changes and the stages of your life. When you're caught up in the day-to-day struggles of separation and divorce, you often can't see beyond the next week, or day or even the next minute. Just after a parting ceremony, if you pay attention, you may find yourself free of those struggles and distractions. Your old life has ended, and your new life has yet to begin. It's like toiling through mountains to arrive at a peak where, for a moment, you can see clearly where you've come from, where you are and where you might choose to go in the future. If you take the time, the view can be enlightening.

As inspiration and encouragement for this time of emptiness, we offer some compassionate advice from the poet Rilke (1984) that has often inspired and comforted us:

> Be patient with all that is unsolved in your heart and try to love the questions themselves, as if they were locked rooms or books written in a foreign language. Don't search for the answers, which could not be given to you now, because you would not be able to live them. And the point is, to live everything. Live the questions now. Perhaps then, someday, far in the future, you will gradually, without even noticing it, live your way into the answer. . . . (pp. 34-35)

Recommendations

1. After the ceremony, take some time to be alone and integrate your experience. Find a place that will nourish you. While we don't think it's necessary to go into the forest or the desert, there is wisdom in the idea of going someplace new and unfamiliar, away from the temptation of old habits and routines. If that's not possible, do your best to set aside time every day. Perhaps you could get up earlier in the morning or use your lunch hour. In these quiet moments, reflect on the

141

past and the future. Apprehend your truths. Allow the emptiness. Flow. Be patient.

2. Continue your journal. In the same way that you described your experience of "crazy time," write now about your experience of emptiness. Before, you wrote about your chaotic and shifting feelings. You may do that now, too, but you're also looking for what's really going on within you. How will you know? Imagine yourself sitting on a river bank watching the river flow by, or watching the shifting patterns of clouds in the sky above. Imagine yourself in the river with the water passing through you, or in the sky as the clouds drift through the emptiness of your body. Stay quiet. Pay attention to shifts in mood. Sometimes these will be quite subtle. Notice vagrant thoughts. Take note of things that puzzle or intrigue you. Remember your dreams. Write it all down.

Colette's Story

The whole experience of my marriage and the decision to part was one of the greatest initiations of my life — but not one I would have chosen consciously. For me, the decision to leave my marriage came after I'd been married only ten months. It was heartbreaking. I didn't get married frivolously. My partner and I were in the same spiritual community. There were many aspects of the relationship I felt were strong. We were both 32 years old and ready for partnership. On paper everything looked good. Of course, there were warning signs before we got married, and I was concerned about them, but I also thought, well, maybe it's just fear and resistance coming up. I was the one holding the stable ground in the hope that things would settle down after we got married. Instead, they just got worse. It was devastating. I'd never been even close to getting married before. I really felt ready for a committed partnership. But there's something about a ritual container — that's why the marriage ceremony is so important; it's a container that's a reflector of the deepest truth.

I knew when I walked down the aisle that there was something wrong. Seriously wrong. And I was devastated. But what do you do? People come from all over the world, everything's in motion. I felt in my body that J. was not really there for the commitment and yet we got married, we went through with it. Immediately, there were problems. I didn't want to jump ship at the first sign of trouble, and at the time it was very alarming and destructive for me. I had a very hard time focusing on my own life because I felt like I was in a battlefield and I didn't know where the mines were going to go off.

After eight months, J. and I separated. At this point, I didn't know if we were actually going to part forever. I just thought that maybe we needed some time apart to kind of create a new foundation for our relationship, to focus on our own lives so that we could come together in a clearer way. I felt like I still loved him, I still felt committed to the marriage; I felt like we just needed to separate, to get clear about what we needed next.

143

So it wasn't like I just severed it and cut off. We were in couples' sessions for about two months. Again, it was the same cycle — feeling at times like we were coming toward greater intimacy and feeling like there may be some hope, to feeling completely cut off and in pain. There was an abusive quality to these cycles that I realized I had to step out of. There came a point when something in me knew that if I stayed in this marriage, I would die. On some crucial level, I would lose myself. It might not literally kill me, but it would be like a soul death. I really felt like I had given my best, but there was part of me that realized that I could have stayed in the marriage five or ten years and then wondered, what happened to my life? There was a crucial moment where I realized, I could choose life or I could choose death. I chose life, painful as it was.

There was one point when I suggested that we do a ritual to end our marriage, to somehow honor and acknowledge our passage together. And I remember that J. was in a particularly cut-off place, and he said, "Well, what's there to honor?" Like, I don't love this person, there's nothing there, so there's nothing to honor — which was hurtful and wasn't the truth. But, I realized that although I needed some ritual in order to complete, he would not be able to participate with me.

Much of my work at that point was involved with creating rituals for other people using movement as the springboard for a deeper exploration. I knew I wanted to create something for myself, but I wasn't sure what I was going to do. During the whole year I was married and then separated, I was involved with a group called Transformational Energetic Arts, which used energetic work combined with movement arts. It was a wonderful and very supportive community for me. I met with them once a month. They had really witnessed my whole passage, from showing up as the newlywed bride to, at the end of the year, being with me in the midst of a divorce. They had really supported me through that entire passage. So I felt like they could be the people who would be the witnesses and could hold the space for the experience.

We held a kind of anything-goes creative forum on Friday nights. We were meeting for the last time that year, and I'd just made the decision to file for divorce. As I was preparing to go for that week-end, something told me that I needed to take my wedding dress with me. I didn't know what I was going to do exactly, but I had a sense that if I took my wedding dress and just went there and created a ritual space, something would unfold. I tried on my wedding dress for the first time since my marriage, and a phrase kept coming to my mind, "Ten months ago I took on the veil, ten months ago I took on the veil." That's all I had to go on. I just knew that that was the starting point for me.

When I went to the retreat center for our meeting, I told the group that I wanted to share something with them. I asked them to come into the space and wait for me. I didn't tell them anything about what was going on. In fact, they didn't yet know I was filing for divorce. During lunch, I'd collected flowers and made a bouquet for myself. I put on my wedding dress — the dress was from India, a Muslim wedding outfit. I played some music from Sheila Chandra. This is an Indian woman singing Sanskrit songs in a very expressionistic way that connects to an earlier time in my life when I studied dancing in India — a kind of Sanskrit lament. Using the Indian music conjured up the whole energy of the wedding, as well as a deep part of my soul and my experience through dance. I knew that the music would take me to a deep place. It was music that I had moved to before. Those were the only elements that I had decided on in advance. I would enter the sacred space in my wedding dress, carrying the flowers, to this music.

I entered the space as if I were entering a wedding procession. One of the women acted as a spiritual gatekeeper. The group sat in a half circle around votive candles like those I'd had at my wedding. I started moving. I didn't know what I was going to say, I didn't know what was going to come out of me besides that first line: "Ten months ago I took on the veil, ten months ago I took on the veil." In my movement, what came out was a longing to embrace the mystery of the Beloved. I said:

"I took on the veil because I wanted to soar.
I wanted to soar,
I wanted to love,
And this is my lament."

At that point I fell down to the ground, and I covered myself with my veil. I sobbed. So much grief poured out of me. I'm just astounded at how broken open I was. Being married for just ten months, it felt like something had been aborted. Regardless of what had happened between us, it didn't feel like we had lived out the life of the marriage. And that was one of the hardest things for me to let go of, the feeling that there were so many potentials that had never been lived out.

After the grieving, Sanskrit just started coming out of my mouth. I didn't even know what any of it meant. But I started singing with the song. The loose translation is, "I'm lost on an ocean of loneliness. Why has my beloved forsaken me?" Again, a lot of it was in movement; so much of what needed to pass through me was energetic. And I think that for me, someone who is primarily very mental, it was very important to really just stay with the body and follow the body's own wisdom about what needed to pass through me at that time. That's why, if I had created too much of a structure beforehand — it could have been powerful as well, but I think I would not have gotten to that same visceral level that I needed to, for my own healing.

At the very end of the ritual, I returned to the phrase I had started with: "Ten months ago I took on the veil, ten months ago I took on the veil." And then I said, "Now it's time to say good-bye, and now it's time to say good-bye." And I removed my wedding ring for the last time. I left it in the center of the circle. And then I left the space.

That was probably as exposed and visible as I've ever been, in the depths of myself. And yet I felt a safety and a trust in the group that allowed that. This is where the witnesses are such an important part of a ritual because I could not have gotten to that level on my own. Even with the experience I've had and the ease creating rituals in my own life, I could not have touched that level, I could not have opened up to such a profound place of

146

grief in myself. I've learned over the years, working with myself and with others, just how crucial it is to have a supportive container for a ritual, to have people who can bear witness and support the experience.

Some time later, once I filed for divorce and J. had moved away, across the country, I had a lot of anger come up, a lot of resentment around what had happened in the marriage, and also because I didn't feel like my husband took responsibility for his part. To this day he still continues to blame me for a lot of things. There've been times when I've felt a certain bitterness and resentment about that. It was at a Lakota Sun Dance, when I went through another deep piece around forgiving him. I could feel his anguish and his pain, and I think because I was in a sacred ceremony, there was a part of me that was able to open my heart with compassion. Even though I felt angry that he still blamed me, I was able to move beyond to a deep place of compassion and forgiveness.

After the divorce from my husband, I'd made the decision not to have contact with him any more. This wasn't out of bitterness or trying to punish him — I kept my heart open, but I had a lot of feelings I needed to move through. A lot of anger. A lot of really shadow material that was not appropriate for me to bring to him. This angered my former husband to no end. But each time I've tuned in, I've realized that it's not safe and not appropriate for me to be in contact with him.

Later, my husband sent me his wedding vows. The wedding vows that I had written and given to him — we had exchanged wedding vows in our wedding. He sent them back to me and basically said, "This is bullshit, so here you go, have this back." And what was interesting — I felt there was angry intent on his part, but I was actually glad to have them back because I had his vows and now I had my vows, too. As I read over my vows, I realized that my love in my heart was true. That I had received him and that I did give my best to the marriage. I was actually grateful to have those returned to me. And then, when I reread his vows, I took in that he had loved me to the extent he was capable; there was a way that he did the best that he could, too. But it was not what I needed. . . .

147

Two years after the first ritual, some time after the divorce, I traveled to Peru. I had been trying to sell my wedding ring and could not sell it. It's interesting; where do all the divorced wedding rings go? I didn't feel like I wanted to keep it, but what was I supposed to do with it? Then the thought of creating a ritual came to me. Perhaps I would bury it in Peru. Again, I trusted that a spontaneous ritual would emerge that would bring closure to another level, and that would mark a healing process and the final letting go. Again, I didn't exactly know what was going to happen, or when I was going to do it, but I knew that the moment would come to me. And it did, when we were on Lake Titicaca.

We'd stopped our boat between the Island of the Sun, where the ancient priests lived, and the Island of the Moon. We were at that conjunction point between the sacred feminine and the sacred masculine. In Inca tradition, Lake Titicaca is considered the birthplace of creation, where Mother Earth and Father Sky consummated and created the earth. So it's a very sacred place. We stopped the boat to do a meditation there and suddenly I knew, this was the place. This was the place to return the ring and the vows to the Mother. So I grabbed a friend of mine and went out in the boat — again, it was a very spontaneous ritual. I basically just said that I honored the time we had shared together and that it was time to let the rest of this go so that my true beloved could come forth in my life. I cast the vows and the ring into the waters and watched them sink.

When I went back to my friends, they immediately noticed an energetic lightening. Because I'd done a lot of processing and a lot of healing work during those two years, I didn't even realize that I was still carrying residue from all of this. It felt like a really important piece to ritualize.

For me, I felt like returning to the Mother Earth — meeting in the Ground of the Body —allowing whatever needs to come forth into the body and into consciousness to be absorbed back into the All and find healing there, and transformation.

My intention with all the rituals was to really honor this passage and to move through whatever I needed to, for my own

148

healing. But there are so many layers. It's not a linear process. I'd go through a very powerful ritual and think, great, I won't have to revisit this territory. I'm done, yeayyy! But that's just not the truth of it. It's been hard for me to go, oh, shit, I'm back here again. I think that's probably one of the most important things for people to realize. I know for myself, I've nursed the hope: OK, I'll do a ritual and then I'll be done. That's just not how it works. A ritual may be a crucial passage, it may be very important, but there are going to be many layers that emerge through time, and it's important to create space for those layers — all of them. There are many turns on the spiral.

Kurt's Story

During my divorce, I found I was having real difficulty dealing with guilt issues about breaking my marriage vows. I'd taken a vow "til death do you part." It wasn't just emotional, it was spiritual, too. I had sworn before God and my family and friends that I would not separate. I was also feeling tremendous guilt about my daughter, H.. I was breaking the commitment I'd made to bring her into this world in a marriage with a mom and dad together.

I did not initiate the divorce. L. and I been married almost seven years when the process began. The whole process was a surprise to me. I had no forewarning. It was August 2nd, our anniversary, when the topic first came up, and it was just thirty days later, Labor Day weekend, when we decided we needed to get the divorce. By that point it had become a mutual decision; I realized that L. had already made up her mind. In retrospect, talking to friends, she probably had made up her mind six months before. She'd been in counseling by herself and when I was finally invited in at the end, it seemed to be really more to confirm her decision. There was no interest in fixing this. For me, it was a shock.

We lived together for the months of October and November trying to sell the property we owned. We physically separated starting in December and the ceremony was held in May, six months later.

I discussed the difficulty I was having with guilt with a Methodist minister. L. and I didn't really share a religious background. I'd been raised Methodist. She'd been raised Catholic but had abandoned the Catholic church. We'd tried to find a church together. We finally decided on a Methodist church, but when I joined, she didn't. We seldom worshipped together because she'd go to the service and I'd end up helping in the nursery. We didn't really share a faith.

150

Anyway, the minister I turned to reflected that there are ceremonies for birth and death and graduation and marriage and yet we don't have any publicly recognized ceremony for divorce. He turned me on to these readings in Rituals for a New Day. *He said that he knew someone who had participated in a divorce ceremony to help break the emotional bonds and suggested I explore the possibility. That's when I talked to Julie Griffith, who was in seminary at the time. We talked about it and she said, "If you want to do it and L. wants to do it, I'll help you do it."*

I think some of my interest in ritual came out of my experience hunting. If you've done any reading about Native Americans you can see the respect they show for the animal they kill. When I hunt, although the killing is significant, it's also the most insignificant part of the hunt. I don't hunt to kill but killing is part of the hunt. A couple of friends I hunt with share the same feelings. When we kill a deer, we give thanks. Nothing dramatic, nothing weird, but we often will bow our heads and in the joy of the kill put our hands on the animal and thank it. Sometimes we put sprigs of greenery in the animal's mouth as a sign of respect. And when we do our butchering we don't just throw the head in the garbage can. We return it to a wild life area so it can be taken by other animals. Ritual isn't something I was raised with, but when I read about it I thought, yeah, this makes sense. When I use rituals hunting, it really brings me an inner peace.

So even though divorce is a completely different context, I did go to Julie with some understanding of ritual from hunting. It wasn't a foreign idea. It made sense to me. As soon as we started talking I liked the idea, and the more we talked the more I knew I needed to do it.

Julie really took the bull by the horns. She asked for my input. What did I want to do? I wanted to undo my vows. I wanted to reverse them. She came up with a ritual that included not only that, but also what we wished for each other, what we wished for ourselves, what L. wished I hadn't done, what I wished she hadn't done. That forced us both to reflect.

151

L. didn't physically participate in the ritual but she agreed to participate in writing. I wish she would have been there to participate because then it would have been even more significant. But I was willing to take anything at that point. Truthfully, I thought her responses were very pat, taken out of psychology 101: "I should have communicated better." I felt like I was searching my soul for my responsibility. But, of course, I had a lot of anger at that time. And, I don't think she had resolved the issues. I don't think she understood herself why she had left the marriage. Her only explanation was, "I'm still searching for myself. I've been following your dreams my whole life. I haven't had any dreams of my own and still don't know what they are, but I'm not going to follow yours anymore."

We held the ceremony at Julie's house. There weren't that many people at the ceremony. It was just my sister, Tamera, Joel, and Julie and Julie's then husband, David — he's my hunting partner and my best friend. He was also my best man when I got married again.

By that time, I was involved with my current wife, C., but I didn't ask her to come to the ceremony. She had a hard time understanding why I was doing a divorce ceremony in the first place and was hurt that I didn't invite her. I didn't invite my other brothers and sisters, either. Not because I don't care about them but just because, at the time, I couldn't handle it; it was emotional overload. But in the end, C. said, "Even though I'm not exactly sure what this is about, if it means this much to you, I'll support you." She even did the music tape — twice; I accidentally erased the tape the day before the ceremony. We chose the music for its symbolic meaning. It was very powerful for me to go from a song of sad loss to one about rising again.

In the section "Ask, Knock and Seek," we said what we hoped for each other and for ourselves. For myself, I asked that I could move on, that I could forgive, that I could heal, that I could love again and be in another relationship and another marriage. For L., I asked that she figure it out. I remember saying, "I hope you find yourself."

Julie read the questions. I read my responses and my sister, Tamera, read L.'s responses. It was a public proclamation of both the negative and the positive. That was good. It was hard but it was good to say publicly, "I wish this good thing for L. and she wishes this good thing for me. I acknowledge that there are things I didn't like about what she did and also that I did things wrong." Of course, I wasn't as specific as I could be today because at the time I was still trying to figure out what it was I'd done wrong.

In the ceremony, when we came to the text about removing the speck and the log, we tied the responses L. and I had written (to the questions Julie had asked) onto a set of sticks and floated them in a ceremonial trough of water. We live near the Mississippi — it runs through our cities — and later I took them to the river and floated them away. When I took off my wedding ring, we said a prayer with a blessing. We placed it in a box for H. to do with as she pleases when she's older. This way, she'll know that there was a love bond between us when she was conceived and born. And that there was never a question that we'll always love her and that she'll always have parents. Later, I placed the ring in a safe deposit box.

And, finally, we reversed the candles. From the unity candle we lit two individual candles and then blew out the unity candle.

There were a lot of tears. After the ceremony we had a reception in Julie's living room. My sister brought home-made tortes and we had wine and coffee.

Later, when I talked to people about it, I found I had a lot of explaining to do. For the most part, no one really knew what I was talking about. No one had heard of a divorce ceremony before. No one had gone through one. No one had heard of anyone else going through one. Some people thought it was odd in general, and some people, well, they'll just support you because you're you. The people who were spiritual or who had some understanding of ritual seemed to understand best. But even the people who said, "I just don't get it," understood that I needed to do it to get over the breaking of the vows and the end of the marriage.

153

Always, there's the legal divorce and the papers. But that's all financial — you just split up the stuff. For me, it was very anti-climactic when it happened later, in July. I needed to deal with the spiritual part of it, and when I explained it that way, a lot of people seemed to get it. Later, when I was getting my annulment, the church counselor I was working with took a look at the ceremony and said, "Well, clearly you've dealt with your issues of faith. You've resolved this and are ready to move on."

Truthfully, it's hard for me to imagine anyone getting a divorce and not doing a ceremony. People walk around with so many burdens from divorce. In a society where we often scoff at ritual or scoff at acts of faith, I hurt for the people who haven't done something like this. This ritual healed me in ways that nothing else was able to.

Rev. Julie Griffith Reflects

As Kurt's divorce was occurring, he felt the need to do something beyond the legal process to ritualize the event. He spoke with his own pastor at the United Methodist Church, who encouraged him to pursue creating and enacting some ritual of separation around the divorce. But the pastor didn't have a lot of ideas and resources to help Kurt. So Kurt asked me if I knew of any resources that could help him create a service of this kind — would I help him? I was in seminary at the time, and it just so happened that I was taking a class in preaching and worship in which one of the assignments was to design and enact an "alternative" ritual. So I said, "Well, Kurt, if you wouldn't mind being exposed to this class, let's work on this together because it sounds like a good project, and a necessary one."

I think Kurt's experiences hunting influenced his interest in ritual. Hunting was a family tradition for generations and was often used as a way to supplement the family groceries and something the men of his family looked at in a ritualistic way. There was a clear understanding that they were part of a cycle of life; that when they killed an animal they should not take it for granted but see it as the blessing that it is. I don't know what Kurt's rituals around hunting are. I do know that he's a very

154

thorough, thoughtful and careful hunter. He's honed his physical skills so that he can always kill an animal immediately. In the process of gutting and quartering an animal, I know there's a series of prayers and ritual things that he does. So even before the divorce, ritual had been a part of Kurt's life.

Kurt didn't have a clear idea of what he wanted, except that he wanted it to be Christian-based and that he liked the idea of some active participation. We agreed that he would choose the music because there were specific songs that helped him remember specific rites of passage in his relationship with L..

We considered a variety of settings for the service, including the Mississippi River, but in the end we held it in our home, out of concern for weather and comfort.

When I started researching the ritual, I found only one book that had anything at all about rituals of divorce and separation: Liturgy in Learning Through Life *by Westerhoff, Willamon and Crouch (1997). Another proved inspirational:* Human Rites *edited by Hannah Ward and Jennifer Wild (1995).*

As Kurt and I talked, he said that he wanted to include his ex-wife, L., in the ritual. I talked with L. on the phone. She had no desire to be present for the ritual itself. She was willing to send some written responses to the questions you'll find set forth in the ritual. By doing some writing, she participated, and I think that was useful. During the ceremony, Kurt's sister, Tamera, stood in as a proxy for L. and read her responses to the questions. Then, when the Matthew scripture was read about the log and the speck, we each took a set of responses to the questions — Kurt's responses and L. responses — and wrapped them around two different sticks and tied them with ribbons. I had made a little stream of water in a long tray and, as a way to let go of that conversation between the two of them, we floated those answers away... down the river of life, so to speak.

They had also lit a unity candle as part of their wedding ceremony. We tied each set of responses (to the second set of questions) to two individual candles. Then, at the very close of the ceremony, Kurt took a candle and I took a candle and we lit two single candles and blew out the unity candle, symbolic of the separation and the ending of that relationship.

155

It was a small group that attended, a mix of family and friends. Kurt had a wonderful support system of people who were there for him. Everyone brought food for sort of a potluck after the ceremony — we thought of it more as a wake after the ritual — a sad occasion, but happy, too.

I think that this kind of ritual is something that should be done more often. Each loss in our lives is its own rite of passage. Divorce deserves as much ritual recognition as events like birth and marriage. I also think that in our culture, most losses are not seen as a small death and a cause for grief. Many people think of death only as the actual departure of someone you've known and loved for a long time. Yet, there are a thousand daily deaths that hold tremendous importance for us, deaths that we never acknowledge — not that we do a very good job acknowledging the big deaths either. I believe that this kind of ritual is very valuable because it offers the kind of recognition that helps a person to go through the process of grieving, coming to re- member themselves and then to resurrect themselves into wholeness.

6

Ritual and Children

Memories And Regrets

Phil remembers two experiences of separation and divorce:

"My parents had been fighting for years. One summer they sent us — my brother, my sister and me — to our grandparents' Iowa farm for vacation. They'd done this before and we didn't think anything of it. Then one day, a letter arrived announcing that when we returned to California our mother would no longer be there. She had left. What's more, my father told us, we would be moving to a new home and a new school in a different city.

"I remember everything about that moment. That's how powerful it was for me. I remember where I was sitting in the back seat of my grandfather's car. I remember the smells of dry pig manure on my grandfather's boots and my grandmother's perfume. I remember the damp powder in the cracks on the back of my grandmother's neck. I remember looking out the window of the car at passing cornfields and a golf course. I remember feeling utterly bereft, stunned into silence.

"Later, when we went back to California, it was as if my mother had just disappeared. Oh, we saw her every once in awhile, for day visits, but it was always difficult because my father felt she had betrayed him, and I understood that affection for her would be considered disloyalty to him. Though this was back in the '50s when a father assuming custody was almost unheard of, he was so angry that he vowed a court fight to prevent her from getting us kids — this was also in the days before no-fault divorce and he was prepared to charge her with adultery.

"As is the case for many children, my parents' divorce was one of the most painful and defining events of my life. I would like to be able to tell you that the experience made it easier for my children when the time came for my separation and divorce from their mother. Regretfully, I cannot. Although perhaps not as brutal as my parents' separation and divorce, it was no less traumatic from my children's point of view. They were young (six and four), and I was less aware than I am today. At the time, all I knew was, I had to leave. All they knew was, one day I was there and the next day I was gone. Though I did my (imperfect) best in later years to be a good father, and have asked for and received their forgiveness, looking back, I still feel remorse about the unconscious, hurtful way I ended that marriage and left my children."

Children And Divorce

It's no secret that divorce is difficult for children. Even when parents are reasonable and civil, its disruptive power is well documented. In their book, *Second Chances*: *Men, Women and Children a Decade After Divorce*, Judith Wallerstein and Susan Blakeslee (1996) describe the negative consequences for the children of divorce. In regular follow-up studies of the same sixty families, Wallerstein found 41% of the children of divorced parents doing poorly — depressed, acting out, with low self-esteem and sometimes abusing alcohol or other drugs. Another 14% she found "strikingly uneven in how they adjusted to the world."

There is disagreement about the advisability of preserving a conflict-ridden marriage "for the sake of the children." A recent study by Ronald Simons, et.al. (November, 1999) published in the *Journal of Marriage and the Family*, "failed to find an association between parental conflict in nuclear families and child emotional or behavioral problems" (p. 1031). However, in his book *Helping Children Cope with Divorce*, Edward Teyber (1992) noted, "In 1985, a nation-wide survey of 1,423 children conducted by the National Institute of Mental Health found that children who live with a divorced parent have fewer behavioral problems than those who live with married parents who fight" (p.19) — *if the parents stop fighting*. Most experts agree that it is the children of parents who continue their conflict after divorce who are at the greatest risk.

We all know that difficult feelings are part of divorce. These feelings are often compounded by economic stress. Research has shown that after divorce, a woman's income declines on average between 15% and 30 %, a decline that adds yet another burden to the loss of father and family and fuels a mother's anger.

If your divorce is acrimonious, your children may be a captive audience to your relationship drama, and also the subject of intense competition between you and your partner. If your kids are older, you may find them escaping, into peer groups, for example, or books or hobbies or part-time jobs — anything to get them out of the line of fire until the dust settles and it's safe to re-emerge. Your younger children do not have such options. They must endure. Also, in your anger, you may find yourself tempted to distort their perception of your partner or to betray the secrets of your partner's heart.

We urge you to do your best to resist such temptations. Research tells us that nothing is as damaging to your children as conflict that follows, or even escalates, after a divorce. Teyber (1992) speaks for many other experts when he says, "It cannot be emphasized enough that children will be hurt when they are exposed to parental fighting or are forced to take sides or choose between their parents" (p.21).

In the absence of continuing conflict between parents, a good divorce is possible. A good divorce as defined by Ahrons (1994) is "one in which both the adults and the children emerge at least as emotionally well off as they were before the divorce" (p.2). This often includes the creation of what she calls a "bi-nuclear" family — "any family that spans two households."

Teyber (1992) found that "divorce does not have to harm children or cause long-term problems. The same parenting skills that lead to good adjustment in intact families will lead to good adjustment in divorced families. The quality of parenting you provide and your response to your child throughout the divorce are the most important determinants of your child's adjustment" (p.14). Simon and his colleagues (November, 1999), confirm this wisdom:

Our results suggest that children of divorce are at risk for adjustment problems because their parents are less likely to engage in competent parenting and are more likely to engage in parental conflict than parents who are married to each other. This is good news because it indicates that parents who divorce can substantially reduce the probability that their children will experience developmental difficulties by engaging in effective parenting while avoiding hostile exchanges in the presence of the children. (p. 1031)

What is essential for children is that they be parented well. If the parents continue to persevere in their parenting, are warm and supportive, monitor the children and are consistent with discipline, the risk for behavior problems is no greater than in two parent families (see Kurt's Full Spiral in Chapter 10). Even Wallerstein's (1996) findings support this possibility. At the ten-year follow-up of the families in the *Second Chances* study, 45% of the children showed no evidence of any long-term psychological damage. In fact, Wallerstein herself described them as "competent, compassionate and courageous people."

What's the difference, then, between those children who suffer from divorce and those who emerge as "competent, compassionate and courageous"? In general, the answer seems to be quite simple: the child's parents act in his or her best interest. This simple answer, however, isn't always easy to put into practice. Many of the worst battles between parents often have to do with defining just what *is* a child's best interest. Research identifies two essential factors that seem to make the critical difference between children who are damaged by divorce and those who are not.

First, it is important to do all you can to help your child maintain any relationships that were important to them before the divorce, including extended families, such as grandparents.

Second, the more supportive and cooperative you can be with your ex-partner, the more your children will benefit.

How divorce is perceived also has an effect on children's adjustment. Given the statistical fact that 50% of marriages now end in divorce, we wonder what good it does to continue to describe a divorced family as a "broken home." All too often such a pejorative description becomes part of a child's identity; she thinks of herself as the "child of a broken home." In their hurt and anger, parents may often reinforce this identity by forcing children to choose between them — in effect, further "breaking the home." This makes it difficult for children to think of themselves as still belonging to two parents, an identity conflict exacerbated if one of the parents remarries, as statistics tell us is likely, especially for men.

If you'd like to read more about the effects of divorce and the potential of bi-nuclear families, we strongly recommend the several books we've listed in the Appendix. Here, we simply want to remind you that, although most children are not happy about their parents' divorce, the negative and destructive outcomes can be minimized if you are willing to work with your anger — and your partner. We repeat: *How* you handle your separation or divorce will have at least as great an impact on their well-being as the divorce itself. Ask yourself, is yours going to become a bi-nuclear family — a family that spans two households, where children continue to be lovingly and consistently parented even though you and your partner no longer live together? If so, wouldn't it be best to find ways to make the change as positive and life affirming as possible?

This brings us back to ritual. As we've seen, a ceremony can be a powerful way to effect a transition from one way of life to another. By making your parting more conscious you can create a divorce that is healing for children and helps them adjust to the new reality.

How Ritual Helps Children Cope With Divorce

When we parted, our children were adults with children of their own, and they lived in other states. We included them in the process of planning the parting ceremony by telling them what we intended and encouraging them to share their feelings with us. Our son declined to share his feelings, but our daughter and

161

daughter-in-law did. We also sent them each a transcript and a videotape of our parting ceremony. Because, as adults, they were able to understand what we were doing (even if they did not understand or agree with our reasons for parting), we believe that this degree of involvement was probably sufficient. However, if we had it to do over again, we would also invite them to witness the ritual and create a way for them to actively participate, if they so desired. (Both have said since that because they didn't think we should part, they probably would have declined.)

If our children had been younger, however, we would definitely have tried to create a way for them to join in our parting ceremony. As we've seen, divorce is a family event that has a profound, long-term effect on a child's life. It will almost certainly result in the creation of a bi-nuclear family. Children will be related through remarriage with step-parents and, perhaps, step-siblings and step-grandparents. This situation is complex enough without the added complications of bad feeling — bad feeling which a ceremony of parting can help assuage and heal. As we noted earlier, some of the most poignant responses to our parting ceremony came from young adults of divorced families who wistfully remarked that they wished their parents had handled their parting in a more creative and loving way. Imagine a ceremony that includes children during which they can be told that the divorce is not their fault and their parents can make a commitment to continue to raise them in a healthy family, even if that family lives in two separate households.

There are several good reasons to involve your children in your process of conscious parting and your parting ceremony. All of these will contribute to a healing divorce. All, however, are secondary to this first and most important reason:

- **It allows you to demonstrate to your children by thought, word and deed that you will continue to be — and act as — their parents.**

162

Other reasons include:

- **It relieves children of their sense of responsibility.**

At one time or another almost all children feel responsible for their parents' divorce. Involving them in the process offers the opportunity for age-appropriate explanations and discussions beforehand. During the actual ritual, it gives both parents an opportunity to make explicit that this is an adult decision for which the children are not responsible; that while the parents are divorcing each other, they will never divorce their children.

- **It allows children to feel a greater sense of control.**

One of the problems children face in divorce is feeling as if their lives are spinning out of control. This creates anxiety and depression which many children then act out. By including them in the process, and perhaps the ritual itself, they gain a sense of control through their participation.

- **It allows parents to model for children a way to work through and resolve conflict, and demonstrates the cooperative way their children can expect them to relate after the divorce.**

As a relationship comes to an end, children often witness escalating conflict between their parents. In such circumstances, what they learn is that difficult feelings lead to rage and abandonment. This is terrifying and often leads to separation anxiety and depression. By including them in the process and the ceremony, either as participants or witnesses, they have an opportunity to see their parents practice what most parents preach: disagreements don't have to end in rage and that even rage doesn't have to lead to abandonment. They observe their parents cooperating, despite disagreement and difficult feelings. Through their own participation, they gain a sense of continued love and connection with both parents.

163

- **It gives children a chance to express their own feelings.**

Though lip service is usually paid to giving children their say, in a divorce adult partners are often too consumed with their own feelings to pay much attention to their children's. Preparing for a parting ceremony offers a structured opportunity for children to explore their feelings and for their parents to help them cope.

- **It makes the parting real.**

Children are seldom involved in the formal and arcane rituals of the divorce court. There's a certain unreality about the situation, and this tends to promote fantasies that Mom and Dad will someday get back together. Including children in the parting ritual makes the entire process more real. While children may still fantasize about reconciliation, they (and you, their parents) will have a concrete event to remember that clearly symbolizes your parting.

How can you include your children in a ceremony of parting? Clearly, their age will to some extent determine their level of interest and participation. Again, we emphasize that the most important thing is for you to affirm that you will continue as their parents.

Pre-schoolers

Our research and the experience of others suggests that children age five and under probably will not understand enough of what's happening to participate in the ritual itself. They will, however, feel the tension and the loss, and in their anger and sadness, may regress. What children this age fear is that because one parent has left unexpectedly, the other parent may also disappear. What matters to them most, therefore, is the uninterrupted and nurturing presence of both parents. Reassuring them, individually and together, that both you and your partner

164

love them and will nurture them is critical. Reading some of the excellent age-appropriate books about divorce with them will help them to express their feelings. Their involvement in the planning and preparation of the ritual might include conversation along the lines that this is a way for both parents to promise that, even though they will no longer be living together, they will always love and care for their children. If a child of this age wants to actually participate, allowing him to choose, say, a photo for a remembrance collage could also be healing.

School Age

Children age six through twelve will understand a lot more about what's happening and, if given the opportunity, probably be a lot more articulate about their feelings. Like their younger brothers and sisters, school age children will definitely benefit from uninterrupted nurturing from both parents. Discussions about what's happening can also be helpful.

Teyber (1992) and other experts note that for six to eight year olds, the primary reaction to divorce is sadness. Boys this age miss their absent fathers intensely and often show more distress than girls. Regardless of gender, children this age are most susceptible to feeling rejected by the parent who left, often resulting in lowered self-esteem, depression and declining school performance. Worried about their parents, such children might try to prevent the divorce and restore the family.

For children of this age group, conscious parting and a ceremony of parting can be helpful. It can encourage their expressions of sadness and demonstrate through words and deeds that, although you will be living apart, as their parents you will continue to care for them. Witnessing a ceremony can also help your children adjust to the new reality and let go the fantasy of reconciliation. If they show interest in the ceremony, it may be in much the same way as they'd feel excitement about participating in a wedding. If so, care should be taken that their involvement in no way suggests any responsibility for the divorce and, perhaps, should be limited to receiving their parents' assurances of continued love and support.

Children nine to twelve are sad, too, but the emotion they express most is anger, toward both parents and, especially, toward the parent who has left. If encouraged — or even without encouragement — these children typically assign blame and take sides with one parent against the other. At this age, boys sometimes prove all but impossible for a single mother to discipline, and boys and girls often angrily reject their absent father's (or mother's) attempts to spend time with them. Along with sadness and anger, these children feel powerless, helpless to influence the enormous changes going on in their lives. These feelings may show up in poor school performance, difficulty getting along with friends, physical complaints such as headaches, and even an exaggerated concern about taking care of one or both parents.

Conscious parting and a parting ceremony can help these children express their feelings. Also, if they so choose, it offers an opportunity to interact with your process of parting. Planning for the ceremony can model caring and cooperative behavior between you as parents. Despite feelings of sadness and loss, you and your partner can demonstrate caring for yourselves and for them, your children.

Children this age probably won't be as enamored of actually participating in the ceremony as their younger brothers and sisters. But affirmations of love and continued support by you, their parents, in front of witnesses, may offer even greater comfort and healing than for their younger siblings.

Adolescents

How teenagers respond to their parents' divorce and to a ceremony of parting has much to do with their special stage of life. Already moving away from their parents, many distance themselves and become more involved in their own plans. Mostly, they worry about how the divorce will affect their future — their immediate future in terms of high school and college and, later, their ability to create a good marriage. How they feel about this disruption of their life varies. Some will feel betrayed, angrily disengage from the family and act out. Like school-age

166

children, such teenagers will probably have some strong opinions and judgements about one or both parents, which they may express with the brutal frankness that is an adolescent's age appropriate prerogative. Others, though they may feel and express the same anger and judgements, will also rise to the occasion with compassion and helpfulness.

Your adolescent will be able to clearly understand the intention of a parting ceremony. He or she may, however, reject it as hypocritical or pointless. Or, he may not. After some time to feel hurt and anger, and after some reflection about how savagely and destructively divorces are usually handled in a society that believes in the Myth of the Bad Divorce (say, among his friends' families), he may decide that his parents' loving intention and the healing potential of a parting ceremony far outweighs his own embarrassment or discomfort about participating in something so "weird" (see Marcy's Story). But make no mistake, it is he who will decide. That, too, is a prerogative of becoming a young adult. Trying to force your adolescent (or any child) to participate in a parting ceremony will only cause more pain and estrangement.

Recommendation

Invite children to participate in the process of conscious parting and the parting ritual itself in an age-appropriate way that communicates clearly your intention to continue to be — and act as — their parents. Design what you say and what you do in a way that relieves them of any sense of responsibility for the divorce; encourages them to express their feelings; reassures them that your divorce does not mean the loss of either you or your partner; and helps them understand and accept the reality of the divorce.

A Model Ceremony That Includes Children

Several of the people whose stories appear in this book had young children at the time of divorce. None of the children were included, usually because no one was quite certain how to do so. Marcy, however, did include her two young adult children, and several models of parting rituals also include children (see Chapter 11).

We offer an outline for a ritual that uses our own ceremony as a template while at the same time synthesizing highlights from other rituals that include children. Even though the outline describes a ceremony done by a couple, you can easily adapt it for yourself and your children if you are a single parent. It can also be adapted to a more religious service.

- **Setting Your Intention.** If you include your children, one of your intentions will be to offer them solace, healing and encouragement toward a new life.
- **Before You Begin.** When preparing for the ceremony, spend some time talking with your children about your intention to create a healing divorce and the reasons why you believe this is important. We also suggest that children be given a choice about whether they want to participate in the ceremony, even as witnesses. If they are present at the time of the ceremony, they will hear the commitments you will make to them. If they choose not to be present, whatever commitments you make can be shared later, either in person, on tape or in a letter.
- **Speaking an Intention, Invoking Sacred Energies.** You will want to acknowledge your children's presence or participation in the ceremony, or both. You may also want to call upon a power greater than yourselves to help you realize, through this ceremony, the highest good of all concerned.
- **Open, Honest, Transparent and Undefended.** If your children are present, as you share your personal truths it will be important to temper your honesty with grace and

168

discernment. They should hear nothing here that you haven't already discussed with them. Taking responsibility for your part in the ending of the relationship — and not blaming your partner — can serve as powerful modeling behavior for your children. Especially if they are adolescents, your willingness to tell the truth and accept your individual responsibility may go a long way toward maintaining their respect and ensuring family stability.

- **A Tribute to the Relationship.** Our children were a large part of our tribute. In the video we created, we made a point of including photos of them (and of us with them) as they grew from little children to adolescents and then to adults with children of their own. However it is done, some explicit acknowledgement of your children and their importance in your life is vital.

- **Letting Go of the Past: Sharing Gratitude.** Your children are surely part of what you're grateful for. Please tell them this.

- **Releasing the Future.** One sadness you'll share with your children is the loss of the nuclear family, living together in the same house and sharing each other's lives on a daily basis. It will be helpful for your children to hear you express your feelings of loss, as well as your hopes for a new bi-nuclear family.

- **Forgiveness.** This will serve to reassure your children that you and your partner still care for each other. It will also model for them a healing way of being in the world, the antithesis of the Myth of the Bad Divorce.

- **What About the Rings?** Even small children understand the symbolic nature of wedding rings and what it means to take them off. It will be healing for your children if you and your partner can find a way to make explicit and understandable the changed symbolism of your rings.

- **Vows and Commitment: An Intention for the Future.** In addition to the vows and commitments you and your partner make to each other — say, of mutual affection

169

and support in your lives to come — it is even more important for you both to make vows and commitments to love and support your children.

Here is where the children can be active participants in the ceremony.

Let them come forward to stand between you.

If you have an officiating clergyman, she can say something like this to the children:

> Sean and Lara, you are a blessing to your parents. They wanted you and they love you. Their decision to part is not your responsibility. You have had no part in this decision. It is a choice that your parents have made and you are not responsible. Even if they are living apart, your presence in their lives remains most important. You were a joy to them when you were born and you will always be a joy. They will love you forever.

Here is a general commitment you as a parent might make to your children and your community, spoken separately by each of you:

> Sean and Lara, as your father (mother), I promise to love and support you in any way I can. I ask all of you [your community] to help and encourage me to fulfill this commitment. I promise to place my children's welfare over any personal conflicts that may arise.

Here's a specific explanation you might offer to younger children:

> Sean and Lara, I know that this is difficult for you. This is a sad time for you and for our family. It's hard to understand, I know, but sometimes even people who love each other very much grow apart.

170

This is what's happened to your daddy/mommy and me. It hurts us to grow apart and I know it hurts you. But I want you to know that your daddy/mommy and I both love you very much. Even though we won't be living together, we'll still be a family — just a different kind of family. We both believe that once some time has passed and we have learned to live in this new way, a lot of the hurt we all feel now will go away and we will all be happier. Remember, I am always going to be your mommy/daddy and love you. Your daddy/mommy is always going to be your daddy/mommy and s/he loves you, too. You are an important part of my life and your daddy's/mommy's life, and you always will be. I love you. We both love you. You are the joy of our lives.

Here's a specific commitment you could make to your older children:

Sean (Lara), even though your mom and I have decided to divorce and live apart, I want you to know how grateful I am that you are my son (daughter). You have brought joy to my life. I love you and will always love you. I will always support you in any way I can. As a symbol of the love we share and of my continued support, I give you this gold necklace (or pin or other symbolic gift). Each link represents a happy moment we have shared and, when it's fastened, it forms a circle, a symbol of my love for you that never ends.

If you and your partner are performing the ceremony as a couple, you can give a gift together to your children. It can be the same gift for each. For example, you might fasten a chain around each child's neck. Or, you can select and give different symbolic gifts to each child to

171

commemorate the occasion (see *A Ceremony for a New Family* in Chapter 11).

- **Leaving Sacred Space**. You and your children can leave the ceremony together as a sign that though you and your partner will now be living apart, the (bi-nuclear) family itself remains intact.

- **After the Ceremony.** Besides taking some private time with your partner and for yourself, take some time with your children to answer questions, share feelings and to mourn. Perhaps go out to eat together or do something else that's "normal" to reinforce the idea that, despite your parting, their relationship with each of you remains intact.

Marcy's Story

My husband and I met each other at the age of 21 and were married on my 22nd birthday. We had both been married before. He was married at 18 years of age, a teenage pregnancy situation. The marriage lasted less than three years, with his first wife having an affair. I was married at 20 and the marriage lasted ten months. I knew my first husband for only six weeks before marrying him. So much for young, foolish mistakes.

W. and I met in the fall of 1971. Through mutual acquaintances we were introduced and he pursued me relentlessly. I had no desire to enter into a serious relationship at that time. W. was madly in love with me, and he was a kind, honest and gentle man. I did not enjoy the singles scene and after nine months of dating, I finally said, "Yes."

Our backgrounds are different. W. was raised in the Christian faith and I was raised in the Jewish faith, at least for my first twelve years. Our families were not comfortable attending either a church or a synagogue, and so we chose a Japanese Tea Garden restaurant in Northern California. We had a Baha'i wedding. Our reception followed with a celebration at the condominium party-house of my new in-laws. For our honeymoon, we borrowed the house and swimming pool of a relative out of town in the mountains. Money was scarce and love (passion) was plentiful.

The marriage started with financial problems, debts, child support and an ex-wife who rejoiced in causing pain. My husband found solace six months after we were married by joining a religious group that lives strict lives of service. I had not intended to join him, but my need to make the marriage work and to change my life was significant. I joined him and we spent approximately thirteen years raising our two children in this faith. I finally broke out of the religion and he followed a couple of years later. I had a lot of anger and pain around this. Our marriage was laden with financial struggles. W. was a hard worker, but he lacked enough self-esteem to pursue any real

173

career or successful business. To compensate, I created a career that supported our family with most of the necessities and a few things above that. W. contributed to the monthly bills, but rarely had anything extra to offer. We both brought to the marriage our issues, and I finally understand that part of relationship is the ability to see those issues and work on them individually and together. Instead, our time was filled with "surviving" and our growth together was stifled. Our love over the years was about dependency and neediness on both our parts. Coming from broken homes, we did not want our children to experience the same situation, and so we endured. W. wanted to look at life with simplistic eyes, and I deserted the call of my heart by simply falling "asleep" for 25 years.

I write this not to blame or accuse. We both played our parts and chose our roles. Those choices were based on our own personal upbringings and what we brought into this marriage. Every marriage has its baggage, and if we don't recognize our personal "stuff" and work on it, we simply carry it into the next relationship.

I made a decision in 1997 to return to school and left a relatively lucrative career to do it. That decision altered our lifestyle tremendously, and already the marriage was under duress. Eight months later, W. moved out into his own place. We talked occasionally, but not often. I didn't want to rush into signing the divorce papers. I wasn't interested in finding another relationship. I was interested in working on me. W., on the other hand, used the Internet to connect with others in hopes of finding another caretaker. And he did, but not who I expected.

W.'s first marriage brought with it a son, who is now close to thirty years of age. Despite paying child support all those years, visitation was impossible. His ex-wife had married the man she'd had an affair with while married to W.. She did everything possible to discourage a relationship between W. and his son. Over a fifteen year period of time, W. saw the boy only once.

After our separation, W. attempted once again to see his son. His connection brought him together with his first wife. She was in the middle of her divorce from the man she had been married

174

to for 22 years. I signed divorce papers nine months after our separation not knowing that they had been communicating. Within three weeks, he moved her to our state and in with him. She brought with her a tremendous fortune from both her divorce and her family riches. I became aware of the situation and suffered great distress.

I find it difficult to express my anguish on paper. Half my lifetime had been with this man and now to imagine him growing old in the arms of another woman, this particular woman, has been heartbreaking. There is hardly a human emotion that I have not felt in great intensity these last two years. My peace comes in understanding that there is a bigger picture here that I can't see. And that God is in charge of everything, even this.

W. and I never told each other that we didn't love each other anymore. I told him my spirit could not be free in our relationship and he told me I would be better off without him. Our journey had ended and the lessons for both of us were significant. I saw our marriage as a holy relationship all those years, and I had wanted a holy ending. I had sought out a rabbi from the synagogue I attended periodically. It was my desire to give W. my blessing for a happy life. It took great courage and understanding to continue with the ceremony, even though all of this had transpired.

The rabbi I asked to help us suggested that we perform the ceremony around the time that the divorce would be final. He also helped us carefully choose the day for the ceremony. He wanted to be sure that the dates would coincide with some of the spiritual activities on the Jewish calendar. I picked one day, and he said, "I think we should do it two days later."

The rabbi also recommended some specific procedures for us to follow. He sent me the information and I forwarded it on to my ex. He asked us each to write a letter of thanks to each other. Then we were to list the positive things that were in the relationship and that had come out of the relationship.

He also asked us to write a paragraph of release giving permission for the other to go his or her own way, and to create a new life. Finally, we were each to write the other a closing blessing, to bless each other's new journeys.

175

We held the ceremony in our home because I felt that my ex would be most comfortable coming there, rather than going into any kind of spiritual building. I thought if I asked him to go anywhere else, he probably wouldn't. I also felt that it would be easier for the children to be in a more comfortable, homey kind of environment. The other people present were my two children, and my toddler grandchild, and the rabbi.

I didn't change the house a lot to create sacred space. After a year, it was not the same place as when he and I had lived there together. My home is a holy place to me and everything there was as it should be. It felt right. We did have candles and lit them as part of the ceremony.

We didn't use any music. I had some CDs I would have liked to play, angel type music. But the opportunity wasn't there, I felt, because my ex was extremely nervous. I just wanted to manage to get through the ceremony.

What we had prepared at the rabbi's request was the heart of the ceremony. Using Marianne Williamson's book Illuminata *as a guide, I had written a combination of things. In my part of the ceremony, I said: "We came to each other at a young and painful time in our lives. Through love and commitment we created a life and family together. I experienced a safe feeling for the first time in my life, and we worked very hard to survive difficult circumstances. Through our experiences together I learned to be brave, to have faith, and to work for a common goal. Through the tests and endurance we faced, I found my inner voice and learned to listen to it. I thank you for your friendship and care for twenty-five years. I thank you for providing me with great lessons about integrity, forgiveness and love. I thank you for all your care for over half my life. I thank God for blessing our love with two beautiful children and now a grandchild."*

I also said: "Marianne Williamson writes regarding divorce: 'Relationships are eternal. Separation of our bodies does not mean separation of our souls. We are healed by this knowledge because it reminds us of the oneness of our relationship regardless of the needs or conflicts that tear us apart. Someone leaving sometimes feels like the greatest pain we

176

have ever suffered. But our relationships do not die, they just change form. Faith means knowing that no one is ever really gone.' I give you my permission to go your own way and to create your new life. W., I bless you and release you. Please forgive me. I forgive you. Go in peace. You will remain in my heart."

It was difficult to do this. It was hard to look him in the eyes and to read this and try not to show any emotion. Because my children were observing, I didn't feel that some sobby kind of crying was appropriate. I felt it was important not to break down. The emotion was in my eyes and my voice. When I looked at my children I saw tears in their eyes. I could feel my lower lip quivering near the end. There was such a finality to the whole thing. When I said, I give you permission to go your own way and to create your new life, it was freeing. It was also frightening. There were a lot of mixed emotions. But I decided that any tears I needed to shed, I could shed later. That was my thanks to him and my permission for him to go on with his life. Then he read his to me.

My children also participated. The rabbi asked them if there was anything that they wanted to say to either of us, or to share with us about how they were feeling. My son didn't have too much to say. But my daughter had been very supportive of the ceremony. She shared that it meant a lot to her, to see us end our marriage in this way. I felt very good about that. And even though my son didn't speak, I could see emotion in his eyes. I felt that his heart was being touched. Sometimes the whole journey is just to undo the hardening of the heart. I think ceremony can help with that. Ceremony can not only honor the past relationship but also bring some peace and God's spirit into the situation. Even if both people are not on the same path, a ceremony can represent a circle closing.

The rabbi's involvement made a big difference. He knew what we needed to do and he knew what prayers to use. He was definitely in control of what was going on and was able to help us move through it. He said prayers in Hebrew. One prayer he said holding each of our hands as he stood between us, as a link. At the beginning, when the first prayer ended, no one said,

177

"Amen." But by the end of the ceremony, when the last prayer ended, everyone said, "Amen." This told me that the hearts present had received what they needed.

When the ceremony was over, I said to my ex, "Let me give you a hug." We hugged. I hugged for us but I also hugged for the children as well, to make the closure more personal. True, it was kind of an impersonal hug, but a hug is always a good way to say good-bye.

Given what's happened since, I'm really glad we did the ceremony, for the sake of the family, for the sake of my children. Even though I still have a lot of emotion, I feel finished. The ceremony brought a spiritual closing that you don't get when you're just signing papers. I think the soul requires more than documents. The mind may get along with that, but the heart and soul need more. Of course, a ceremony is just a part of that. There's a lot more healing that needs to happen — but a ceremony is a good beginning.

Rabbi David Zaslow Reflects

There is a profound process in a traditional Jewish divorce whereby the man writes a bill of divorcement, called a get. *In the presence of witnesses he drops it into the cupped hands of his wife. Although the writing and delivery of a get is complex, it's underlying psychological benefits can be profoundly beneficial.*

Just as all beginnings have a sacred nature in Judaism, so should all endings. In the case of interfaith couples, I have used the underlying infrastructure of the traditional get *process as a way of asking God to bring some degree of holiness to the ending of the marriage.*

Ritual, by its very nature, has a powerful psychological impact. Good ritual can bring healing in times of distress, and the divorce rituals I have had the honor of conducting have one goal — healing of heart and soul. Gratitude for the love that was once there is the key to developing such a ritual. Through letters, poetry, and simple spoken words, each person will be asked to thank the other for what was once good in their marriage. We bypass the negative and leave that to counseling later on. By

178

invoking God's presence and sharing words of gratitude, the future is left open to God's continuing work in the lives of the husband and wife getting the divorce.

Civil divorce (an oxymoron?) procedures often leave couples in worse shape psychologically after the property is divided and child custody matters have been resolved. A transpersonal ritual led by rabbi, pastor, or priest is often very important medicine at such a time. Even when a couple no longer will speak to each other, the presence of loving family members and a trusted pastor can have a healing impact.

Through simple ritual — lighting a candle; invoking God's presence; sharing words of gratitude; a statement of mutual release; mutual blessings for the future; blessings read to each parent by older children; extinguishing the candle — the pastor, priest, or rabbi can repair some of the damage done by the civil, legal procedures.

J. , Marcy's Daughter, Remembers

As I pull the car into my parent's driveway, I take a deep breath and pray I get through this night without crying. This is the night of my parents' divorce ceremony. As I walk up to the door, my father, who no longer lives in this house, is standing outside. He greets me with a hug and kiss and so does my brother. My mom opens the screen door, and we all enter with the rabbi.

I feel so weird looking at my two parents in the same house I grew up in, standing so far apart from each other, trying to make conversation with either my brother or me. We all sit down in the living room. The rabbi has a soft, gentle but strong voice. He begins with a prayer, which seems to make everyone relax a little. As the rabbi continues, I realize how beautiful having this ceremony is. How lucky I am to have all my family together again without fighting.

My mother and father exchange words of forgiveness and memories, good and bad, and it almost feels like everyone is their real selves. No walls protecting insecurities, no unforgiven deed not absolved. The rabbi continues his ceremony with such

179

love and spirituality that at that moment we all begin to feel more peace inside.

My brother and I then exchange words with my parents, letting them know we know they tried their best and longest to make their marriage work. They were great parents to us, and we support their decision to be separate because we want them to regain the inner happiness that we feel they lost so long ago. As the ceremony ends in prayer, my brother and I know my parents love us very much, and behind those loving eyes, I know they hope with all their hearts that they have not let us down. We hug our parents strongly. My father shakes the rabbi's hand. He gives my mother one last hug as if to say he is happy for coming to the ceremony and what peace it has brought him and leaves. As my brother and I observe all of this, we know this was the only way to have dissolved this marriage of my parents with love, understanding and peace. Being able to resolve these matters in such a spiritual way makes me feel a lot closer to my God and helps me see who my parents really are, two people who will always love each other. But the lives they need to live in the future cannot be done together, for each one will handicap the other. This ceremony has broken the reins of their marital bond and allowed all of us to see that we can go on in love and have a bright hope for the unknown future.

7

A Ceremony Planner

Now that you know something about preparing and performing a parting ceremony, and how you can include your children, we'd like to back up a bit to help you move forward. This chapter is a brief review of what you've already read as well as a practical step-by-step guide for putting what you've read into practice. This ceremony planner will help you focus on what you need to do while at the same time reminding you why you are doing it.

Although we have written this planner for a couple, it will also be helpful if you are single and performing a ceremony alone or with family and friends.

Here are the steps we recommend:

Familiarize yourself with the process of parting, with what's happening to you now or what happened to you before.

We suggest that you

- Read a book about the process of parting — *Crazy Time* (Trafford 1992) is our favorite.
- Read Chapters One and Two of this book.
- If there are unresolved practical issues (money, custody), consult a mediator — we prefer mediation to adversarial law — and/or read a book that combines straight talk with compassion, such as M. Sue Talia's (1997) *How to Avoid the Divorce from Hell and Dance Together at Your Daughter's Wedding.*

Remember, the more consciousness you bring to the process of parting, the better, for you and for your children. If you're feeling overwhelmed by loss, pain and grief, familiarize yourself with the "crazy time" process of parting. Even if it's been awhile since your actual separation or divorce, when you reflect on what you've gone through, unresolved feelings might arise as a parting ceremony brings you around another turn on the spiral. The more you know about who you are, how you feel and the process of parting, the better you can plan a ceremony that will meet the needs of you and your children and contribute to a healing divorce.

Familiarize yourself with the experience others have had preparing and performing a parting ceremony.

We suggest that you

- Read the rest of this book. Note particularly the essentials of preparing and performing a ceremony of parting, as well as how the people who have told their stories have made such ceremonies personally meaningful.

Before you start planning specific details, review what we mean when we talk about preparing and performing a parting ritual. Also, how can conscious parting and a divorce ceremony help your children? These are subjects found in Chapters 3 to 6. Chapters 8 to 11 offer personal reflections and examples of ceremonies, along with a discussion about how to make the transition from marriage to friendship.

Arrange to spend some quiet, reflective time alone, either a little time each day or perhaps a longer time at a retreat.

We suggest that you

- Keep a daily journal.
- Do exercises to help you get in touch with your feelings (see Chapters 2, 4, 5, and the Appendix for recommendations. Our favorite is Daphne Kingma's (1987) *Coming Apart*).

- Do exercises to help you own 100% responsibility for your separation or divorce (see Chapters 2 and 4, and the Appendix for recommendations).

Are you having difficulty feeling your feelings? Are you still struggling with anger and bitterness and a sense that you're a victim? Are you still blaming your partner? Does allowing yourself to feel the depth of your emotion seem to throw you back into "crazy time?" If so, we suggest that you also

- Attend a divorce recovery program (check with your local churches).
- Seek assistance from a spiritual adviser or a professional helper.

Ask, why do I want to perform a divorce ritual or parting ceremony?

We suggest that you

- Write in your journal what outcome you want a parting ceremony to have in your life and in the lives of those important to you. Be specific.
- Write in your journal what symbolic meaning you want a parting ceremony to have in your life.
- Discuss these issues with your spiritual adviser, a professional helper or a trusted friend.
- Write your intention in your journal.

Decide if you want to prepare and perform the ceremony with your partner. If you do, ask yourself, is this possible? Is your partner willing? Are you willing — really, are you? Are your feelings and your partner's feelings under good enough control for the two of you to cooperate?

We suggest that you

- Tell your partner that you want to do a parting ceremony. Do this in person, if possible. If not, write a letter. (We don't recommend the phone; studies show that less than 30% of what you intend to communicate gets through over a telephone line.) Share with him the effect you intend a ceremony to have for the two of you and your children. Invite him to participate. Share this book with him. Give him some time to consider your proposal. Ask him to respond with a yes or no by a specific date.
- If he is willing to participate, review with him the ceremonies in this book. Ask him how he would like to participate. Would he like to help you prepare the ceremony? Would he like to prepare parts of the ceremony for himself? Would he prefer that you prepare it and he simply participate? Even if it's minimal and begrudging, accept his level of involvement. Just his participation will be healing, for the two of you and for your children.
- If he says no, or does not respond, proceed with preparing the ceremony on your own. It will still offer healing for you and your children.
- Even if you end up doing the ceremony by yourself, keep your partner informed of your planning as you proceed. There's always the chance that he might change his mind.

Decide when you want to perform the ceremony. At the time of your actual separation? At the time your divorce is final? Sometime later, after your separation and divorce? Each time may have a different symbolic meaning but all share an intention to end the relationship with forgiveness and healing. Remember, sooner will be more difficult because you're closer to "crazy time." On the other hand, preparing and planning a ceremony may help you work through a lot of your "crazy time" feelings.

If you want to do a ceremony but don't feel entirely clear, that's OK. You can always do one ritual now and another later.

We suggest that you

- Discuss your feelings about the timing of your ceremony with your spiritual adviser, a professional helper or a trusted friend. Make the decision based on what you want the ceremony to represent and on your emotional readiness (and your partner's, if participating).

Decide on the kind of ceremony that will be most meaningful to you. Do you want it to be spiritual in nature? Do you want it to be religious; more like a church service? Remember, there is no "right" way. It can be as simple or as elaborate as you choose.

We suggest that you

- Reread the stories in this book and review the ceremonies in Chapter 11.
- Discuss the nature of your ceremony with your spiritual adviser, a professional helper or a trusted friend.

Begin to prepare the actual ceremony itself. Remember, ritual is an art that rewards patience and attention to detail.

We suggest that you

- Write your ideas in your journal. Just write notes at first, or doodle. It doesn't matter. Expect to change your mind as new ideas occur to you.
- If you have decided on a religious ceremony, consult your minister or rabbi.
- If your church or synagogue does not seem sympathetic to your intention, contact a minister from one of the Christian denominations that supports the use of ritual for divorce, or a rabbi from the Reform Jewish tradition.

185

- If you cannot find a minister or rabbi in your area, consult other people and clergy who have prepared and performed parting ceremonies (see the contact list in the Appendix).

Sketch out the first draft of your ceremony. Don't worry if it's rough. This is just to get you started.

We suggest that you

- Spend some quiet time alone. Meditate. Pray. Open yourself to inspiration. Whatever kind of ceremony you've decided on, we suggest including the following. Write them down in your journal.

    - Declare a statement of intention. If you haven't completed this, it's important to do so now, before you go further. Write it down. If you still can't get clear about your intention, you may want to consult with your spiritual adviser or seek professional help.
    - Invoke sacred energies. As you imagine your ceremony, how do you see yourself invoking whatever is sacred to you? What images or words come to mind?
    - Commit to be open, honest, transparent and undefended. This is an opportunity to tell the truths of your heart. In the end, you may not include all these truths in the ceremony. Discernment is important, too. But as you create the ceremony, telling these truths can be helpful and healing. Consider sharing them with your partner, your spiritual adviser, a professional helper or a trusted friend.
    - Give tribute to your relationship. What about your partner and your relationship are you grateful for? What will you miss? Be specific.

186

- Release the past. This is an opportunity to let go and mourn all that you shared in the relationship, the good as well as the bad. Remember, it's important to feel these feelings; you can't let them go until you do. The more specific you can be, the better. The more specific the memories, the more they will evoke feeling. Do you want to release the past in some symbolic way?
- Let go of the future. Here is an opportunity to let go and mourn what you'd dreamed together and now will not be. As you release these hopes and dreams, remember to be as specific as you can. Do you want to release the future in some symbolic way?
- Offer statements of forgiveness. Here's your opportunity to forgive your partner, or to express your willingness to forgive. This is also a chance to ask for forgiveness. Offering and asking for forgiveness implies an intention to release resentments and to give up the role of victim.
- Plan for your ring(s). Now is the time to consider a symbolic action. Do you want to remove the ring(s) during the ceremony? Do you want to exchange the rings for safekeeping, or each keep your own? Will one of you keep both rings? Do you want to bury the rings? Cast them into the sea? Or would you prefer to transform the metal and the energy of your ring(s) into something else? What might that be?
- Include your children. Do you want to involve them? Do they want to participate? How? Reread Chapter 6.
- Prepare vows and commitments. Do you want to explicitly release each other from your wedding vows? Do you want to make vows and commitments to support each other in your new lives? Do you want to make vows and

commitments to your community? To your
children?

- Design a way to end the ceremony. How will
  you leave the ceremonial space? Together?
  Apart? With your children?
- Create a way to benefit from "the Neutral Zone."
  After the ceremony, what plans do you have to
  spend time alone, to reflect and integrate this
  important experience?

Now that you have sketched out your ceremony, set it aside.
That's right, put it away and forget it.

We suggest that you

- Allow God and your unconscious to work with what
  you've imagined.

**If you have decided that you want to perform a ceremony,
choose a date.**

We suggest that you

- Decide if you want the date to be symbolic, such as the
  day of your divorce, or the anniversary of your divorce.
- Select a date far enough in advance to give yourself
  plenty of time for continued reflection and thoughtful
  and heartfelt planning.

**Working back from the date you have chosen, make a
schedule of all that you must do to prepare for the ceremony.**

We suggest that you

- Create a ceremony planner to keep track of the details.
  This can be your journal, if you would like to combine
  the logistics of planning with entries about your feelings.
  Or, you could buy or create a special notebook.

188

Decide whom you want to witness your ceremony. Your children? Your immediate family? Your extended family? Your intimate friends? Your casual friends and acquaintances?

We suggest that you

- Ask yourself, whom do you really want to be there? Listen to your heart. Trust your intuition. While we believe witnesses are important, remember, this is a personal, sacred ceremony, not a social event.

Decide where you want to perform the ceremony. Even if the location doesn't hold symbolic meaning, it should at least help create the mood you want. Do you want to use a church? A private home or garden? Will the space accommodate the people you want to invite?

We suggest that you

- Arrange for the space as soon as possible. If necessary, make a reservation.
- If you plan to be outside, arrange for an alternative in case the weather is bad.
- Consider how you will make the space sacred.

As part of the tribute to your relationship, decide if you want to create anything special such as a photo collage, slides, a video or stories. Again, get quiet and allow inspiration to speak through you. Remember, a tribute can be simple or elaborate, and as planned or as spontaneous as you choose. (If you plan to speak your tribute extemporaneously, however, be aware of the possibility of stage fright.)

189

We suggest that you

- Find any personal mementos you may need, such as photographs and letters.
- Consult any professionals whose help you may need. If necessary, reserve their services.
- Allow yourself time to grieve.

After several days (or longer), take some quiet time to reread the ceremony you sketched out in your rough draft. How does it strike you now? Have any new ideas? Now that you have some sense about what you want to do and say, who is it that you want to participate with you? Your partner? Your children? Clergy? Family? Friends? What do you want them to do or say?

We suggest that you

- Rewrite the ceremony in more detail, adding anything that has occurred to you since you sketched out the first draft.
- Include anyone you would like to participate and indicate how.
- Type up the ceremony and share it with your spiritual adviser, a professional helper or a trusted friend. Remember, this is your ceremony. You're asking for feedback, not approval. However, because others are not as emotionally involved, they may bring a different perspective that can help you clarify issues and see things you've forgotten.
- Put the ceremony away again. Go ahead, put it away. Trust the process.

Begin to work with the details and tone of the ceremony.

We suggest that you answer the following questions:

- Do you want to use music? What music? Live or recorded? Before the ceremony? During? After? Do you need equipment? Is there electricity available?
- Do you want the ceremony to be formal? Informal? What clothes will you wear? What clothes would you like other people to wear? Does it matter?
- Do you want candles at your ceremony? Flowers? Will you need a burning bowl or some container for water?
- Do you want to use a program to guide the witnesses or to help those participating?
- Do you want to send out invitations? If so, what will they look like? What will they say? If you invite guests personally, what will you say?
- Do you want someone to take pictures?
- Do you want to hold a reception, a party or some other gathering after the ceremony?

Ask for help. If the ceremony is public and reasonably elaborate, you will need help to not get bogged down in the logistics and lose sight of the event's emotional and spiritual intention. If you're still dealing with "crazy time" swings of emotion, you may need help even if your ceremony is simple and small.

We suggest that you

- Explain to a trusted family member or friend what you intend to do and ask for help with the logistics.

If you include your children and intend to make a commitment to them, perhaps offering a symbolic token, now is the time to consider what you will say and what you will give them.

We suggest that you

- Write out your commitment to each child individually. In the end, the commitment you make may be the same for each, but focusing on the individual children can help you find what you want to say.
- Choose the tokens you want to give each child. As with the commitments you make, these can be personalized or the same.

Now (several days, weeks or even months later), reread your ceremony again, adding in your commitment(s) to your children and anything new that has occurred to you. Delete what no longer feels right.

We suggest that you

- Write another draft of your ceremony. Make it as complete as you can. Is this the final draft? Maybe. Maybe not. Remember, there's no hurry. Give yourself plenty of time.

Consider what you will do after the ceremony? Where will you go? Can you be alone? Remember, once the ceremony is over, many feelings might arise. Some may be old and familiar. Some may be new and surprise you. You need time to honor and integrate what you have done.

We suggest that you

- Plan time alone after the ceremony. Don't go to work. Ask family or friends to take care of your children. Ideally, go to a retreat center. For certain, go to a place where you can relax and feel nurtured. This is a vulnerable time for you. If you stay at a friend's house, advise your friend that you may not want to talk and be social. Take a full day and night, and longer if possible. Make reservations or arrangements in advance.

- If you are involved in another relationship, explain to your new partner that you need time alone to honor and integrate the ending of your previous relationship. If your partner is dubious, explain that such honoring and integration will serve you both well as a foundation for any new relationship.
- Once you return home, reaffirm the commitment(s) you made to your children and encourage them to talk about their experience of the parting ceremony and their feelings.

Honor the one year anniversary of your parting ceremony.

We suggest that you

- Take a quiet day by yourself.
- Revisit the place your parting ceremony took place, either with your former partner or by yourself, depending on what feels most skillful for each of you. This could be an actual visit or, if that's not possible, a symbolic visit using pictures, photographs or even your memory and imagination.
- Relive the experience of your parting and the parting ceremony. You can reread what you wrote in your journal, look at pictures or watch a video, if you had one made. What's important is to give yourself the opportunity to feel so that residual emotions of grief, pain and loss can rise, pass through you and then be released.
- Spend some time praying and reflecting. Give thanks again for the life you shared with your partner and for the new life you have found.
- In remembrance and in gratitude for the consciousness, healing and forgiveness you brought to the end of your relationship, take one life-affirming action. What do we mean? Listen to your heart. Be spontaneous. You'll know what to do.

I guess you would have called my ex-husband and me the ideal Methodist young couple. My husband was lay leader, I was church secretary. If there was anything going on at the church, we were there. But all of this time, I knew we didn't have a marriage.

My husband had many, many girlfriends, and I knew that. Still, I felt it was God's will for my life to stay in that marriage. It was not by accident I stayed; it was a conscious decision. I was a real good actress and, although a few people close to me knew, nobody really knew. Some time passed. One day I called Reverend Maze and said I will be late coming into the office. And I started to cry. On this particular day I had exhausted all the options; nothing worked. Finally, we talked a while and he said, "Come into the office when you're ready and we'll talk more about this." And so I shared the truth of what was really going on in our life. Some more time went by after that — I don't really know how long — and I finally came to the conclusion that I would be the person I wanted to be, regardless. I've pretty much lived my life like that since.

Finally, my husband fell in love with someone, and we were divorced. I thought I would die. In the process of that, when I shared with David Maze that the divorce was going to happen — I remember sitting in the office — he said to me, "How will you tell people?"

And I said, "You know how! The grapevine will take it, of course, just like it takes everything else."

And he said, "What would happen if you told people?"

"Oh, there's an idea! How would I do that?"

David was very creative. He said we could do a divorce ceremony.

I said, "You've got to be kidding."

"No, you could write an announcement and then follow that with an act of reconciliation."

I said, "Well, let me see what I can write."

194

The book Rituals for a New Day *was very important for me. I started out saying "Dear friends and family, our lives that were going in the same direction are now going in different directions and because of this we will divorce. You have supported us."*

You see, he and I had both grown up in this church. I asked the congregation for their support, as they had always supported us in our lives, I asked that they support us now. (The text of the service appears in Chapter 11.)

I was not present in church that day; neither of us were. But David read what I wrote and I felt good about that. Rather than letting the grapevine go around and buzz, it gave me the opportunity to tell the story in my own words. I think it took people by surprise. Even my brother didn't know before it happened. I remember, people were shocked. One of the church patriarchs called me immediately after church to say, "Nancy, it isn't true, and you really are not going to go through with it, are you?" And I just said, "Yes I am." I think that people didn't know what to do, and after that they just left me alone. I continued to go and worship every Sunday, but usually I sat by myself. I think they just didn't know what to do. It was sad. People who'd called me "Nancy" forever now called me Mrs. F., and it made me furious because now that I was divorced, who wanted to be Mrs. F. for cripe's sake? I'm kind of a rebellious lady. When this would happen I would say, "Mrs. F.? I beg your pardon, what happened to Nancy?" I said, "My name is Nancy, and I'm the same Nancy you've talked to for a long time." If I hadn't had children I would have changed my name. Our sons were 17 and 19 and they were torn apart by their own grief — they didn't even realize that we'd done a ritual — so I needed to keep my name, for their sake.

Afterwards, there was some publicity about it. This was back in the '70s so it was pretty unusual. Anyway, there was an article in the Methodist Reporter *[October 22, 1976], and one of these tabloids called* National Enquirer *[January 25, 1977]. But for me, personally, the most important publicity came about three years after the divorce, when I had a chance to speak in church on Lay Sunday. Here's what I said to the congregation:*

195

"How many times in your life have you said, 'that won't happen to me' or 'I'd never do that.' More times than you can remember, I'm sure. The same was true for us. C. and I married with similar thoughts in our mind. It was to last forever. Then we began to live our lives, and almost from the start something was missing. For several years we struggled with that realization and then made the decision that we would dissolve our marriage.

"We continued to struggle. How do we tell our family and how do we tell our friends and how do we share with you, our church family? Because God was guiding and directing us, we decided that we would write an announcement of our divorce and Rev. David Maze would share that with you from this very pulpit.

"It is exciting for me to be able to share with you this morning what far-reaching effects this announcement has had. It was written for one express purpose: to share with you the decision that our lives would go in different directions. But God used it for another purpose. He knew that all over the world Christian people, like C. and myself, were struggling with how the Christian deals with divorce.

"About that same time, in New York, a clergy person by the name of Jeanne Audery Powers had started collecting rituals to be published in a book, called Rituals for a New Day. *We were contacted to see if we would give permission for our service to be printed in her book. It is impossible to tell you how pleased I was to share with you the good news that the divorce ritual might be able to help other lives. How do you share the fact that out of our struggle and agony something good has come? Also, for me it was one more affirmation that God is at work in all areas of my life and can use all situations for good in His Kingdom. Because of this ritual, I have had trans-Atlantic phone calls and it has been written up in several publications. It was used on the United Methodist radio program* Connections. *It is exciting to think how many lives have been touched by this very simple message.*

"The sad thing C. and I discovered is that we, the church, have no idea how to deal with people when they really hurt. We are prepared to give our blessings at the baptism, the confirmation, the marriage and even at death, but we don't know how to react when someone tells us that life is not taking the normal, socially accepted path. For the most part, as a church family, we have been hesitant to ask any questions about something that might not be any of our business. We have not learned how to be supportive of people where they really hurt.

"If this morning you asked someone, 'How are you?' and she said, 'Not good at all,' what would you really do or say? We need to make the decision that it is OK to get involved in the lives of people we really care about. Don't be afraid to ask meaningfully if everything is OK, or if there is something wrong. Often there will be nothing you can do to help, but when you're feeling bad it sure feels good to have someone ask and be supportive of you.

"Not too long ago I was falling apart at work one afternoon, well aware that coworkers were close by and would probably know that something was the matter. But I couldn't help that. I had to deal with my hurt on the spot. Later on, one of my coworkers looked up from what she was doing and asked, 'How are you?'

"I answered honestly: 'Not as good as I would like.' Some things in my life were not going the way I needed them to go.

"With a big smile, she replied that she hoped this time would pass quickly for me. 'We need your smile around here.'

"How good it felt to have her support. Ecclesiastes tells us that 'for everything there is a season.' Grieving is a natural part of life.

"Where I am today may not be all that different from where some of you are in your lives. Sometimes I am very lonely. Sometimes I appreciate my freedom so much that I'm not sure that I ever want to be with someone again. The greatest struggle for me is that there are some times when you are 'supposed to be a family.' Many years of training have instilled that in me, but this is no longer possible for us. I try, but it does not come

easily. I never thought that at 45 I would wake up in a home completely alone on Christmas morning.

"In closing, I just want to affirm for myself, as well as for you, that I know God has a plan for my life, and that the divorce was allowed to be part of that plan. I believe that He will continue to use me in His plan for the world as long as I remain a faithful steward and look to Him for His guidance and direction. This probably won't be easy, but then neither was the cross."

Rev. David Maze Reflects

Ours was really an inner-city church, and there was always a concern for the dispossessed. A third of our congregation was African American, so it was Polish, black and European. It was an interesting congregation. It was my first real pulpit and we struggled together.

That was a time [early 1970s] of experimentation for the church. We were coming up with all sorts of new rituals and I sort of had the bug. At the same time, we had taken the sanctuary and made a church-in-the-round out of it; for $60 we remodeled the sanctuary. We moved all of the pews, put the pulpit on the floor, put the choir on the floor, but we didn't spend any money. We used the same old carpet, just relaid the runner down the center; they still have that arrangement. We had a food co-op. It was just that kind of church.

Nancy — Mrs. F. — was the church secretary. Her grandfather had been one of the founders of the church. She traveled across town to come to this church. She was married to C., the man who headed the men's group. C. frequently prayed in church. I loved the way he prayed; it was just so right from the heart. So they both were active in the church, actually grew up in that church; they were children of that church. They'd been married in that church. This was their home. It seemed to me that we were almost forced to do something to acknowledge this change in their lives. Or should we never mention it and just ignore it?

No one knew that they were getting a divorce until Sunday morning when I announced it and did this service. There was a shock wave through the congregation – jaws dropped.

Nancy basically wrote the service — I tidied it up and made it liturgical. One of the important things that she said was, "We hope that you will still care for C. and me after this as you did before." Those are the words she used, those are her words. But sometimes it's easier to say than do. She said later that she had trouble with people not wanting to sit near her — you become a leper. Of course, this was 22 years ago, but even today, to many people a woman like Nancy is different just because she's divorced. What do you say? How do you talk to this divorced person?

Some people might have thought we were endorsing divorce. Not true. I despised it. I still despise it. I always say it's a little bit like surgery — it may be the best choice in the situation, but it sure is going to hurt. And, like surgery, you ought not to do it casually. Nancy didn't. And she remained a faithful church person. The divorce did not change her commitment. She stayed in that church for years and years, until she ended up marrying a Roman Catholic.

Looking back, I find myself wondering, what if we put a flower on the altar for divorce as we do for weddings and funerals? What kind of flower would it be? You can't say it's to celebrate, exactly, but in recognition. Christ says we are all made one, in spite of our disunity. In spite of the things we do to each other, the way we harm each other, all are one in Christ. There's neither male nor female, married nor divorced nor single. We all are one in Christ, and a divorce decree cannot, should not, break this unity.

8

Lovers to Friends

Friends? With My Ex?

The December/January 1999 issue of *Time* Magazine carried a profile of home run hero Mark McGwire. Discussing McGwire's friendly relationship with his ex-wife, Kathy, the authors seemed a bit dubious when they mused "And why shouldn't his ex-wife hug him after his record-breaking home run?" They went on to quote McGwire: "No divorce is ever peachy keen. But Kathy and I are two grown adults." However, later in the same article, the discovery that McGwire's girlfriend, Ali Dickson, is also friends with Kathy, and that McGwire and Dickson sometimes "hang out" with Kathy and her second husband, proved finally too much for *Time*: "Who *are* these people?"

We think Mark McGwire said it well: two grown adults — adults, we might add, who clearly have lived and loved beyond the Myth of the Bad Divorce. These are the kind of adults therapist and researcher Scott Nelson (1991) discovered doing research on post-divorce relationships between ex-partners. Many couples remain on friendly terms after a divorce. They are able to create a balance between the needs of each ex-partner, the post break-up friendship and any new relationship that follows. In our opinion, such people are actually healthier than more "normal" couples whose anger continues to blight their lives and the lives of their children. There comes a time — hopefully sooner rather than later — when healing and wholeness become more important than blame and resentment. As Ahrons (1994) succinctly stated in *The Good Divorce*,

> At some point, to lay down the swords and make a peace agreement will benefit you greatly. In addition to helping your children, cordiality will heal you. Over time, being able to integrate our past history into our

present life provides a wonderful sense of wholeness. Those who adapt well to the stresses of divorce and develop amicable relationships with their ex-spouses are better able to appreciate their own history and to understand how it has prepared them for the present. (p.83)

In his book *Happily Even After* Alan Cohen (1999) offers many stories by couples who have remained or become friends after the end of their relationship. He observes, "As a culture, we are participating in an all-important cultural shift from torturous endings to more soul-satisfying connections. We are paving the way for relationship completions that add to the quality of our lives, rather than destroying them.... Nothing is so botched up that it cannot be restored to kindness and dignity through sincerity, caring, and love" (p.3).

We find it comforting to know that in our desire to remain friends we are neither as unique nor alone as we'd feared — and neither are you. If your friends and family insist that you're crazy, we suggest that you share with them the following benefits for remaining friends with your ex which we've adapted and amplified from a list by Nelson (1991).

1. You share a warm sense of deep, enduring intimate connection.

All of us long to be known. Truly known. In a separation or divorce, no matter how angry you may be, remember, your ex-partner is a person who knows you *as you are*. This depth of intimacy — an "emotional openness and availability that we usually share with only a few others" — is rare and can be the foundation of a friendship. For a lot of couples — this was true for us — intimacy may actually increase after a divorce because both partners cease having expectations that the other will change. You no longer need fear rejection and are free to be yourselves. Also, once you've actually parted, you may be less fearful that your ex will use personal, inside knowledge against you or leave the relationship because of what you tell her. As you move from being lovers to being friends, you may find yourself more willing to risk honesty and less likely to withhold important thoughts and feelings. This further contributes to intimacy.

2. You have special knowledge of each other that can be helpful.

Some divorced people feel fear because their ex-partner "knows things." But reflect for a moment about how much time and involvement it takes to get to know someone. Do you really want to throw all that away? Besides, because you're now no longer a couple and there's no fear of break-up, perhaps your ex could offer helpful feedback — assuming you're willing to listen — about your old, self-defeating patterns, feedback that might improve your chances in your next relationship.

3. Forgiving your partner helps you forgive yourself.

If you don't remain friends with your partner, odds are that it will be because one or both of you continue to blame the other for the break-up, either piling on guilt or assuming an inordinate share of guilt yourself. As we mentioned before, one key to forgiveness is mutual acceptance of responsibility — 100% responsibility. Taking such responsibility helps develop empathy and compassion and this, in turn, leads to forgiveness, for yourself as well as for your partner. It is also wonderful modeling behavior for your children.

4. Someone continues to care for you.

Ours is a mobile and rapidly changing society. This increases our sense of loss as we move from place to place and our partings multiply. Too many friends disappear. Sometimes, especially if you live alone, you may find yourself wondering, who out there cares about me? There is something to be said for knowing that at least one person, your ex-partner, cares about you through all the changes of your life.

5. You share a valuable and unique history.

Knowledge and acceptance of your past can give you a fuller perspective on who you are now and who you want to become. We're all familiar with how difficult it often is to see ourselves. In an ex-partner of goodwill, you have a mirror who can reflect back to you how you have changed and grown.

6. Without the threat of break-up, your differences can be worked through.

Certainly this was true of us. During our marriage we prided ourselves on our honesty and our ability to communicate. But after our parting, we realized that without the fear of loss it was easier to tell and hear the truth. Working through differences can help you both build self-esteem and contribute to your sense of well being.

7. You have a chance to grow and work through psychological distortions.

We all project our own fears, angers and worries onto our partner. Usually, the closer the relationship, the more frequent and more powerful the projections. This is a large part of what goes on in the "blame game" after a separation or divorce. Many of these projections are manifestations of shadows, darker aspects you project outward onto others because you find it difficult to accept them in yourself. After a divorce, you may also see how you brought unrealistic (and often unspoken) expectations to a relationship, and how this resulted in disappointment, anger and bitterness.

In a relationship, it's often difficult to recognize and work with shadows and expectations. We know from sad experience how humbling it is to see all you missed when, at the time, you were convinced you were fully conscious of what you were doing. The more of these unconscious aspects of yourself you can bring to consciousness, the less likely you'll be to act them out again in a future relationship. Also, taking responsibility moves you out of the victim role.

In all this, however, trust is critical. Partners must trust each other if they're going to acknowledge unrealistic expectations and projections and learn to cope with uncomfortable feelings. Unfortunately, trust is often an early casualty of divorce. But holding on to anger and resentment can cause you to miss the opportunity to work through your psychological distortions. For this reason, we suggest that you actively seek out ways to reestablish trust, for yourself and for your children. Of course, if your ex is truly untrustworthy, this may not be possible or advisable. However, we believe it's worth the effort. Most people want to trust and be trusted. Even if your ex doesn't reciprocate, you'll benefit because later you'll know that you honestly tried.

8. You can enjoy simple, relaxed companionship

It's easy to underrate companionship until you remember how anxious you often feel around new people, no matter how exciting you may find them. Sometimes your anxiety increases because you *do* find their presence exciting. If you and your ex-partner remain friends, there's at least one person with whom you can relax.

9. You develop a pride of accomplishment.

This has certainly been true for us. Many conversations since our parting have focused on what we each now recognize as our respective contributions to the difficulties in our marriage, as well as what we have learned and how we can apply those lessons to new relationships. For example, Barbara once called Phil to report with some chagrin that a new lover had complained about her "lack of presence" in language almost identical to statements Phil had used during their married years. Another time Phil called Barbara to say that he found himself sometimes falling into an old pattern of perceiving his partner as an "enemy" and then withdrawing. Although pride in such

205

insights is often tempered with sadness and regret, the accomplishments of personal growth and a sustained friendship remain real benefits you and your ex-partner can share.

10. You continue to enjoy the psychological and physical benefits of a social support network.

Few things are more distressing as a consequence of an acrimonious break-up than the loss of family and friends. People either feel that they're forced to choose between the partners or break off contact with both — and sometimes with their innocent children as well. It's after a break-up that you and your children need your family and friends the most. The more you can show that you and your ex-partner remain friendly, the more likely it is that you'll both keep the social network you value and that can support you and your children through a difficult transition.

What Does "Friendship" Mean?

Among the couples he interviewed for *Lost Lovers, Found Friends*, Nelson (1991) found that the "ideal" friendship includes a connection with another in which there is a measure of trust and caring; a willingness in both friends to share intimate aspects of their lives; a kind of mutuality or give and take; and a mutual acceptance of each other for who they are. In her research, Ahrons (1994) found two basic ways that ex-spouses relate as friends. She called these "Perfect Pals" and "Cooperative Colleagues."

From the beginning of our decision to part, there was never any question that we wanted to remain friends. We had, after all, shared twenty-five years of marriage, including coparenting children who now had children of their own. Even though we felt we needed to part in order to change and grow in some crucial ways, that in no way diminished the many wonderful experiences we had shared or our friendship and willingness to support each other's soul journey. We aspired to be "Perfect Pals." These are people for whom Ahrons (1994) said,

206

... the disappointments of a failed marriage didn't overshadow the positive elements of a long-standing relationship. Most explained that the strength of their marriage had been that they were basically best friends, and they still called themselves good friends. They spoke with each other at least once or twice every week and were interested in each other's current lives. They asked each other how their work was going, what they were doing that week, and even how they were feeling. They trusted one another, asked for advice, and helped each other out, as friends do. (pp. 52-53)

This describes us well in the two years after our parting ceremony. Except for several months when we decided to forego contact in order to let go and begin to establish our new lives, we spoke an average of once a week on the phone. Our communications continued to be open and tended to focus on many of the same concerns as when we were married: personal growth, experiences and books each thought the other might appreciate, mutual friendships, ongoing family issues and, eventually, writing this book.

We also saw no reason that our parting should disrupt our family's life any more than necessary. This was especially true of our children, and grandchildren, who related to us as a unit — Grandma Barbara and Grandpa Phil. After we parted, we agreed to continue several long-standing customs. While we each took responsibility for sending our own birthday cards to friends and adults (one of Phil's responsibilities during the marriage), we continued to send the grandchildren birthday cards and gifts from both of us, and also shared the expense of those gifts. When our granddaughter was christened, we both attended the ceremony and both stayed at our son's home. The only difference was the sleeping arrangement — our granddaughter, Melanie, was delighted to have Grandma Barbara in her top bunk. We took some pride in our son's and daughter-in-law's comment that, despite their initial misgivings, our visit felt like old times. We both continued to send cards, and birthday and

207

Christmas gifts and other remembrances to each other and to members of the other's immediate family. Eventually, we decided to write this book together, which made us business partners, too, at least for a time.

While "Perfect Pals" is one model for an amicable post divorce relationship, another is perhaps more common. If you continue to share custody or coparenting of children, or both, with your ex-partner, you may be what Ahrons (1994) calls "Cooperative Colleagues."

> Unlike "Perfect Pals," ["Cooperative Colleagues"] didn't consider each other to be close friends but for the most part they co-operated quite well around issues that concerned the children. Some of the couples talked fairly frequently, while others had only minimal contact. For the most part, they usually were able to compromise when it came to dividing up the holidays and vacations, though they were more likely to split the time rather than spend it together. Some couples, however, did spend occasional time together — usually special occasions such as birthdays, school plays, or parent-teacher conferences ...
>
> A common denominator for "Cooperative Colleague" couples was the ability to compartmentalize their relationship: they separated out issues related to their marital relationship from those related to their parenting relationship. Their desire to provide the best situation for their children took precedence over their personal issues. Unlike the "Perfect Pals," most of the "Cooperative Colleagues" said they wouldn't have much, if any, personal contact with their ex-spouse if not for their children. (pp. 54-55)

Clearly, the degree of intimacy is different between "Cooperative Colleagues" and "Perfect Pals." However, whether you want to preserve a friendship with your ex-partner for its own sake or for the sake of your children, you may find many important similarities in how you go about doing that.

How Do They Do That?

Our reasons for wanting to remain friends had to do with maintaining our family relationships and also preserving what we could of a relationship that was important to us both for its shared history and its mutual support. To some degree, Carolyn and Kurt (each of whom share custody with an ex), Jessie, Nancy, Lea and David, Marcy, Matthew and Anne, and Jim, in his own way, also managed the transition through separation and divorce and maintained either a cordial, cooperative relationship or a friendship with their ex-partner. For Jessie, Lea and Kurt, this friendship also included cordiality with their ex's new partner. Scott, Anne and Colette all affirmed their desire to eventually establish a more amicable relationship with their ex-partners.

How can a friendship rise out of the ashes of a marriage or other love relationship? It can't — that's the wrong metaphor, drawn from the Myth of the Bad Divorce. A marriage doesn't have to end in scorched earth. Instead, the new can grow from the old. Remember the symbolic image on Scott's program? A young sprig grows out of the stump of a tree that's been cut down. It's a new tree, yes, but the roots supporting growth are old and sunk deep into the earth.

In the early days after your divorce, it may be difficult to work out a friendship. Patience is important here, with your ex and with yourself. How do you nurture new growth? First, you must avoid doing those things that make remaining friends with anyone problematic. Many of these may seem commonsensical — and we believe they're worth remembering. For example, it will be hard for someone to be your friend if you're judgmental. It won't help if you're indecisive about what you want from the friendship and waffle back and forth. Blaming, dishonesty, unfairness (say, in distribution of property) will also make it difficult, as will dragging out the divorce or allowing a third party to interfere — especially a new lover.

It's also wise to be on the lookout for several troubling attitudes and behaviors that might call for at least a temporary suspension of an attempt to be friends. Clearly, as Nelson

(1991) points out, if mental or physical abuse is a part of your relationship, any friendship is ill advised. Also, you may want to reconsider if one of you is avoiding the reality of how your relationship has changed or if friendship proves to be an unhealthy obstacle to personal growth or inhibits forming new relationships. Certainly, there's little point in remaining "friends" just to save face or preserve an idealized self image, or when efforts to be friendly repeatedly evoke bad feeling or end in disappointment. And, of course, one or both of you may simply decide that being friends is just not something you want to do.

But if you and your ex-partner decide you want to try to develop a friendship, it's important to remember that it will take two of you. That's right, you'll need each other's help. Despite the "dos and don'ts" in this chapter, there are no hard and fast rules about how to manage it. Relationships are dynamic and constantly changing, and this is particularly true of a friendship that follows a break-up. What your friendship will look like is for you to decide. Cohen (1999) put it well when he said, "A mutually empowering relationship does not require any particular form; indeed, the belief that it is supposed to be a certain way is the source of much unnecessary angst. The only form required is *whatever works*" (p.185).

As a friendship develops, it will be helpful for both of you to keep track of a number of subtle psychological dimensions simultaneously. This requires attention, practice, goodwill and a sense of humor. As Nelson's research suggests, first you must decide what aspects of the couple relationship you do *not* want as part of the friendship. This may evoke feelings of loss because one of you — or both — can no longer have something that you valued in the relationship and may still desire. Honesty is important here; there's no way to work with these feelings if they remain hidden. Then, it's equally important to decide just what aspects of the previous relationship you *do* want to preserve, and to find ways to support these. For example, we had always valued our conversations and, with a couple of exceptions we'll discuss later, made it a point to continue these as a way to build a foundation for our friendship. Most

210

important of all, however, it's vital that you each begin to move toward your own separate futures (see the Full Spiral updates in Chapter 10).

When asked what they and their ex-partners could do to help ease the transition from lovers to friends, Nelson found that his subjects had a difficult time making the distinction between helping themselves, helping their ex-partners and helping their changing relationship. Our experience bears this out. Here are some ways we've found that create a synergy between your own personal growth, supporting your ex-partner and nurturing a friendship between the two of you. (Again, for a fuller discussion of these issues we recommend Nelson's (1991) book, and also Alan Cohen's (1999) *(Happily Even After.)*

Set Limits. Firm and compassionate limit setting is a balanced way for you to take care of yourself. Taking care of yourself is as essential to establishing a friendship with your ex-partner as it is with anyone else.

The most obvious example of limit setting has to do with sex. Many ex-partners report that they continue to feel sexual desire. Sometimes desire actually increases after they're divorced, for the same reasons it becomes easier to tell the truth: lessened expectations and a diminished fear of loss. The quandary is, what do you do with this desire? Although most people decide not to act on it, there is no hard and fast rule.

In our case, we kept wondering if personal growth and change might enhance passion and intimacy between us. But each time the subject came up, one or the other of us was involved in a monogamous relationship with someone else.

Despite occasional desire, almost all the others we've talked to also refrained from resuming a sexual relationship with their ex-partners, and those who didn't usually regretted it. All were fearful of creating ambiguity in the process of parting that might throw them and their ex-partners back into "crazy time." Those with children were also concerned that resuming such a relationship would muddy the waters of custody and child support and, even more important, confuse their children. How would children understand Mom and Dad sleeping together but not getting remarried?

211

Whatever you decide about sex, do your best to be conscious about it. This probably means not acting in the heat of sexual passion. Easier said than done, we know, especially if some sexual desire arises from the very process of trying to work out a friendship. But there are ways to work with this energy so it doesn't complicate your parting or — worst case scenario — reopen old wounds and throw you back into the "crazy time" feelings of ambivalence, betrayal and loss. Talking helps, about your feelings and about the potential consequences for you, your partner and your children. When in doubt, don't act. Talk.

Another way to keep sex conscious is to avoid situations that carry sexual associations from the past — candlelight dinners, conversations in front of the fire, anything that feels like "dating." Also, carefully limit physical contact to that which you can manage without a rise of sexual desire that's hard to control. This could mean A-frame hugs, just shaking hands or no physical contact at all. Only you know. But whatever you decide about sex — and this is vital — be certain that the decision is coming from a place of honesty with yourself and with your partner.

While sexuality may be the most obvious subject of limit setting, it is by no means the only one. We found we also had to set limits about how much we would talk about other personal relationships. Transferring loyalties from an old relationship to a new one is never easy and can be confusing. What, if anything, about new relationships is it appropriate to share with an ex-partner who continues to be a good friend? What does an ex-partner wish to hear? It's important to talk this through lest sharing too much violate the confidence of a new relationship or cause unnecessary discomfort in the old.

Others have also found it necessary to set limits around prior relationships. Scott set a limit when he refused to accept what he considered his ex-partner's revisionist history of their relationship. For a time, it was necessary for David to see and talk to Lea less in order to establish the integrity of his new marriage. Colette had to set limits that refused her ex-husband's angry demands for contact because she felt that it was not good for her.

Be Sensitive to Timing. We knew that we wanted to be friends and set out to accomplish this. Most people we've talked to, however, were more ambivalent about friendship with their ex. Once they decided, it took a longer time to work out how to be friends. Many factors contribute to right timing, including simply enough time for anger to cool and hearts to begin to heal. Patience is definitely a virtue. This is another opportunity to make haste slowly.

Honor the Natural Complexity and Uniqueness of Your Friendship. In unusual circumstances, we often look for models about how we should behave. Unfortunately, in a culture made cynical by the Myth of the Bad Divorce, there are few examples to follow as you try to work out a friendship with your ex. Remember, your friendship will be different than anyone else's. What we've found most important is that you keep careful track of your feelings and ask that your ex-partner do the same — and that you both be willing to tell the truth. What feels comfortable for you? For example, does it feel comfortable for you to talk on the phone? What are you willing to talk about? News? Family? Kids? Feelings? Other relationships? How about exchanging occasional cards or letters? Personal visits? If you get together, is there sexual tension? How do you feel about that? Does such tension lead to the temptation to resume sexuality? Is that something that you want? If not, how can you handle such desires? How do you feel hearing about your ex-partner's new relationship? About seeing your ex with someone else? All these questions and many more will arise as you work out your friendship. Some things you'll find easy, some more difficult. Let go of your expectations that things will just simply fall into place. Also, let go of any expectations that your friendship must evolve in a particular direction or end up looking a certain way.

Change Involves Mutual Effort (Including Individual Rights). What this means is deceptively simple: if one of you wants to do something — say, get together for dinner — and the other doesn't, then you don't. You're no longer partners, constrained to compromise. Of course, partners don't have to compromise about such things either, but most do. Now you're friends, and as friends it's important that you honor each other's

213

wishes. Besides, times change, and so do people's feelings. The same invitation your ex-partner and friend refused today she might accept next week.

Communicate, Communicate, Communicate. If you didn't learn this in your relationship, and you haven't yet learned it during the process of parting, here's another opportunity. Remember, *how* you communicate is as important as what you say. If communication with your ex continues to be a problem, we strongly advise that you get some help — you, not your ex. There are excellent books and helpful workshops on the subject, including Cohen's (1999) *Happily Ever After*. The basics of good communication include:

- **Using "I" Statements**. If you know what this means, this reminder will probably suffice. If you don't, we recommend the books in the Appendix. For now, just remember how different it feels when someone *blames* you for their feelings ("You *made* me angry when you didn't call me back") and when they simply *own* the same feelings ("I *feel* angry when you don't return my calls").

- **Actively Listening.** This bears repeating: listen, listen, listen. Active listening means that you pay attention to what your ex-partner is saying rather than thinking about how you plan to respond. Remember, you're not together anymore. There's nothing to win or lose — not even an argument. Ask yourself, how would I listen to a friend?

- **Taking Care What You Say.** We all know that words have great power to hurt or heal. Using confidences — the secrets of another's heart — as weapons in an argument is as fast a way to end friendship with your ex-partner as it is with anyone else. Also, what you say about your past relationship can in many ways limit or expand the possibility of a friendship. If one or both of you insist on announcing that the relationship (or the other) "failed," then there's probably going to be a continuing temptation to find fault and blame. This is

214

something that no friendship can long endure. On the other hand, saying that "things didn't work out as we'd hoped" or that "we're trying to find a new form for our relationship" leaves you more options.

Focus on the Positive. It's inevitable, and probably even helpful sometimes, for you to remind yourself of why you are no longer with your ex-partner. But once you're separated or divorced, dwelling on the negatives makes the transition to friendship far more difficult. Obsessing on problems — even if they're real, such as issues of custody and money — takes time and energy. This is time and energy you won't have for working out a friendship with an honest and respectful exchange of views about problem issues. For example, instead of telling your ex what you don't want — "Don't call, OK, it upsets me" — tell him or her what you do want: "I'm having some trouble with my feelings, and I'd appreciate it if for now you'd only call me once a week."

Act As If You Are Friends. Remember "fake it 'til you make it?" If you treat each other as if you already are friends, then when you disagree — especially when you disagree — such cordial behavior will go a long way toward sustaining a friendship of mutual respect and caring. Honesty is important, too, but use care and discernment. The Golden Rule definitely applies: do and say unto your ex as you would have your ex do and say unto you.

Laugh About It. While making jokes at your ex-partner's expense probably isn't a way to enhance friendship, agreeing between you to do your best to see the light side of your missteps and stumbles toward friendship is another good way to help the friendship along.

Clean Things Up. Essentially, this means taking 100% responsibility and working out what you'll say to your children, your family and the world. As Nelson (1991) pointed out, it also may mean spending time with each other after you part "trying to understand in a nonjudgmental way what happened, to tie up the loose ends — unfinished business." Clearly, a parting ceremony of some kind can be helpful with this.

215

Cope with Emotional Dependence. For many people — for us — the loss of emotional dependence was one of the most difficult problems we had to face. Plain and simple, we missed each other. We missed both the day-to-day contact with someone else who cared and we also missed each other as individuals. There's no "right" way to handle weaning yourself from your ex-partner. We tried limiting conversational topics, no contact for awhile and no visits for quite a while. You can make rules, but because your relationship is evolving, the rules must evolve, too. This involves constant renegotiation.

In the end, the most important thing we could do to help ourselves and each other is exactly as described in numerous self-help books about divorce and in divorce recovery programs: learn to live alone and learn to care for yourself. For us, this was a particular challenge. Neither of us had lived alone since our early twenties.

If you are a parent, you may face other challenges. You may have little time to yourself and even less time for reflection and self-care. In some ways, this can be a blessing — you don't have the luxury of brooding. But the business of life can also encourage you to deny your feelings, which then get buried only to surface later. Again, knowledge about how the process of parting works gives you some power. We encourage you to read books like *Crazy Time* (Trafford 1992) and attend a divorce recovery program. Even more important, encourage each other.

Beware of Advice. Don't be surprised if family and friends scoff at your intention to remain friends with your ex. Many people still believe in the Myth of the Bad Divorce. They'll even quote statistics that sound convincing. We half believed them until we began to research this book. Phil met discouragement even in a divorce recovery program he attended. The idea of a post-divorce friendship met with puzzlement ("If you can be friends, how come you divorced?"); skepticism ("You're fooling yourself."); cynicism ("You're just trying to manipulate her."); and hostility ("Why would anyone want to?"). In our experience, most advice you'll receive will be well meaning and misguided.

It also may come tinged with envy and *Schadenfreude*; if others couldn't do it — or didn't even consider the possibility — well, neither should you. When "friends" whispered such doubts in our ears, we wondered if we were fools. At such times, the memory of our parting ceremony became very important. We had vowed to support each other on our souls' journey, and we both felt that friendship was one way to do this.

Develop a Mutual Explanation About the End of the Relationship. If you haven't managed to work out a mutually acceptable explanation about why your relationship ended — including an acknowledgement of differences of opinion and your partner's point of view — now may be a good time to try again. In *Uncoupling*, Vaughn (1986) reminds us:

> Through the social process of mourning [we], too, eventually arrive at an account that explains this unexpected denouement [of our relationship]. "Getting over" the relationship does not mean relinquishing the part of our life that we shared with another but rather coming to some conclusion which allows us to accept its altered significance. Once we develop such an account, we can incorporate it into our lives and then go on. (p.174)

As we've seen, the preparation and performance of a parting ceremony can contribute to developing such a mutual account. In the end, even if you continue to disagree about some particulars — and we still do — the more honestly you can say to yourself, to your partner and to the world that *we* broke up, the easier it will be for you to remain friends.

Give the Gift of Distance. Listening and empathy are important, but for a time, you both may find it more helpful if you listen and empathize from an emotional distance — a warm distance, not an icy distance, but a distance just the same. You need time and space to grieve the loss of your relationship. Paradoxical as it may seem, some distance between you now may make it easier for both of you to let go and gradually grow to an emotional place where you can be friends.

217

Recommendations

1. Ask yourself, do I want to be friends with my ex?
2. If the honest answer is yes (or even maybe), read *Lost Lovers, Found Friends* (Nelson 1991) and *Happily Even After* (Cohen 1999).
3. Discuss the possibility with your ex. If she's interested, share what you've read with her and begin a dialogue about issues raised in this chapter.

Anne's Story

As the date came near to my divorce, I intuitively knew I had to do something to mark the day. I had to make the divorce more real, so it really felt like an ending. My marriage had ended abruptly. My husband took off and left to live 3,000 miles away from our home. I wanted him to stay, so we could figure out together if we were parting or continuing our relationship. It was as if my marriage had disappeared. I had not seen my husband in nine months. It made sense to do a divorce ritual, though I had never heard of such an idea before.

All my soul searching and therapy within that year was used as a springboard for the ritual. I had closely examined my ten-year relationship, including the three years of marriage. What did I like? What did I not like? How had it affected me? What had I learned and discovered? My relationship with my husband since the separation had been mostly distant. We had to talk about practical and financial matters, yet I felt very guarded during those talks, always watching out for what "he might do to me." I felt I had lost my sense of self. I was trying to hold on to bits and pieces of my identity. I felt extremely tense.

On the day of the divorce, I gathered close friends, three men and one couple. As the sun was setting, we drove out into the wilderness. We hiked up a mountain in silence, except for the slow beat of a lone drum, until we reached a fire ring in a clearing. I was gathering myself, my thoughts and my feelings. I was wearing the same dress that I was wearing the day I proposed to my husband.

I made the ritual space on a blanket and spread out candles, incense and percussion instruments. The ritual began. The tone chime, a high-pitched, clear sound with a strong vibration, signaled the beginning. We sat down in a circle and lit the candles and incense. I sang "Birds Are Flying," a song I had composed during my marriage.

219

Birds are flying in the sky
You behind the fence.
Electric wire.
Connect and be burned.
Sun is shining — it is cold
let me in...

It illustrated well how trapped and suffocated I felt, how great the distance had become between my husband and me, and how difficult it was for me to find room for myself.

I gave a brief talk about why we were gathered. I described my greatest fear and my core dilemma. I had always had poor boundaries with my husband. In our relationship, we had had many break-ups and reunions. I illustrated my difficulties in maintaining my boundaries with a song I wrote called "Why?"

Why is it so hard
to say what is on my mind?
It's better running away
than face your angry face.
Should I run away or should I stay?
Should I run away or should I stay?

I was afraid that I would not be able to assert myself, not be able to say, no, and that I would get married to him again.

To symbolize the end, I burned a photo of him; his eyes would no longer be able to seduce me. I also burned a recent card he had sent to me; his words would no longer lead me to act against what I knew was healthy for me.

We buried my wedding necklace. It wasn't very expensive, but it meant something because I'd worn it the day we were married. It was a tough job to bury it. The earth was very hard. I sang another song, "Stop," to signify the end of my marriage.

I need a long, long break
To gain myself and my respect
Away from you.
Some day the door will open again

220

and you may be my friend
just my friend.
May I feel as light as the clouds in the sky
Feel like dancing, feel like saying, hi,
to the sky
And to look at people's eyes.

I asked each of my friends to give me a word or a sound of support. We closed the ceremony with a chant: "Oh, let it go, oh, let it go…" and then everybody began to sing and play one of the instruments.

To celebrate the end we had snacks, bread and champagne.

It was a powerful experience that also affected my friends. One friend described how being part of my ritual helped her to address certain issues that had been unresolved for years. It gave her strength to seek her own closure. By opening up and showing my vulnerable side, it also made the bond between my friends and me stronger.

9

Bearing Witness

Parting through divorce involves your entire community —
you, your children, your extended families, your friends and,
often, even relative strangers, such as doctors and therapists,
teachers, PTA members, your minister or rabbi and the
congregation of your church or synagogue. If your divorce is full
of acrimony, bitterness and conflict it can have a negative,
deadening effect on all of those it touches. Worse, by confirming
the Myth of the Bad Divorce, it seeds despair, making it that
much more difficult for people to imagine parting in a caring and
forgiving way. On the other hand, a parting ceremony can have a
healing and life affirming effect far beyond what you might ever
have imagined. What few realize — we didn't until later — is
how profoundly a parting ceremony may touch the hearts and
lives of those who witness it.

The following are reflections from people who witnessed
one of three ceremonies described in this book — ours, Scott's
and Kurt's. The comments were drawn from interviews
conducted by Phil in person or by telephone.

Witnesses to Our Parting Ceremony

Charles W., early 40s, married and divorced, remembers:
It was just so amazing, that you and Barbara were dealing
with your feelings related to the separation in public. Because
my impression of a separation in a romantic relationship in this
culture is that it's shameful; that somehow this is a failure; that if
you're not together for life something serious must have gone
wrong. And there you were, standing up in front of fifty people,
talking about the reasons why you're parting, how you're feeling
about it. You're talking about your futures, you're talking about
your spiritual evolution together, you're talking about how great

223

it was to be together, asking for the support and the blessing of the community.

I had always been brought up to believe that this is something you should try to sweep under the rug. What you did opened up the possibility of healing with community support, which I don't believe exists for a whole lot of people. It's always seemed to me that if you break up with someone, particularly a wife or a husband, it's got to be acrimonious, it's got to be difficult, you've got to be estranged for the rest of your life — hey, that's the model, at least that's the way it worked with my parents, and with me, and with so many other couples I know. This ceremony was a loving gesture. It was not a renunciation or denial of what had come before; it was more a change in form; another opportunity to continue all the great work that you had done with each other.

The ceremony has been a catalyst for me. What does loving mean? What's my own personal definition of love? I've come to appreciate that there are really a lot of negative beliefs that I have about love. Love means staying with somebody forever, love means not telling the truth when you think that telling the truth will hurt the person that you love, love means putting up with a hurtful situation because that was your commitment, to stay. The ceremony helped me focus on those images, and the discontinuity between what was going on in your case and what I expect would ordinarily happen in the real world.

We have a fancy ceremony to get married, but what's the fancy ceremony that goes along with parting? There's no equivalent. It's so joyous and relatively easy to get married and so hurtful and painful and difficult to get separated. Now why is that? Why shouldn't separation also be joyous? Why shouldn't it just be another part of life? Why should there be so much trauma and so much pain and so much drama associated with separation?

Sheila J., early 40s, married, divorced and living in partnership, remembers:

Because we were in group together and you had been working on your relationship issues over the years, I had such a

224

great sense of compassion for the longing that each of you had to be met in a relationship. I think what struck me most was seeing just how much you guys had experienced together and seeing you and Barb in a really different life than the life I had experienced with you in group. When you showed that video during the parting ceremony I could see your happiness, your joy, the life that you had created together, family — I can feel my emotion with it now. I felt tremendous grief and confusion. I could see all of these places where you were meeting each other — how could it be that in the deepest place of longing you still weren't meeting each other? So the parting ceremony was, for me, in that moment, premature. I wanted to say, hold it; now I know more about you guys, let's see what we can do to preserve the treasure you had created together over a long period of time. That made the parting more painful for me, more bitter-sweet. I was feeling that ache, that ache of loving and creating and still not being fully met.

And, on top of that, I'd had enough conversation with Barb to know that she didn't really want to dissolve the relationship. That's another reason I wondered, is this premature? I felt like she still really wanted the relationship — and when I saw the video, I could see a lot of the reasons why she would. Because of all the good things that you had experienced together, I could see the pain of letting go.

And, at the same time, it feels like the ritual was very much a part of the transformation process. It's good to know that partings can really be done with love, even in the midst of anguish.

Barbara L., early 40s, married, divorced and living in partnership, remembers:

The idea of a conscious ritual to mark the ending of a relationship was initially appealing to me. During the courting phase of a relationship, much time and energy is expended to nurture the budding romance. Even more time and energy is given to the planning of wedding ceremonies, which mark the initiation of the passage into union. It makes sense to me that the dissolution of a union deserves similar time, energy and

225

conscious intent. A dissolution ceremony, similar to a funeral, may celebrate the achievements and attributes of the union, as well as allow an avenue for grief to be expressed over the loss of a once loved form. It has been my experience, witnessing the dissolution of my own relationships and the dissolution of the relationships of some of my friends, that the grief over the loss is not allowed an outlet. Many times it is translated into a smouldering anger — held against the other. I was excited over the inherent possibility of handling these dynamics in a loving and understanding way when I initially spoke about the parting ceremony with Phil.

During the weeks prior to the ceremony, I began to feel conflicted. I really enjoyed the first part of the ceremony, as the highlights of Phil and Barbara's union were acknowledged and celebrated. However, sadness crept in as I noticed that Barbara didn't equally reciprocate Phil's desire to part. In the dissolution of every relationship I've witnessed, one party wants the parting more than the other. Maybe it's because I'm a woman and have had that same experience myself, that my heart went out to Barbara. I have also had the experience of having a third party involved, which compounds the grief, so I empathized with Barbara in that area as well.

In the end, I wished it would have been more private — in front of close friends and family instead of within a circle of less familiar acquaintances. Afterwards, I felt a bit of embarrassment, as if I had been a voyeur. But I think the ceremony succeeded very well in providing a vehicle for conscious grieving.

Diane R., early 40s, married and divorced, remembers:
On the emotional level, it was just incredibly painful for me. I had so much remorse about my two divorces. So many of the things that you and Barbara had done together and had accomplished in your lives — I've never stayed with a partner long enough to get there. Both of my marriages were eight years. I just never had the kind of friendship that the two of you really displayed in that ceremony. It brought up such deep pain and remorse for me in my own life and my own relationships. It was

226

very painful in that way. Not bad, but that was part of my not wanting to be there to witness the ceremony.

The beauty of it and the acknowledgement of each other — that was heartbreaking for me. It was beautiful to witness and it just tore me open. Because the things you were saying to each other were the things I know I'll never hear from my first husband. And I don't know if I'll ever make the gesture to do that with my second husband. So hearing it from both of you was wonderful because I could take it in through osmosis. And it was also painful because I knew that I'd never hear it for myself.

In the end, the biggest impression I was left with was of the healing between the two of you; to have a public forum, to witness each other and be witnessed by others — it wasn't just a completion but an acknowledgement and a healing.

Nicola C., 40s, married, remembers:
I have been married and stay very practical in my outlook about marriage. I'm not a romantic. That's the way I view the whole marriage package in our culture. I felt very much aligned with Barbara. I'm an "older woman," too, and the whole situation was initially very irritating to me. At the time, my irritation distanced me from my feelings.

When I thought about it afterwards, I certainly could see the benefit of ritualizing and acknowledging the passage. It seemed like a really positive and constructive idea. Usually, you have so much drama around the tragedy of divorce. It was hopeful to see another way of doing it.

Barbara G-C., early 60s, divorced, remarried, remembers:
I didn't see the ceremony, but I heard about it and then I saw the video later. I think it's so incredible. I showed it to six people, people who had been together for a long time, working with me individually and in a group. Two couples were really touched by it and it helped them. They're still in the process – they may never even separate – but it gave them permission to try something different.

I met my husband when I was thirteen. So we did high school, we did college, and when I saw you and Barbara in the

227

video, all the pictures, everything that you went through, it was just so wonderful. "Grow old with me, the best is yet to be" — that just broke my heart. And yet I felt you tried beyond imagination to keep this marriage going. But if intimacy and passion are missing, well, there's no way you can fix that. My degree is in sexuality, but I don't understand it. You can do exercises, you can do marriage encounter, you can go away for a weekend and learn how to pet, but it doesn't make one person hot for the other. I have intimacy with a lot of people, but it doesn't mean I'm going to have a celebratory, heart-singing thing.

It's very difficult, separation with love and consciousness. Even more if there's another person involved. So I really felt a lot of compassion for all of you. The ceremony reminded me of a quote that I love from Emmanuel: "Sometimes two souls come together to learn how to separate."

Janet R., mid-40s, married and divorced, remembers:
I found the ceremony to be somewhat confusing. What I observed energetically was that despite the words of parting and separation at the beginning, once the slides [tribute to the relationship] started, it was hard to accept that the relationship I had seen was to be put aside.

I had been married 24 years, 25 by the time the divorce paperwork was done. I was married at 18, in the heady year of 1967. I did not have the joy that you and Barbara had. I watched with alternating waves of envy and shame. I cried, not for your consciousness but for my lack of it. My married life was black and distorted where yours had, for a time, been light and straightforward. True, your faces became slowly mask-like, but in my marriage I was covering bruises with makeup, avoiding family and not allowing friendships. I envied what may have seemed like entombment to you, and at the same time understood that my life has served me as yours served you. I envied your ability to have ended your relationship the way you seemed to have begun it — as friends, with friends and family. I can't say enough about how much more sane and caring your relationship seemed to me than the relationship I had participated in.

In some ways, I suppose it's the same reaction that people have at weddings — they cry, not out of sadness, but out of the memories of relationships that began with the same high hopes and yet didn't work. That may be a critical factor in rituals like this: what it brings up more than what it is. What I observed was a roomful of people rocked to their cores on primal issues.

Peg H., early 60s, divorced and remarried, remembers:
Like everybody else, I was very moved by the ceremony. I was moved by the fact that you and Barbara would do it, that you would share all that with us, that you would share your lives. I was moved by the juxtaposition of love and pain. This was a painful event, particularly for Barbara, although I could see that it was for you, too, in making the choice. I could see respect for each other, respecting the relationship you were leaving. The ceremony caused me to look at my own relationship with my husband. And I could feel being the leaver and being the one who was left. I could identify with both of you. That was painful for me.

Another part for me was watching two people who once loved each other — and still do. Even if you've made the decision to part, even if you've decided that the relationship isn't working or isn't doing what you want it to do, love doesn't vanish, love is still there. My sense of it was that the love would always be there. That this was something that you would hold forever. That just because you were choosing not to stay with each other didn't mean that this was the end of love. It was very clear that your love was permanent; that it would never cease to be even though the relationship might be different.

For me, the ceremony did away with dualities. It showed how loving and parting can live side by side, that they aren't opposites. Even though there was pain, it felt like sharing what had been was very meaningful — not only sharing with us but also sharing between yourselves; all you had done, and been, and how that led to who you are today. I felt privileged.

229

As a witness, I was certainly encouraged to look at my own relationship — where I might be careless or dishonest. In that sense, the ceremony was a gift to the people who were watching, an encouragement to be conscious and vigilant and not careless in their own relationships. Watching people part, watching two people decide that their relationship hasn't made it, that really encourages you to pay attention.

I was left — I think we all were left — with a feeling of respect and gratitude that you guys would have the courage to expose yourselves in this way and to let us all share the experience with you. It was like a gift.

Gene H., late 50s, divorced and remarried, remembers:

I was deeply affected by the integrity of the ceremonial process, and also by all of the different feelings that I experienced. I appreciated and admired the integrity of both of you in what you had created, and I contrasted it with my own first parting. I felt deeply saddened that my first wife and I had not done anything like this. We parted in anger and numbness, and I'm sure that there were consequences for each of us personally and, I believe, probably deeper consequences for our children. Because the fall-out from not having done the kind of work you and Barbara did meant that there was on-going tension and occasional anger that my children experienced. My ex and I, being adults, were strong enough to either deal with those feelings or defend against them. But my children, who were four and one and a half at the time, were much more vulnerable, and as a result felt torn whenever that tension came up between their mother and me.

After your ceremony, I called my ex and suggested that I come to Toronto where she is currently living, to create that kind of ritual with her. Her response was "Why?"; our divorce was now 24 years ago. So I regret to report that my enthusiasm diminished quite a bit. I thought to myself, if she isn't really a willing party to this, I wonder what the benefit would be? I can deal with my own lack of consciousness about the way that I left my first marriage, and the animosity that I bore toward her for years after. But I realized that had I done the kind of work that

230

you and Barb did, either that animosity would have diminished or not been there at all. So even decades after the fact, seeing what was possible encouraged me to try to heal an old wound. Had I been received with greater encouragement, I would have gone there and created a ritual with my ex-wife and my children. I think it would have benefited everybody.

I know from talking to people subsequently that there was a deepening of people's commitment to work on their relationship issues. I think many people were deeply touched by the images from the history of your relationship, and in a way they — and I — were saying, "Now how can it be so beautiful and so apparently nourishing for both parties in the relationship, and not work?" It is a mystery. I think wrestling with that mystery is very important. To be willing to stand in pain and deal with it instead of running away from it is one of the strengths of the work that we do, that you did together.

Wouldn't it be wonderful if, as a part of their preparation for marriage, people could agree that if a divorce happens they will take steps to seek counseling for their relationship? And if, at the end of all their work to save the marriage, they still find that it's not going to work, they agree in advance that they will work together to create a conscious parting, for themselves and for their children?

Witnesses to Scott's Service of Recognition, Resolution and Renewal

Claude S. (Scott's father), 60s, married, remembers:
I'd never heard of anyone doing a divorce service before. Going into it, not knowing what the ceremony was about, I thought it was more like an unhitching, more like an uncoupling. But I really think — after experiencing it — it was necessary. There was none of the negative, blaming of one person, none of that. It really wasn't that kind of thing.

I think a lot of the people who came didn't have any idea what it was. They were there because of their friendship with Scott, and out of curiosity. I think some of them thought it was

231

kind of weird to have a church ceremony. I really hadn't thought that much about it myself and it turned out to be different than what I thought it would be. Mostly Scott's friends came, about thirty people in all. Scott's ex didn't come. She did write us a farewell letter, but we don't have much contact with her anymore. Overall, I think it was a good thing to do. I'd recommend it to other people.

Lee B., 50s, married, remembers:

As I recall, I sent Scott an opening draft of the service. I was familiar with the liturgical terms. I'm a United Methodist and our version of *carisio* is called the Walk of Emmaus. It's a spiritual renewal, and one of the features of the walk that I have always loved is the part called dying moments. It is a special communion service at which each of us is asked to declare a piece of ourselves that we want to become dead. It seemed to me that a service around divorce was a great time to offer that, not just to the ending marriage of Scott and M., but to the body of Christ. I said, "Why don't we try to do a dying moment kind of thing?" The form that took for Scott — his take on it — was to encourage each of us to write down on a sheet of paper that piece of ourselves that we wished to go away. During the service those individual pieces of paper were deposited in a metal cauldron at the front of this little chapel. And then Scott and somebody else burned those pieces of paper in front of the congregation.

After my initial suggestions, Scott worked on it with his minister, Dorothy, and several friends, and it became very much his service. The service itself was designed to be healing, in contrast to some more judgmental points of view. That's not what Scott's service was about. There was no blaming of his ex-wife.

Whenever I describe a divorce service to people, they assume it's going to be somber; "Ew, oh boy, I don't want to go to that." That was not the case with Scott's service. The time during which we gathered before the service, the service itself, and the time we gathered after the service were all pleasant, upbeat, a time to be enjoying good friends.

Dorothy S., 40s, married and divorced, remembers:

Because I also officiated at Scott's service, it's interesting to think of myself as a participant. My general experience with worship is that I feel like a participant in a worship service I'm leading only during breakthrough moments. It doesn't always happen because a lot of times my role as leader overshadows my ability to acknowledge where I am personally, what's going on in my own self. Not this time. I led the communion but there were a lot of other people — Scott, his father, Claude, his friends, Lee and Alison — who were leading also, which meant I was able to be more participatory than I ordinarily would have been.

My divorce had been final about a year at the time of the service, and clearly I had not — have not — quit grieving. So participation in the service certainly came at an apropos moment in my life.

When my husband first left, I wanted desperately for somebody to tell me what to do. On all kinds of levels! I have not done anything like a divorce recovery workshop and I do not have a whole large support group of divorced friends. I kept saying, "Isn't there a book that tells you what you're supposed to do?" What do you tell your kids? Who gets what furniture? I wanted directions on everything. Spiritually, I certainly struggled on my own on a lot of levels.

My hobby in life is tree scriptures. Those are scriptures in the Bible that refer to trees. So the image of the cut-down tree [used by Scott on the cover of the program for his service] was very powerful to me. It's an image that's related to other things in my life. What that picture says to me is, something that was strong and beautiful and living has been cut down. But out of that thing — not separate from it but out of that very tree stump — new life has come. It's the same root. Some of the roots have died, but from that same rooted place new life has come. In my own personal life, that's one of the things I'm trying to claim. When we did the part of the burning, the thing I wrote down — which I hadn't told anybody because nobody asked me — was to give up my dislike of being single.

233

Like many other people, a part of me was angry after divorce that my life wasn't going to be what I'd envisioned. During Scott's service, it was a very good thing for me to say, "I'm not going to resent this quite as much because it is what is." Sometimes you have to say, "This is what is so let's live with it and quit worrying about what isn't anymore." We all come to an event like this with our unique regrets and pain and hurt, and what I liked about that part of the service was that it gave everyone an opportunity to express their own personal needs. Scott introduced that part. He did a really good job. He didn't tell you what you had to be feeling but just said, "I don't know what's going on in your life, and I'm not asking you to tell me. Whatever it is you want to give up, here's the opportunity." I thought that was great. And since the ceremony, in the months that followed, I have found days when I wake up and I think of reasons why being single is not the worst thing that ever happened to me!

Witnesses to Kurt's Service of Lamentation and Healing

Joel L., 30s, married and divorced, remembers:
At the time, Kurt and I worked together. We did similar jobs and we shared an aisle between our cubicles. As luck would have it — if you can use that term — we both began ending our marriages on the same week-end, unbeknownst to each other. So we went through this entire process together and became pretty close friends.

When Kurt asked me to participate, I had never heard of such a thing. When we got there we were wondering what was going to occur. I don't believe anybody there had ever participated in that kind of ceremony before. There was some small talk in the kitchen and when everybody had arrived someone said, well, let's go into the living room and do this. I felt a little nervous because I wasn't sure exactly what was going to transpire. Kurt and I had talked a little bit about it and it sounded interesting, but I didn't know any of the details. But very quickly, all of the nervousness went away because we were all very much into the ceremony and the symbology of the breaking apart of a relationship and a marriage.

It was a very emotional, extremely moving experience for me, especially because of my own divorce. I can remember where I was sitting in the room, I can remember my tears, I can remember the symbology of extinguishing the one candle and lighting the two — that was particularly poignant for me because my wife — my ex-wife — and I had done the opposite when we got married: lit one candle and then extinguished the two. I think it was particularly moving for me because my ex-wife and I didn't do anything like this, never even talked about it. But it really helped me put my own relationship behind me, especially the symbology of the candles. Even though I was a guest, it was almost as if it was partly my ceremony.

Tamera El-S., 40s, married, remembers:
My brother Kurt's divorce completely blindsided him. He's the youngest of five, the baby of the family, and it grieved us tremendously. We've never had a divorce in the family. So it was really a devastating experience for all of us. It was complicated by the fact that he and L. had a toddler daughter. It was especially painful because it seemed from the onset that the relationship wasn't reconcilable in thought, let alone action; L. wanted a divorce and that was the end of it. It was a very painful process for all of us as we watched him really hurt by the experience.

As will often happen in a situation like that, there were some very strong feelings of animosity we all had to process. We had always tried to be respectful of L. because Kurt had chosen her as his wife. We had to continue that because she is the mother of our niece, H.. But we still had our own hurts and unresolved painful issues which had been problems in our family because of this relationship and then because of the divorce. It was a real struggle. How could we process those feelings when it was clear from the outset that L. didn't want to?

When Kurt approached me about the ceremony, I thought, oh, this is a good way of trying to bring acknowledgement and resolution to this whole process. We acknowledge weddings, baptisms, graduations, funerals, but there really isn't any way to mark the passing of a marriage relationship. I thought it was a really useful and innovative way to express the grief we all felt because this relationship had failed — even more so because it was done from a religious perspective.

Julie did a tremendous job using the parable of removing the log from your eye (see Chapter 11). We all have fallen short of what we ought to do and so we shouldn't be particularly harsh on one party of a failed marriage. It's always a two-way situation. It made me pause and reflect on how easy it is to hold a grudge and be part of that negativity. The marriage was over; there was nothing to be gained by rehashing the he-said-she-said scenario.

It was a very moving ceremony. It felt like an emotional catharsis for everyone who was there. We all had been a part of Kurt's life from the beginning of the relationship, through the marriage and the years of faltering, and then the final end of it. I felt badly for L. in that she had declined the opportunity to be part of it. Actually, I read her written comments at the ceremony as a proxy. But I really felt that she missed out by not having been there. It would not have been comfortable. It wasn't comfortable for any of us, but it gave everyone a chance to grieve the loss and acknowledge each other, including L., as still important and valued persons in the network of family and friends. There was so much forgiveness. I think it would have been good for her. I also wish that someone in her family had been there. I think they would have seen that although we all felt sad about it, we still valued them as people. I felt that there was a hole because no one from her family was part of the ceremony.

The people who attended were Kurt's family and friends, all adults. If my children were then the age they are now — thirteen and ten — I think I would have had them come, especially if I had known how it would turn out. It was very beautiful, very emotional; certainly not a ceremony where you're just a bystander. I still remember it intensely. It was as sacred as any church service I have ever been in, even more spiritual than most. It was very personal, very intense. It left me feeling completely drained, and not in a negative way. It was as if the ceremony gave me a way to acknowledge that this was a

236

marriage that had given us a beautiful niece and for that we would be forever grateful to L.. We wished that the marriage had turned out differently, but it hadn't. Since L. will always be part of our life, the ceremony was helpful in letting go of a lot of anger and frustration and a sense of violation. There was no going for L.'s emotional jugular in her absence, no blaming, but it allowed Kurt to pour out every disappointment and hurt and let it go, not just verbally but also symbolically by sending a little piece of wood down the [Mississippi] river.

The wood made visible that both Kurt and L. had come with logs and splinters that they'd added to the relationship, just as we add logs and splinters to our relationships every day. One was not more to blame than the other. If we are to ask for forgiveness and receive it then we also have to give it. It was a wonderful visual symbol; it tied everything together, failure and forgiveness. For me, it was reminiscent of the old testament Jews who sent the sacrificial ram out into the desert with the sins of all the people. This is it, the symbol said; we're letting all of this go. It's not going to help any of us to hold onto these logs of hurt and resentment. We have to move forward. We have to weigh what's really important. And number one in importance was that H. be raised in a family that did not make one parent a villain. A family that could love and support Kurt, H. and L. in whatever way they needed. The process was very comforting and freeing. I strongly recommend it. It was much more personal and spiritual and emotional than just getting a registered letter announcing that the divorce decree is final.

Since the ceremony, I've talked to quite a few people about it. Some have been fairly skeptical. It's unfamiliar and there simply isn't much out there about it. But most have been interested, and even people who don't have a traditional Judeo-Christian focus could see how it might fit with their own spirituality.

I work in an inpatient hospice. Over and over again I see people struggling with unresolved family dynamics and losses, filled with woulda-shoulda-coulda regrets. I always tell my hospice families that the one gift they don't have much of is the gift of time. If they are going to get anything resolved it's got to be *now* because you won't have later.

I feel that the ceremony was a very supportive and nurturing way to resolve the end of Kurt's and L.'s relationship, and to help bring emotional closure for our family.

Jessie's Story

I had a four-year relationship with a man whom I had hoped to marry. When we parted, at his choosing, I had a lot of anger towards him. After much thought, I created a ceremony that I shared with a close girlfriend. I gathered mementos of the relationship — photographs of us together, small gifts he had given me. I also wrote a list of each instance in which I was harboring resentment towards him, being as specific as possible. The emphasis was on my need to forgive myself for my part in each situation. I used a model I have found helpful.

When you did thus and so (I named what he'd done specifically) . . . I felt (and then I named the emotion I'd felt — angry/happy/sad) . . . because I assumed/judged that you were (I named what I had perceived his attitude to have been — disrespectful/cruel). What I want to forgive myself for is (and then I named these specifically — for example, giving you the power to override my self-respect/allowing your actions to upset me. . . .)

The list was extensive because I had a lot of blame toward him that I wanted to dissolve, and I wanted to consciously release the hold self-anger and self-hate had on my life.

My girlfriend and I took the mementos and the list up to a large ceremonial plateau that we have on our mountainside. We built a large fire and I burned the mementos while reading the list. I then tossed the list into the fire.

The most powerful part of the ceremony was when I released my anger over an abortion that I had had with this man. He wanted it but I did not. I went ahead and had the abortion to "save" my relationship with him. I needed to forgive myself for compromising what I desperately had wanted to keep — the baby — for the sake of keeping the relationship with him. As I read this portion of the list, I burned a small rag doll as the symbol of the unborn child. This was an important statement for me because, as it turned out, I will never be able to have another child. It was my way of making amends to myself for my responsibility at the loss of motherhood.

Very shortly after our relationship dissolved, my ex-boyfriend fell madly in love with a mutual acquaintance. They married and had a child a year later. I was privileged to hold their newborn son a week after his birth and, two years later, held their second son a month after his birth. I believe that the ceremony I performed played an essential part in the genuine joy I felt when holding those babies. It is also ironic that, while watching the challenges of their new parenthood, I thought, "Boy, better her than me." This was especially true for me after they had the second child. My ex-boyfriend's wife — now a friend of mine — was trying to manage a two year old who was screaming and throwing food around the kitchen while my ex-boyfriend, a somewhat inept father, was trying to manage a squalling newborn in a toy-strewn apartment. I would not have traded places with his wife for anything, and I uttered a prayer of thanksgiving to God for the circumstances of my life, just as they were.

10
Full Spiral

We like what David, Colette and others said to us about the spiraling nature of grieving and letting go. In this emotional process you never come full circle — that is, back where you started. Instead, in David's inspired phrase, you come "full spiral"; you come around to the same emotions again and again — sadness, anger, jealousy, acceptance. But when you do, you're higher on the spiral, experiencing them in a new way because you are a new and different person. Of course, it's always possible to slide back down the spiral. This would show in an inability to let go of your past relationship, manifested by continuing resentment, depression and stagnation. However, we believe that if you commit to conscious parting and a healing divorce, then you and your community can travel up the spiral toward greater consciousness, acceptance and love. As we have seen, ritual and ceremony can help you make this important life transition.

We asked people who shared their stories to bring us up to date about their lives, and to include any comments they wanted to make about their experience with ritual. Most responded. These reflections were either written by the storytellers themselves or are drawn from personal interviews.

Barbara
It has been almost four years since the parting ceremony with Phil. I woke up the morning after the ceremony out of a dream in which I was saying two lines from the 23rd Psalm: "Yea, though I walk through the valley of the shadow of death, I will fear no evil, for Thou art with me. Surely goodness and mercy will follow me all the days of my life, and I will dwell in the house of the Lord forever." It felt like a promise that somehow I would be OK.

Between January and April following the ceremony, Phil and I sold our home, divided everything up, packed up everything and moved to different parts of the state. I moved into a little house in the Carmel Valley in northern California and began working in my garden. I think I spent the whole first six months crying. Being outside so much really helped. I had the blessing of being able to take a year off from work so I had time to really grieve. There was such an enormous sense of loss. There was also a lot of anger and jealousy that came up for me to work through. There were times when I just thought I would die — that it was just too much — that my heart would never heal. Then one morning, I felt a sense of release and I knew I would be OK — I was really through the worst of it. The rest of the year was spent looking at what I really wanted in my life and putting my new life together. In December, at the end of the first year, I spent two weeks by myself in silence reviewing all my journals, letting go of all the little residual pieces of anger and grief that I could find, and getting ready to come out into the world again.

In the first part of January, I answered ten personals ads in the paper and went on ten dates in ten days. The intent was just to practice meeting people and to reassure myself that I was still desirable. It was not to find a permanent relationship at that point. However, from that beginning, much to my surprise, I met a wonderful man with whom I am now very much in love. I have restarted my healing practice and am assisting people in developing rituals for life transitions such as coming of age, parting and becoming an "elder." My life is really full, happy and satisfying.

Phil

After Barb and I sold the house I moved to San Diego. I lived alone in a condo not far from the sea — the first time I'd ever lived by myself. For a time, I felt cut off, lonely and scared. Had I made a huge mistake? These feeling were exacerbated by another life transition, this one unexpected. The screen writing I'd been doing for fifteen years came to an end, the result of changes in the marketplace and aging in a business that puts a premium on youth. Money got tight, and I could see a time coming when I would have to live off of my savings. It was

242

difficult. I often felt bereft and at sea. I continued to feel ambivalence about the divorce, as well as a lot of nostalgia and regret. This was intensified by the fact that Barbara and I remained friends. A reminder of all I had given up was always just a phone call away. I spent many days crying. Despite this inner turmoil, however, I remained convinced that I had made the right decision. A chronic disease disappeared and my physical health improved. I found I liked living alone and learning to do for myself. I joined a yoga class and a gym. My creativity flourished as I began to write more from my heart and soul. Now that one career was ending, I decided I would reinvent myself artistically. I wrote short stories again, and a novel, and began this book. I joined a writer's group and gradually made friends. I also started going to church, to keep connected with spirit and with beauty through an early morning music service, and with spiritual questions through an adult Sunday school. I attended a Divorce Recovery program and found it healing. On the first anniversary of our parting ceremony, I relived the experience through the video. On the second anniversary, the day of our official divorce, Barbara and I performed a second ritual at her home in Carmel. Each of us wrote wishes for ourselves and each other, tied them to helium-filled balloons and then let them go, to rise and disappear into the clouds.

My long-distance relationship with Chris did not last. Although we spoke often on the phone and exchanged e-mail almost every day, we saw each other only every other month, and then only for a few days. It was a romantic, loving and passionate relationship, and it was also stormy, fraught with misunderstandings, hurt feelings, fears, doubts, jealousies, betrayals and several break-ups and reconciliations — darkness as well as light. Chris was convinced that all this was no more than a normal period of adjustment; that, indeed, the turmoil was positive evidence of our connection because intimacy "brought up our stuff." To me, the ongoing turmoil was a sign that despite our love for each other, living together was not going to work. Much as I loved Chris and mourned the loss of her spirit, passion and beauty in my life, I chose to end the relationship.

We saw each other one last time a few months later in San Diego, where we performed a simple parting ceremony on the beach. We chose the night of December 31st as symbolic of an ending. We intended that midnight would represent a new beginning for our relationship, a transition from lovers to friends. Together, we built a sand castle to symbolize the hopes and dreams we had shared and, once it was built, we sat together and watched as the rising tide washed it away. But then we made love again. More confusion and heartache. Within a few weeks, Chris decided she needed to break off contact in order to heal. From the relief I felt, I realized that I did, too. Although I look forward to the day when we can resume a more active friendship, for the time being it seems most skillful for me to have no contact.

After parting from Chris, I lived alone and waited to see how life developed. I chose not to date. I did my best to stay open and protect an inner emptiness. That's what I was doing when one day an e-mail inquiring about this book arrived from S., a friend of my sister. They both lived on Guam, the same South Pacific island where Barbara and I first met and where our son, Geoffrey, is buried. A correspondence developed, and then a cyber relationship. Not wanting to waste precious time, S. and I did our best to be open, honest, transparent and undefended. Neither of us wanted a long-distance relationship. At S.'s invitation, I made a trip to the island to meet her and her two children. Later, I met her extended family when she came back to the States for a visit. Though we were both nervous, given the love we felt we decided to take the risk. I stored most of my belongings and returned to Guam, where I now live with S. and her children, engaged in intimate relationship, family and the reinvention of my artistic life. It's not all perfect. I feel isolated so far from my friends and my family, and sometimes I long for a life alone. Sometimes, too, I feel grief about all I've let go. Still, I am glad that I answered the call. Living here feels like a "full spiral" affirmation of life's mystery and wonder. And I trust that, as Rilke says, if I am patient with all that is unsolved in my heart and try to love the questions themselves, sooner or later I will live into the answers.

244

Carolyn Elizabeth

It has been three and a half years since our divorce ritual at the gazebo. I am grateful I initiated the ceremony, and that my husband participated as he did. As a result, B. and I shared unexpected tenderness and intimacy which felt very healing. Reflecting back on the experience, I would have to say that the last hour of our married life was the most conscious and loving of our twelve years together.

It is a paradox how we could share such closeness and still be certain we needed to end our marriage. I remember thinking during the ritual that if our hearts could meet here, now, why couldn't we do so in our marriage? I knew our situation would be very different if we were able to meet in this tender, undefended place where love resides. But, this is the way it is, and I accept this mystery of relationship.

Following our divorce, each of us plunged into other exclusive relationships. Now I see how we unconsciously used these new relationships to comfort us from the intensity of divorce. We were able to postpone the grief we held deep within. When our respective romances ended, we were broken open once again. Fortunately, some time had passed since our divorce, and we were strong enough to stand on our own. Separately, we faced the deep-seated grief we had avoided.

B. and I are still learning how to have a successful divorce. Our children are beginning to heal, to grieve their own losses, and to accept that their mother and father will not live together.

Recently, B. and I came together in celebration of our children's Baptism. It was the first time the four of us had met in body and Spirit. During the ceremony, B. stood behind our daughter and I stood behind our son. As prayers for our children were being read, B. extended his arm around me and touched my shoulder. As soon as I met his hand with mine, he was gone again. I will always remember the sweetness of that moment, and I trust we will share other intimate moments of mutuality in the future.

We love our children and we want to give our best to them as they grow into adulthood. B. and I are learning to respect each other as the mother and father of our children.

Through the divorce ritual, my husband and I created fertile ground in which our seeds can be sown. Like the peace lily plant, our blossoms face opposite directions, but we are planted in the same rich soil.

Scott

I am determined to do whatever it takes not to hurt or be hurt in a relationship again. Statistics reveal that the marriage rate is only about 3% lower now than it was one hundred years ago. That is, 67% of first time marriages remain intact. The difference is the divorce rate. When people divorce now, they are more likely to remarry, then divorce again, then remarry once more, then divorce again, and so on. This is where the famous statistic comes from — 50% of all marriage end in divorce. Once you're divorced, it's easier to do it again. Even though my statistical chances of remaining in an intact second marriage are less than 20%, I won't let this number stop me from trying. In preparation, I am renewing old commitments and making new ones with God and myself that I believe will provide a better opportunity to live a happy and healthy life.

It's been only a few months since my ceremony. I was one of the youngest in my divorce recovery workshop. I just couldn't understand these people who were only out of a marriage a few weeks or months and were starting another relationship. Right now, I know it will be two or three years before I'm ready. There needs to be time for things to blur; I think we all have to kind of get blurry. We have to get to a place where we're comfortable enjoying that sunrise alone, instead of feeling that desperate need. It's not fair to other people you might be in relationship with. Right now, I'm in my infancy. As much healing as I had with this service, I still have dreams and cold sweats about the marriage. There's no substitute for time. It's just going to take time. I know that three months from now, six months from now, things will be different. I've been keeping a journal. And I can see some changes already. However, I also have that daily debate with myself: am I really getting better or just better at pretending? Or maybe I'm just tired of hearing myself talk about it. Then, sometimes, I wonder, where's the progress? It's like watching hair grow. Sometimes it feels like nothing is happening.

There's still a long way to go. But I think about when I got married. Not everyone is married in their heart the day they put on the rings. It took a long time to get to the wedding day, and then it took a long time to get into the habit of having that other person around. A lot happened before the marriage fell apart; little problems festered into bigger ones due to lack of attention or acceptance. And then I had this ceremony to bring closure to the spiritual part of our relationship. But it still takes time.

I'm selling the house that M. and I remodeled together; another piece of closure. I'm now working with a start-up company and starting my own company to export our products to Canada. I'm doing quite a bit of traveling again. I've found a nice country cabin just outside of Knoxville near the Smokey Mountains, a kind of retreat, and am starting to look for an urban condo in Toronto.

If two years ago anybody had told me that this is where I would be, I wouldn't have believed them. I'm really not going to make any predictions about my life and where I'll be in another two years. All I know is that I will keep my faith in what God provides. I will keep faith in myself and what I can accomplish. Then, eventually, I will be able to share this wonderful adventure with somebody who harbors similar thoughts and feelings and possesses the means to achieve them. I pray that I am willing and able to recognize, accept and act when such an opportunity arises.

Lea

It's been a year and a half since the ceremony with David. I continue to be grateful for the experience of that relationship and the opening of my heart. Part of my purpose in ending the relationship with David was to free my energy to allow for the possibility of a more complete and mutual relationship to come into my life. As it turned out, within two days of completing the ceremony with David, a man whom I had met a year earlier called — just to see how I was doing. Within a short time we were seeing each other regularly and are now in a wonderful,

247

deep and very satisfying long term relationship. I know that the experience with David and the ceremony of completion that we did helped open the way for this miracle of love to occur in my life. I continue to practice and teach Tantra with my new found life-partner. It only gets better and better.

I still have occasional contact with David and his wife and we share thoughts and insights about our respective journeys as they unfold. It feels good to know that the caring and affection has lasted and that, even though the relationship ended, the friendship remains.

David

Creating a conscious ending with Lea carried forward into making a conscious beginning in my next relationship. My wife and I got married fairly quickly; we'd known each other about four months. One reason that occurred, I think, was that as a result of having done the ritual of parting with Lea I had a lot of clarity about what I wanted and what I was looking for. I still keep in touch with Lea because there is a genuine sense of caring between us. Because the ending with Lea was so clear and definite, my wife trusts me and doesn't worry that I would leave and return to the past relationship. That's one of the benefits of doing a parting ritual; it makes the former partner much less threatening. At least that's been the case for me and my wife.

If you can end a relationship consciously, then I think you have a greater capacity to create a conscious relationship. The consciousness I was able to bring to the relationship with Lea and to the parting ceremony has carried forward and made me much more able to speak my truth about what I want and need and about where my boundaries are, and to hear my wife when she does the same.

I also realize now that even if you end a relationship consciously, it still hurts and can be scary. In spite of all your best intentions and all your work, you may have to face that a relationship can still not work out, even if it is a good one. People can just grow in different directions. Potentially, I think that's true even of me and my wife. I love her very much and value the relationship but now, having done a parting ceremony, it is not inconceivable to me that at some point she and I could come to the conclusion that our time together has come to an end. Just the thought of that makes me sad. And I know there would be a grieving time, one of those times when you think you'll never be involved with anyone again, that you'll be lonely. But when you end a relationship consciously, really releasing the relationship and wishing the other person well, there is a tremendous amount of energy released, too, energy that will help you to attract someone (or something) else new into your life. You take with you the lessons learned from the last relationship — what you want to keep and what you want to do differently — and that affects who (what) you attract next.

Having done the parting ceremony, I think I'm more open to mystery, a knowing that whatever comes is OK and will unfold in surprising and wonderful ways.

Jim

After we left Raleigh, we moved to Philadelphia. For five years I threw myself into a graduate program in clinical psychology. It was my passion, though looking back it's hard to believe I pulled it off. I really loved those five years of being a student. It was wonderful to have a faculty who challenged me: I wanted to learn these skills, to learn all about the mind, how people think, what motivates them, what makes our lives so irrational? The faculty really wanted to teach me this stuff and I wanted to learn. Of course there were parts that were really tedious. They made me jump through a lot of hoops. But I jumped and now I work as a clinical psychologist in a community mental health center with people who have substance abuse problems and severe mental illness. I also have a private practice. An important part of that is working with rabbis and clergy. The title of my dissertation was "The Unconscious Motivations of the Pulpit Rabbi." Of course, I was writing about myself, but the study also included a literature review and an intensive study of eight rabbis who had been in psychotherapy and, as a result of that experience, came to understand more about their motivations as rabbis. I do some writing, give talks and conduct workshops. I also conduct a supervision group for

249

rabbis. I still feel like I work as a rabbi, just in a different way. Looking back on my separation from the Temple in Raleigh, I realize that even though it was painful and we didn't achieve perfection, in parting there was still a sweetness. There is a Jewish mystical tradition that teaches that God is in everything, even in evil. It sounds like a hideous thought and is easily misunderstood as God sanctioning evil. What this tradition attempts to describe, and what appeals to me, is that you can find God in a place that you thought was going to be only devastation. Of course, to get to that point you have to be open and honest and willing to risk — the things the congregation and I were trying to do in the ritual. If you're willing to make that effort, even in the midst of something as painful as a separation, there can be a real sweetness.

Marcy

Fall of 1999 is here and I will have completed a degree in human services by the Spring of 2000. It has been a difficult road emotionally and financially, but I could always see the light and it is getting brighter. I am dreaming of creating a non-profit for women and also of traveling. I may lease out my home next Spring for a year and work overseas. It is time for a change of scenery and some new life experiences.

Most days are good, some days are lonely. I have chosen not to be involved in another relationship these last two years. I am getting closer to opening up to the possibility of loving again. My heart has awakened to loving on a universal scale and service is very important to me. I want to work at helping others and making this a better world for my children and grandchildren. This life I would share with someone who wants the same and has already shown the spirit of giving.

The healing continues and I can never forget 25 years of living. I pray for the ability to forgive each and every day. I thank God for my many blessings.

Kurt

The divorce and the ceremony gave me an opportunity to reevaluate my entire life and gave me a second chance. L. and I

250

got married young — 21. After eight years of life and maturity and mistakes, you stop and say, what's important? What do I need in my life? You learn that you're not going to change someone. They may evolve with you, but when you get a second chance, you realize it's important not to overlook the major issues.

I can remember being alone in an apartment in a completely different town in a completely different world going, "Wow! Here's a second chance. Don't screw this up. What do I do now?" I didn't know how to date. I didn't know how to do any of that stuff. But I felt this surge of freedom; "Wow, I can do anything. I can go to Africa." You probably won't do something like that, but for the first time in a long time, you realize you can if you want to.

Later, I took a shopping list approach to dating. If you go to a new town to live for a time, you're going to make a list when you go to the grocery store. You'll be getting the big five: bread, milk, meat, fruit, vegetables. There's a bunch of other stuff you want, but because you don't know the store, you may not find them all.

In the same way, you make a list before you meet someone. A literal list. What do you want and need in a relationship? And then you prioritize those. And you make sure, after you're dating someone for awhile, that the big five are there. I wanted someone who had faith, intelligence, who was financially astute — she didn't have to be rich or out of debt, but I wanted someone who could live with an older car and yet appreciate new things. I wanted someone who was passionate — about life, about me; she needed to have a spark. I wanted someone who appreciated devotion. I wanted someone who could sew — my wife teases me that I didn't get that. Whoever I married again needed to understand and support my business. She needed to understand all that was involved in raising my daughter, H. — child rearing, coparenting. What I did not want was someone who had a lot of emotional problems. I put the people I dated through a lot of tests, including my wife. Maybe they were unfair, but this was what was important for me to feel comfortable to move on. Realizing that I'd been given a second

251

chance helped in this process. My wife laughs now. She says, "That obstacle course was a bear."

Getting an annulment before I married again also gave me a second religious chance. Going through the process, you have to write answers to all these questions. I ended up writing a nine-page, single-space response. That made me put a lot of issues into words: What didn't I see when we got married? What was our sex life like? What was wrong with our sex life? What was wrong with our dating skills, our communication skills?

Since the divorce and the ceremony, my relationship with L. has been friendly. The participation in the ceremony was the beginning of our cooperation after the divorce. It clearly served as a transition from one stage of the relationship to another. We don't fight, and especially not about money. We agreed that it was crucial that we not fight about anything to do with H., our daughter. And that commitment helped us resolve a lot of the money issues without a lot of conflict. We agreed that if we fight each other over money, we're only going to hurt H.. In fact, when we were going through the divorce people would say, if you're getting along this well, why are you getting a divorce? Of course, there's a lot more to a marriage than the absence of conflict, but some people don't understand that.

These days, L. and I are not exactly friends but we share joint custody and we're coparenting. We live twenty miles apart — two different towns and two different school districts in a metropolitan area — and H. goes back and forth. From the outside, people would probably say that you couldn't ask for a better relationship after a divorce. We don't fight. The one major disagreement we had, involving where H. would go to school, we settled with an arbitrator. She said that it was clear to her that we weren't fighting over power but only about what we believed to be in H.'s best interest. I agreed that H. would go to the school my ex-wife wanted. But in exchange, I got to arrange for H.'s extra-curricular activities and religious upbringing. I'm by no means right wing or a born again Bible pounder, but at the same time it's a very important part of our life. It concerned me that when someone asked her if she went to church, H. said, "Mommies don't go to church, only daddies go to church."

252

Our coparenting is going along fine. We try to talk whenever needed. It used to be once or twice a week, but it's less now that H. is older. We still have some real philosophical differences about child raising, but we discuss these issues with respect and in the end we've agreed to disagree. H. buys me presents with her mother and my wife and I help her buy presents for her mother. H. calls my wife, C., her step-mom and C. and L. get along. They sometimes go to skating lessons together with H., who's now six and a half.

H. seems pretty well adjusted. This is because of the openness of L's family and my family to the divorce. H. was a flower girl for my wedding with C. and her mother was very supportive and so was my ex-mother in law. Last Christmas Eve, when we had my in-laws over, H. said to everyone, "I've got three grandmas, two grandpas, two moms, one dad and more cousins than I can count. I'm so lucky."

Colette

Three years and a half years have passed since my husband and I parted, and still I feel the longing for a spiritual partnership. Yes, there has been love since then, and meaningful relationship. Brief flashes of union with the divine, that fiery embrace of dissolution and purification. But I have yet to find that level of communion on a sustained level in my life. Perhaps I am thwarted by my own idealism around partnership. But I would like to think that the experience of my short and very painful marriage has brought me the wisdom of greater clarity around what my longings are, and an unwillingness to settle for a relationship that lacks a strong spiritual container and commitment.

The dark gift of my marriage was that it broke my heart wide open, and it left me with a greater capacity for loving. I feel a deepening of compassion towards myself and others with whom I am intimately involved. I allow myself to be more undefended now, to take the risk of loving regardless of outcome. So many times I hear people say they can't open their hearts because of the losses they have experienced in the past, or because of the uncertainty of the future in a particular relationship. My response

253

is that we only have the present moment in which to love, so why miss the opportunity? Admittedly, I have been a prisoner of fear in the past, withholding my love or commitment. The initiation of my marriage and divorce helped to liberate me from those patterns. And so when people refer to my marriage as a "bad experience" because of what happened, I see that as a myopic viewpoint. Yes, it was painful, and certainly I would not make the same choices again, but I have not let those losses harden my heart. I have been made wiser and tempered by the willingness to keep loving in the face of such wrenching loss.

And so I stand, clearer, stronger, my heart open and ready. I know the Beloved within and can embrace the Beloved in so many who have touched my heart. And I know my beloved partner will come.

Nancy

I am very, very happily remarried. My husband is a Catholic. We were married in 1981 by both a United Methodist minister and a Catholic priest. My husband is a wonderful man who God sent to me, and we were married in one of the biggest church weddings that church had ever known. I don't think my husband quite realized what the celebration was going to be, but I felt so much for all these people, who in the ensuing years had loved me and cared for me and supported me, and for a God that had heard my prayers and sent me a precious soul — all this needed to be celebrated by the church. We had five children between us. We wrote our own vows and all five of these children and their husbands and/or wives stood up with us. And at the end of the service, rather than processing out of the church, we all turned around and Larry and I introduced ourselves and the family to the church. Larry introduced the men, which included his son and my sons. I introduced the women, which included his daughter and my daughter. I just felt real good about that.

So that's how God has worked in my life. We've now been married 17 wonderful years. My husband and I are both retired and we do go to a Catholic church now. That's where God wanted us to be. And if you came into our house on Christmas,

254

you would not be able to tell my children from Larry's children. God has been very good to us, very good.

Anne

Today, I am able to maintain a long-distance friendship with my ex-husband. I feel much stronger and clearer about who I am. I don't feel tempted to get back together with him. I don't feel I have to operate in an either-or mode; I don't have to either cut off all contact with him completely or go back to living with him. I feel very relaxed when I talk with him. I care about him, his pain and his joys. I don't feel the need to change him or to change the past. I can be thankful for what we had and accept that we disagree on essential life issues. I don't feel vulnerable or seduced anymore.

Matthew and Anne's Story

The other stories in this book are told in their own words by people who created and performed rituals or ceremonies. However, we found "An Amicable Divorce" by Mary Shideler (copyright © 1971 *Christian Century*) so personal, relevant and compelling that we felt we had to include it. It appeared orignally in the May 5, 1971 issue of the *Christian Century* and is reprinted here by permission. Group responses appear in **bold** and instructions in [brackets].

An Amicable Divorce

How one couple approached their divorce and met certain of its problems — and why they decided to solemnize the dissolution of their marriage with a religious ceremony.

Matthew and Anne Surrey announce an amicable divorce. Their relatives and friends are invited not to take sides and to keep in touch with both of them. For the time being, both are at home at 1492 Columbus Circle, Middle City, Missouri.

An amicable divorce sounds like a contradiction in terms. Usually we assume that either the couple was driven to that step by bitter conflict leading to permanent alienation if not violence, or else they had entered marriage so flippantly that its dissolution leaves them utterly indifferent to each other. Either way, the word "amicable" is not appropriate to describe the process or its aftermath.

Many people indeed, especially in our churches, are likely to feel that if the couple remains amicable, their marriage ought not to be dissolved. Marriage is too serious an affair, they believe, to be terminated unless it becomes intolerable; and when it has reached that stage, the break will necessarily be drastic.

256

Other attitudes toward marriage and divorce are being developed, but are seldom enough understood to make it worth examining how the particular couple whom I have named Matthew and Anne Surrey approached their divorce and met certain of its problems, especially in the light of their Christian commitment and of their desire that the dissolution of their marriage, like its institution, should be solemnized with a religious ceremony.

I

In the dozen years of their marriage, Matt and Anne had separated twice — at least once for more than a year — in order to obtain for themselves and give each other the kind of breathing space they needed in their search for a way to solve their problems without violence. Each thoroughly liked and respected the other. They continued to share many interests. But now their relationship had become destructive of their individual selves and therefore of their union. The details do not matter. Here was simply the not uncommon situation where, in order to grow or even endure, each needed something that the other could not give without destroying his or her very identity as a person, and each was compelled to express in his or her own life something essential which undercut the other's well-being. They could laugh and weep together, but they could not build. The time had come for them to go their own ways, not bound and not keeping the other in bondage. "Nothing short of necessity," Anne told me, "could have pried us apart."

Those reasons did not satisfy the judge who presided over the final hearing. Apparently Anne's testimony that Matt had never physically abused her, that their previous separations had ended with reconciliations, and perhaps the fact that they had no children, conveyed to him an impression that they were treating the institution of marriage frivolously. And, since the divorce was not being contested, he was clearly shocked at Matt's presence in the courtroom — the more because he sat with Anne and her witness before the court was in session, the three of them conversing decorously but in as friendly a manner as if they

257

were waiting for the curtain to rise at a theater. The judge plainly interpreted the case as one of "easy come, easy go," and his moral sensitivities were outraged. In conclusion, he said in so many words that he was exceedingly reluctant to grant this divorce, and did so only because the new laws in that state required him to.

For the legal making or breaking of a marriage, nothing more than such bare formalities is prescribed. The other rituals associated with marriage — the parties before the wedding, the ceremony in the presence of families and friends, the official announcements — are unnecessary. But they are notably enriching; they are means for initiating the couple and their associates into the new conditions of their lives. Far from being merely decorative, these rites of passage are psychologically and sociologically of great importance. Unfortunately, no such rites have yet been established for divorce, which is also the beginning of a new life. So the Surreys, recognizing their value and wanting them, improvised their own rites.

Because the Surreys are not only intelligent and perceptive but also imaginative, their rites accurately reflected their attitudes and convictions. Central for them was the affirmation that their divorce was not the cutting of a fabric but its unraveling. Their marriage was not a rag to be consigned to a trash can, but a network whose threads were to be disentangled and sorted out into those which could be used again and those which should be discarded. Moreover, they wanted to make their affirmation in both secular and religious terms. Between the time they filed for divorce and the time when Anne left town several days after it had been granted, two private and three public forms of expression emerged, not including their appearance in court.

II

First, together Matt and Anne told their closest friends of their intention. Together they received the brunt of the initial surprise and regret, answered any questions, and gave any explanations asked for. Whatever the procedure accomplished for them, it saved their friends from the considerable embarrassments which can follow when one party to a divorce confides individually in someone who has been close to both parties.

Second, the Surreys continued to inhabit the same house, to run their household as before, and to go places as a couple in their usual way. Partly this was because they were not financially able to maintain separate households. But also, throughout they remained friends — possibly better friends than while they were married; and the continuation of their domestic arrangements was a way of demonstrating publicly that extremely important fact. Let those who consider the Surreys' behavior another evidence of frivolity take note that, almost invariably, a request, a criticism, a gesture, will have a different impact if not a different meaning when it is made in the context of marriage and when it is made in the context of friendship or of a professional relationship (as with a priest or doctor or lawyer). Some people can be freer with each other and hurt each other less when they are not married than when they are, especially in the nuclear family where all one's emotional eggs are being carried by a single other person.

If marriage be interpreted narrowly as the licensing of sexual relations instead of broadly as the commitment to become a family, the Surreys' living together after they filed for divorce will appear scandalous. To the Surreys themselves, it was not only natural but upright thus to affirm the mutual love and respect that ensued even when they had discovered that the two of them could no longer constitute a family. To quote another woman, replying to her lawyer's expression of surprise that she should be so friendly with the man she was divorcing, "But I'm not married to all my friends!"

259

One view of marriage which is popular today says that friendship is (or should be) its basis. Another falsely called "romanticism," says that love of any particular kind is enough for a successful marriage. Neither of these views, however, takes adequate account of the blazing truth that above all else marriage in our society is a working relationship, a matter of building together a common structure by working toward a common goal: maintaining a household, bringing up children, serving the community, or whatever. In the absence of a working relationship, neither mutual love (romantic or other) nor friendship nor common interests will make a marriage more than tolerable. The essential is dedication to the same task. Husband and wife can have different vocations and occupations, and still be a family so long as their work is compatible and each is willing — and able — to serve the other in his or her vocation. But the exalted emotions are the icing on the cake, not the substance of the dinner.

III

The third of the Surreys' rites of passage was a party — today, the most pervasive and flexible of social rituals. Because the date of the hearing was postponed at the last minute, the observance preceded the event, but its character was in no way changed because of that dislocation. Like all the Surreys' parties, this one was informal. Twenty or 30 people turned up in the course of the evening, many bringing contributions of beer, to sit on the floor of the tiny living room or gather where they could in the rest of the house. Many commented on how much they liked both Matt and Anne, and how sorry they were about the divorce. None in my sight or hearing criticized either by as much as a lifted eyebrow, or implied fault or blame or seemed to think it out of place for them to announce the beginning of their lives apart with the same kind of fanfare that proclaims the beginning of a life together.

The high point of that party was the cutting of wedding cake, complete with figures of a bride and groom on top. The company gathered about the table. Anne took the knife and Matt laid his hand on hers. They looked up to make sure that the friend who had brought his camera was ready to record the event. They brought the knife down accurately between the dolls, so that one fell over on each side. The noisy chatter started again, not quite drowning Anne's announcement that it was a spice cake, the flavor chosen for its symbolic meaning.

If the divorce had had bitter overtones, the party would have been unbearable for everyone. As it was there was pain, but only the clean pain that characterizes even the happiest of weddings. The wound of separation is deep in marriage as well as in divorce, but it need not fester. And while its presence may give the festivities the tinge of a deeper color, it should not be allowed to dominate the pattern of rejoicing. Appropriately, emotions are mixed in an amicable divorce as well as in a happy wedding. But the priorities are kept clear, and private grief is expressed privately not because one is hypocritical, but from a sensitivity to the fitness of things. It is a grief too profound, too intimate, to be publicized.

IV

That same intensity of feeling led the Surreys to make the religious ceremony a private one. Necessarily it was conducted in a home rather than in a church or chapel: what denomination today would "sanctify" a divorce? Nor has any denomination that they knew of provided such a liturgy as this, which they asked me to write for them, and which they and my husband amended slightly before it was performed on the evening of the day when their divorce decree was signed.

When Matthew and Anne arrived at our house with the two other friends they had invited, they were too keyed up from the hearing to do anything but tell their tale, with its funny moments as well as tense and sober ones. Bit by bit, the sharing of the narrative diminished their tension. When all of us were inwardly quiet, Anne put on the phonograph Egon Petrie's recording of

261

his own transcription of "Sheep May Safely Graze." As it ended, the Service for the Dissolution of a Marriage began.

Officiant: Let us stand in a circle.
[We did so, with Matt on his left and Anne on his right.]
All: **Oh Lord, our Lord, how excellent is thy Name in all the earth.**
Officiant: Dearly beloved, we have gathered here to solemnize the end of one time in Matthew's and Anne's lives, and the beginning of another. We are so made that we cannot live in isolation from our fellow men, but neither can we live too closely joined with them. We are social beings, but also individual selves and it is the rhythm of union and separation that enables us to live in the communion which sustains ourselves, and in the solitude which nourishes our community. As it is written (here he read Ecclesiastes 3:1-8, 11-14).

Thirteen years ago, the time was right for Matthew and Anne to be joined in holy matrimony. Then they needed for their growth in grace and truth the visible bond of marriage. Now the time has come when that bond is hampering both their growth as individual persons, and their common life. They have resolved, therefore, to sever the ties of their marriage, though not of their mutual love and honor, and have asked us, their friends, to witness that affirmation of their new lives, and to uphold them in the new undertakings.

Matthew Surrey, do you now relinquish your status as husband of Anne, freeing her from all claims upon and responsibilities to you except those that you willingly give to all other children of God?
Matthew: I do.
Officiant: Do you forgive her any sins she has committed against you, and do you accept her forgiveness, thus freeing her from the burdens of guilt and sterile remorse?
Matthew: I do.
Officiant: Do you release her with your love and blessing, in gratitude for the part she has played in your life, in knowledge that her part in you will never be forgotten or

262

despised, and in faith that in separation as in union, you both are held in the grace and unity of God?

Matthew: I do.

[The same questions were asked of Anne, and she replied in the same way.]

Officiant: Matthew, what sign do you give to Anne as a token of your forgiveness and your release of her?

Matthew: Her wedding ring reconsecrated to her freedom.

[He placed it on the third finger of her right hand.]

Officiant: Anne, what sign do you give to Matthew as a token of your forgiveness and your release of him?

Anne: His wedding ring reconsecrated to his freedom.

[She placed it on the third finger of his right hand.]

Officiant: Let us pray. Almighty and loving God, who has ordered that seasons shall change and that human lives shall proceed by change, we ask thy blessing upon thy children who now, in their commitment to thee, have severed their commitment to each other. Send them forth in the bond of peace. When they meet, sustain them in their liberty. Keep them both reminded that thy love flows upon and through them both. Sanctify them in their lives, deaths, and resurrections, by the power of thy Holy Spirit, and for the sake of thy Son, Jesus Christ our Lord.

All: Amen.

Officiant: The peace of God which passes all understanding keep your hearts and minds in the knowledge and love of God, and the blessing of God Almighty, the, Father, the Son, and the Holy Spirit, be among you and remain with you always. Go in peace.

All: In the name of the Lord. Amen.

Spontaneously, each person put his arms around those closest him, and for several minutes there were tears and laughter, hugging and kissing, in a glorious affirmation. Awaiting them were home-made bread of that mornings' baking, and wine that flashed red.

263

Two days later, the mail brought the last of their symbolic expressions, the notification printed in Gothic type: "Matthew and Anne Surrey announce an amicable divorce...."

11

Rituals and Ceremonies of Parting

The rituals and ceremonies in this chapter have been drawn from two sources: Those that have actually been created and performed by contributors to this book and those that have been published as models in other books about ritual or divorce. We have selected the latter to be representative of as many traditions as possible. Some other rituals and ceremonies are not included because of limitations of space or because they are similar to a ritual that appears here (please see the Appendix for a list of books and publications that include a divorce ritual or ceremony). Although we have tried to be thorough, we suspect that there are other model rituals we haven't heard about. Also, from what we have been told, we are certain that there are many more couples and individuals who have created and performed a divorce ritual or ceremony as part of a healing divorce. (**Note**: If you know of another published ritual that we've missed, or if you would like to share your own ritual or ceremony, we encourage you to contact us at our webpage: www. healingdivorce.com.)

Ceremony of Parting

This ceremony was created and performed by Barbara and Phil Penningroth to end their marriage on January 27, 1997, at Glen Ivy, near Corona, California.

(A teacher in our spiritual community briefly explained what was to occur. Then, as the music played, we sat holding hands in an attunement as, around us, the members of our spiritual community did the same.)

265

Music

"We Will Find a Way", written by Steve Diamond and Sue Sheridan from the original motion picture soundtrack *Corrina, Corrina.*

(We chose this song because it expressed many feelings and ideas we shared about our parting : "Sun follows rain, strength follows pain ... There is a plan, peace follows understanding ... We will find a way" ....)

Welcome

(We each carried scripts. We read aloud to the community.)

Phil: We've invited you here today to witness a celebration of our marriage and a ceremony of parting. Barbara and I have been together for 25 years and it seems to us that the ending of our life as husband and wife is as important as the wedding that began our marriage, and the ten-year anniversary when we renewed our vows.

We're sharing this experience with you, the members of our Pathwork group, our spiritual family. There are many friends and family who are not here, and it's for them that we are videotaping the ceremony.

Barbara: We planned this ceremony embracing the Pathwork principles we have learned during the past several years. Tonight we will do our best to be open, honest, transparent and undefended. We both feel some fear about this. We ask that you reserve judgement and do your best to hold us in your hearts.

What we're going to do this evening is offer a brief introduction and then show a film of remembrance we've put together as a celebration of our marriage. Then, after that, Phil and I will describe the process we've gone through in making this difficult decision. Finally, there will be a ceremony that will include rituals and vows of transformation and parting.

Phil: During the last several months, Barbara and I have spent a lot of time reviewing the course of our relationship. What

266

we've found is that it falls into eras. The first year, on the South Pacific island of Guam, where we met, was full of romance, life, and the birth and death of our son, Geoffrey. The next ten years, after our return to the United States and our first wedding, were focused on career and family. Then came our re-wedding. The ten years after that was a period of inner and outer exploration and adventure, a time when we discovered and became more of who we really are, who we were born to be. And the last five years, first living apart and then together, has proved to be a time of family again, and grandparenting, as well as a time of spiritual quest in search of meaning for each of us, and an understanding of how we want to live the rest of our lives.

Barbara: Before we watch the remembrance, we'd like to share two insights we've come to over the years that have become especially important these last few months.

The first of these has to do with a quotation we used in our first wedding and then used again in our re-wedding. Today, it still has meaning for us — but a meaning that has changed through the years. It's from Robert Browning's poem, "Rabbi Ben Ezra", and in our first wedding it went like this:

Grow old along with me
The best is yet to be
The last of life for which the first was made...

Actually, in those days we were so confident that we knew what life had in store for us that we even rewrote the last line. Instead of "The *last* of life for which the first was made," we said: "The *rest* of life for which the first was made."

Our re-wedding, on our ten-year anniversary, started out as a sentimental re-enactment of our first wedding and ended up as a heart-wrenching, soul-stirring reassessment of our relationship, a reassessment that set the course of the next fourteen years. During that process, we discovered, among other things, that the quotation we had used in our first

267

wedding was incomplete. What Browning really said turned
out to be profoundly relevant to the pilgrimage to the Self on
which we were then about to embark.

> Grow old along with me
> The best is yet to be
> The last of life for which the first was made.
> Our times are in His hand
> Who saith, a whole I planned
> Youth shows but half; trust God; see all; nor be afraid.

Phil: The second insight has to do with what Barbara and I
have come to see as perhaps the hallmark of our marriage:
our willingness to support and encourage each other in
following our souls' longing no matter where it might lead,
even when doing so caused pain by taking us into situations
we did not fully understand, and into relationships that
others — and we — considered unconventional. This
insight, this support and encouragement, is best expressed in
something said by one of Jung's students, Marie Louise von
Franz: "Fidelity is loyalty to the true essence, the inner heart
of the other." When times have been difficult, although this
insight hasn't eased the pain, it has helped us put the pain in
context.

Barbara: Now, we'd like to share with you memories of the
life Phil and I have lived together.

A Celebration of the Marriage of Phil and Barbara Penningroth
(We darkened the room and showed the video.)

How This Parting Came To Be
(We continued speaking to the community.)

Phil: We'd like to tell you something about the process — the
difficult and painful process — we've gone through in
making the decision to part.

First, although at this point our process is a mutual one, I want to acknowledge that I was the one who initiated it. And so it seems to me that I have a responsibility to try to say why it is that I have made the difficult choice to leave a marriage that in so many ways has been nourishing and supportive for so many years. "Try to say" — I emphasize "try" because there is still a lot of sadness and mystery in this for me, and what I do know I'm not sure I can put into words that others will understand.

For me, in general terms, it all comes down yet again to following my soul's longing. But what is my soul longing for? Here are the three things I know so far.

First, Emotional Intimacy. Such simple words for such a critical and, for me, elusive connection between a man and a woman, a connection that I have felt missing for years at the core of our relationship, and a connection I find I cannot live without — do not want to live without. For some time, I sought intimacy outside of the relationship. We both did, always in an open and honest way; there were no betrayals in the sense of secrets and lies. These relationships were often warm and nourishing, and allowed us to experience and share aspects of ourselves we otherwise might not have. And yet, in the end, they proved an unsatisfying solution to our dilemma. I — we — came to understand that a divided heart cannot commit; that intimacy cannot be half-hearted.

Second, an end to the struggle. Since our re-wedding, as part of our commitment to personal growth, Barbara and I have done more than any other couple we know to work with the issues between us. We have explored our Selves and our relationship in the context of many different therapeutic and spiritual processes, some conventional, some unconventional, some no longer than a weekend, some for years. Pathwork has been one of our most important mutual attempts to find a shared practice that would help us satisfy our souls' longing together. In the end, for me, the result of all this exploration, this process of individuation, has been to bring me to the place where I must finally acknowledge that Barbara is who she is, I am who I am, and that in certain fundamental ways, for certain fundamental reasons, despite all of our work and all of our love and goodwill, we are not going to meet in the deep place so important to both of us. With that insight gradually has come the realization that I do not want to struggle any longer to make things other than they are.

Third, freedom to follow my soul's longing, and the physical health and emotional and spiritual well-being that comes with that freedom.

To explain this I have to tell you a story. As some of you know, for the last several years I've suffered from chronic hives. Most of the time hives are an allergic reaction, but sometimes, in cases Western doctors call *idiopathic urticaria*, no one really knows the cause. My intuition told me that the hives were a message, and I rejected the prescription of massive doses of antihistamines for alternative medical care. None of it worked. In dialogue, the hives told me that the illness was a spiritual issue; that they were here so that I would not forget. Forget what?

Eventually, with Barb's help, I found a doctor and a diet that, by mid-summer 1996, had done a lot to improve the condition. But the hives never completely disappeared, and if I deviated even a little bit from the diet, I would suffer consequences that could be severe.

Now, the second part of the story. A few years ago, I wrote a television movie about the shoot-out in Waco between the government and the Branch Davidians. While it was a skillful work of craft, in the end I felt a lot of remorse about what I came to believe had been my role in demonizing David Koresh and perhaps contributing to the destruction of him and his followers.

Now the timing is important here: it was in early August that I decided to leave the marriage. The hives had improved on the diet during the summer but were still very much with me day to day. In September, I decided to write a play about Waco. To do so, I realized I would have to talk to people who knew more about what had happened than I did. I decided to go to Texas. What happened artistically is another

270

story, one that's not yet ended. But what I want to share tonight is this: when I got to Houston, I expected to suffer a flare-up of hives, as had happened before when I traveled, especially if I couldn't follow my diet and was under stress. But to my amazement, just the opposite occurred. Instead of a flare-up, the hives disappeared. Why? I did my best to be quiet and listen for the answer to that question and one night, lying in a motel room in Waco, I experienced an epiphany: the hives were gone because I had followed my soul's longing. That's what I'd forgotten: to follow my soul's longing. That's why the hives were there, to remind me: in art, in relationship, follow my soul's longing.

Once I understood this, other confirmations came. When I started to follow my soul's longing a synchronicity occurred, a quote by Barbara Brennan to the effect that illness is caused by unfulfilled longing. When I began to follow my soul's longing, I started to feel emotions I hadn't felt in a long time, especially grief and joy. Friends, and even acquaintances who didn't know me well or see me often, began to remark that I had changed, that I looked different, felt lighter, seemed happier. When I began to follow my soul's longing, I discovered new and unexpected feelings for my Pathwork sister, Chris, and she for me, feelings that painfully complicated Barb's and my parting and yet are also a source, for me, of great joy.

Day by day, hour by hour, I have found that if I follow my soul's longing, my heart sings and my body remains without symptoms. But even if I stay on a strict diet, when I do not follow my soul's longing, the hives reappear, sometimes with their previous severity, to remind me. What was an affliction has become a blessing. In the words of a Baha'i' prophet, "My calamity is my providence; outwardly it is fire and vengeance, but inwardly it is light and mercy."

So these three things: intimacy; an end to the struggle; freedom to follow my soul's longing, and the physical health and emotional and spiritual well-being that have come with that freedom. That's all I can tell you about why I have made the choice I have. The rest is a mystery to me, one that is still

271

unfolding. But sometimes ... sometimes the grief and doubt and uncertainty and fear about what I am doing is so intense that I want to change my mind. Sometimes I feel like this is a dream and soon I'll wake up. But it's not. It's my life, and I feel called to change it, although in the midst of this calling I often find myself identifying with Rumi as he reflected:

> Do you think I know what I'm doing?
> That for one breath or half-breath I belong to myself?
> As much as a pen knows what it's writing,
> or the ball can guess where it's going next.

In the face of grief, doubt, uncertainty and fear, I pray to live my life with faith: as St. Paul tells us, "the substance of things hoped for, the evidence of things not seen."

Barbara: How is it that I am standing here tonight? That after 25 years we are ending this marriage? I have asked myself that a lot in the past several months. It was almost 18 years ago when Phil first told me, "There is no intimacy in this relationship." I didn't, and couldn't, understand what he was talking about. After all, wasn't our relationship the envy of everyone we knew? Weren't we considered the ideal couple? My response was, "Tell me what intimacy looks like and I'll do it." Obviously, my response was part of the problem. I have come to know in the past several years that intimacy isn't about doing at all. It is about Being. Being fully who I am, fully centered in myself and able to share that fullness with another in a way which meets that other's Being. For Phil, we don't meet. For me, we do. I don't experience the same need for intensity and relatedness that he does, and this has been a source of pain and frustration for both of us. So my first reaction when Phil told me in August that he wanted to end our marriage was shock and disbelief and incredible grief and fear, and at the same time, to my dismay, there was also relief — a small internal voice which said, "Thank God, the struggle is over."

Now, at this point, I look back at the timing of Phil's decision with awe and gratitude. At the beginning of August,

I was introduced into a spiritual community in Monterey, which is channeled in the same way that the Pathwork once was. For me, there was an instant sense of finding a spiritual home. I then went on my annual summer "same time next year" backpacking trip in the High Sierras. The high mountains have been one of the only places in which I have been consistently able to drop into a slow natural rhythm and connect with myself, with the earth, and with God. On this trip, however, a spiritual practice appeared through a series of dreams and leadings. For the first time, I found myself in an effortless place — a place of coming to my spiritual practice out of desire, not out of will. On that trip, I was given a new prayer — a prayer in which I daily ask God to show me my deepest and darkest fears and ask for the purification and healing of my spirit, my mind, my heart, and my body. I also began to ask daily that I be emptied so that I might have room to receive the love, grace and mercy of God into my life. Ironically, I have gotten exactly what I asked for, just not in the way I imagined. It has been a severe mercy, but a mercy, nonetheless. It was as if God said to me, "I will give you what you are asking for; and I will also give you the grace that will allow you to go through the fire which will take you to your healing and into the service of the Divine."

In August, after the first few days of living in this intensely painful and difficult position, Phil and I decided that we would wait until November to make a final decision about parting. We would try to truly examine again what was here now in the relationship for each of us and to work with our internal guidance, and with our therapists and helpers and Pathwork groups, both individually and together. Initially, what we experienced was a wonderful sweetness between us when we stopped trying to make things work, and could just be in the moment. This was a real paradox as our guidance about ending the marriage continued to be the same.

Also, during this period since August, an intensity of feeling developed between Phil and my Pathwork sister and friend Chris, whom I love deeply. For me, it has been hard to see the intimacy — the soul connection — that I so wanted for us, arise so naturally elsewhere. I — all of us — have worked with these feelings openly and with goodwill and integrity in our Pathwork group. Thanks to the Pathwork process, to Brian's incredible skill, and to the capacity of our group to hold the intensity from a place of love and support, the result has been profound healing for each one of us.

Phil and I came to the decision to part in November, a point that initiated a whole new and much more intense grief and rage as I moved from thinking about parting into actually doing it. For me, my external life is being emptied. I am losing Phil as my life partner and husband, I am closing my healing practice, and I am losing my home and moving to a new area. All the parts of my life which I have counted on for my identity and stability are disappearing. However, internally, I am being called to a place my soul has longed for, but never had the freedom or discipline to fully embrace — a sort of monastic life, a life bounded by bells, working in the garden and prayer — my own cloister, so to speak, my own Abbey. I have found the little house in the Carmel Valley which will become my cloister, but where this process will take me, and who I am in the process of becoming, I have no idea. I only know that I am called to a radical trust, to continually choosing love — love of God, of myself, of others — over fear.

Since childhood, I have carried the image and fear that if I truly followed my spiritual path it would cost me not less than everything. Recently, I revisited T. S. Eliot's *The Four Quartets* and found this same phrase and it's forgotten context. I'd like to share it with you because it speaks so eloquently to my unfolding process.

(Here Barbara read lines 238 through 259 of "Little Giddings" from *The Four Quartets* by T. S. Eliot, p. 59 of the 1971 Harcourt Brace Co. edition; a section that begins "With the drawing of this love and the voice of this Calling. . ." and ends ". . . And the fire and the rose are one.")

I feel blessed and carried in this sacred task, as much as I feel the grief and loss of Phil's and my parting. This is, indeed, a severe mercy.

Forgiveness
(We turned to face each other and each put a hand on the other's heart.)

Phil: Barbara, I forgive myself, and I ask your forgiveness for any pain that I have caused you, knowingly or unknowingly, by my thoughts, words or actions.

Barbara: Phil, I do forgive you, and I willingly release all resentment or withholding toward you which prevents the full expression of my heart.

Barbara: Phil, I forgive myself, and I ask your forgiveness for any pain that I have caused you, knowingly or unknowingly, by my thoughts, words, or actions.

Phil: Barbara, I do forgive you, and I willingly release all resentment and withholding toward you which prevents the full expression of my heart.

Sharing Our Blessings
(We continued speaking to the community and then turned and spoke to each other.)

Phil: Although Barbara and I have experienced struggle in this marriage, we have also experienced companionship, comfort, adventure and happiness. We'd now like to share with each other our appreciation for what this marriage has meant.

Barbara: Phil, my heart is so full as I stand here with you — full of grief, of wonder, of gratitude and of the deepest and fullest love for you, and of the mystery of this time and these extraordinary circumstances. Sharing the last 25 years with you has been a profound gift and privilege. You are a magnificent man — a man of passion, vision, devotion, sensitivity, compassion, strength, courage, and integrity. You have truly followed your path with all your heart and soul, and I see your essence more and more each day as you bring your wholeness into being, and as you have come to love yourself more fully.

How much you've given me! I thank you for the child we had together and for the weekend on Rota when he was conceived. I thank you for taking care of me and him when he died, and for caring for me after the emergency surgery which resulted in the loss of our dream of having children together. I thank you for all the cards and your messages of love and support; for your unwavering encouragement of my growth toward my heart even when it caused you great pain. I thank you for showing me the falling rain of cherry blossoms in the orchard that day. I thank you for the beauty and peace of our home, and for making our home and all the other luxuries and adventures possible with your discipline and dedication to your writing. Phil, I thank you for being a conscientious and responsible father for Sean and Lara under difficult circumstances and for being there at just the right time in their lives as young adults to make the crucial difference in their lives. I thank you for your kindness, your understanding, for your honesty, for your helpful and wise counsel, and for your passion and aliveness. I thank you for being my base camp on the Vision Quest; for going to Tantra with me; for sharing the Jesus Visions; for the revelation of MDMA; and for your emotional and financial support of my teaching and healing work. I thank you for our adventures in internal and external countries; for the perfect curve of your wand of light; for your smiles and your hugs; for your commitment to yourself and to me; and most of all, Phil, for loving me. I feel your love and am sustained by it, even in this parting. You are a gift and blessing in my life. I love you.

Phil: Barbara, I thank you for choosing love in the face of scandal and condemnation from family and friends. I thank you for our first year filled with pain and joy ... for swimming with me in crystal waters over coral reefs filled with fish like jewels ... for the gift of hipbones, our days on Rota and the child we conceived ... for sharing the happiness of Geoffrey's birth and the agony of his death. I thank you for helping me create a family, for mothering my children as if they were your own. I thank you for the beautiful homes we have created together, their warmth, grace and serenity, especially our cabin in the clouds and our Santa Fe Zen. I thank you for your quick, bright mind, for the interests we've shared, for the knowledge and experiences I would never have come to without you. I thank you for encouraging my creativity and living with an artist's temperament, even when I was more temperamental than artistic. I thank you for your smile, for your friendliness and for your courage, even in the face of fear. I thank you for your Vision Quest and for the memory of you dancing naked in the sun on a promontory overlooking the Valley of Death. I thank you for the re-wedding and for joining me on our long quest to discover who we are and where we're going. I thank you for the shared journeys on MDMA, and for your generosity of spirit as we shared explorations that opened our arms and our hearts to others. I thank you for your integrity and for the pilgrim in you that chose to give up security to follow your own soul's longing, even in the face of insecurity and doubt. Barbara, I thank you for your love, for your rage, for the freedom you have always offered me, and for your encouragement to open my heart and follow my soul's longing even when doing so has caused you pain and grief. You have been, you will always be, a healing presence and a blessing in my life, a gift from God. I love you and I always will.

Releasing the Future
(We continued speaking to the community, and then turned and spoke to each other.)

Barbara: As we've been working with this process there has been a lot of grief for both us. It might have been easier if we were angry with each other. There has been anger, and disappointment, and yet we come to the end of our marriage, and to this ceremony, full of love and respect and admiration

277

for each other, and for ourselves. In a way, this makes it harder to let go. We have been together many years and sometimes the idea that we will not be together in the way we have been feels almost unbearable. There are many things we will miss about our life together, and many plans and dreams that will never come to pass in the way we had imagined. This fills us with grief for all that might have been. We've written down some of the things we'll miss, and some of our plans and dreams, and would like to share them with each other now.

Phil: I'll miss your smile … snuggling with you when we wake in the night … how we fit together so well … I'll miss sharing the daily routine and hearing about your life … I'll miss the sense of us as parents and grandparents together … I'll miss seeing you tenderly inspecting each plant and rock in the yard … our walks by the lake … our honesty and conversations … the flowers you place on my desk … your little gifts for no reason … It grieves me that we won't attend workshops anymore … that our first trip to London was our last … that we will never walk the streets of Florence hand in hand and marvel at Michaelangelo's statues coming out of the stone … It grieves me that we will not be a couple who grows old together … that we will never again renew our vows or celebrate a wedding anniversary … that when we join our families for the holidays it will not be as husband and wife. It grieves me that we'll never live together near the sea and that in years to come we'll share our dreams with others. Barbara, I will miss you.

Barbara: Phil, I will miss growing old together and the sweetness and sorrow that we would have shared. I'll miss lying on the patio with you on summer evenings watching the sunset on the mountains with the scent of gardenias, jasmine, and honeysuckle in the air. I'll miss sitting with you in the shade of the trees we planted together, and sitting by the fireplace in the living room each morning reading the paper and drinking vegetable juice. I'll miss walking into your room and seeing you look up and smile at me. I'll miss snuggling with you and falling asleep in your arms, my back against your chest, feeling your breath against my body. I'll miss our shared adventures — the planned-for trips to Florence, and to New Zealand and Australia; sitting on the balcony in the rain in Puerto Vallarta watching the clouds move across the ocean; the advanced Tantra workshop we will never attend together; the cruise to the Caribbean. I'll miss being parents and grandparents together, signing the cards and letters "from Phil and Barbara." I'll miss your aliveness, your wonderful heart, your daily presence and the sharing of our lives and our dreams. Phil, I will miss you.

(We then burned the papers on which we had written what we would miss in a glass bowl.)

Phil: We ask that the energy of these things we'll miss, and of our plans and dreams, be released and transformed into the energy and grace that we will need for the lives that lie ahead for each of us.

Vows and Exchange of Rings
(We turned and spoke to each other and removed our rings.)

Phil: Barbara, I release you as my wife and will love you as my friend. I receive your ring, and will hold it in my keeping as a symbol of my love and support for you on your soul's journey.

Barbara's Vow: I commit to my heart, and with all my heart I will follow my soul's longing wherever it may lead and know that there is nothing to fear ... even when I am afraid.

Barbara: Phil, I release you as my husband and will love you as my friend. I receive your ring, and will hold it in my keeping as a symbol of my love and support for you on your soul's journey.

Phil's Vow: I commit to my heart, and with all my heart I will follow my soul's longing wherever it may lead and know that there is nothing to fear ... even when I am afraid.

279

Grow Old Along With Me
(We continued speaking to the community.)

Phil: Remember the poem we shared with you at the beginning of this ceremony? As we said, it seems as if we've continued to live into it through the years, and its meaning has changed and been informed by the transformations of our lives ... is changing even now.

Barbara: Truly, our times are in His hand. We live in a state of grace and unknowing.

Phil: Truly, it was a whole God planned for each of us. We are marvelous collages of lower self, higher self, shadow and light.

Barbara: Truly, youth shows but half, and isn't it one of life's gentle ironies that it takes growing older to realize this?

Phil: Truly, we must trust God, for life is a mystery, and as Rilke advises, we must be patient with all that is unsolved in our hearts and try to love the questions themselves.

Barbara: Truly, we must see all. For to turn away from the truth of ourselves, even when that truth brings us sorrow and pain, is also to deny joy and creativity and the other gifts of God's abundance. It is as Jesus tells us in the *Gospel According to Thomas* : "That which you bring forth will save you, but that which you do not bring forth will destroy you."

Phil: And finally, truly, we need not be afraid. For as the Guide tells us, if we have the courage to live our lives as honest, open, transparent and undefended beings, we will ultimately arrive "at the experiential knowledge that we are held by God and live in a creation in which there is absolutely nothing to fear."

Both: Grow old along with me
The best is yet to be
The last of life for which the first was made.
Our times are in His hand
Who saith, a whole I planned
Youth shows but half; trust God; see all; nor be afraid.

Music

"You're a Part of Me, I'm a Part of You," from the original motion picture soundtrack *Thelma and Louise*, written by Glen Frey and Jack Tempchin.

(We chose this song, too, because it expressed thoughts and feelings that we shared: "A distant voice is calling me away ... We can never know about tomorrow, Still we have to choose which way to go" ... and, as long as we live, "You're a part of me, I'm a part of you." As the music played we slowly made our way out of the room, embracing members of the community.)

A few weeks after the ceremony we sent the following letter with a video to those family and friends who had not been present at the ceremony.

Dear Friends and Family:

This is a sad time for us, and an exciting one. After many years we have decided to part, changing the form of our relationship for reasons that are best explained in the accompanying "Ceremony of Parting." We're sorry it wasn't possible to ask you to join us for the ceremony itself. We hope that the enclosed video will help you feel a part of what has been, for us, one of the most difficult and important events of our lives, individually and together.

We are embarked on new lives and new adventures. We have sold the house in Bakersfield and will be moving by the end of March. Barbara plans to move to the Carmel Valley. Her new address will be: _____. Phil plans to live near the Del Mar area but doesn't yet have an address or phone. For now you can reach him at:_____.

We realize that this announcement will come as a surprise to those of you we did not get a chance to talk to during our decision process before the ceremony, and may evoke a lot of emotions. Some of you may have questions you would like to ask or feelings you would like to share. We hope you will do

281

this. Each of us treasures you as friends and we both look forward to continuing our relationships with you in the future.

We hold you in our hearts and pray that you will hold us in yours.

With Love,
Phil and Barbara

A Service of Recognition, Resolution and Renewal

The following ritual was created and performed by Scott Small and several of his friends and family in a United Methodist Church to celebrate and mourn the end of his marriage to his wife, M.. Besides Scott, those participating in his ritual were:

- Dorothy, the ordained minister who had performed his wedding to M., and who could offer the sacrament.
- Scott's father, Claude.
- Lee, a friend and mentor.
- Alison, a close friend.

Later, Scott offered this written explanation about the development of the service to people who were interested.

About the Service

I recently created and performed this service with the assistance of several friends. It grew from my need for concrete spiritual closure for my marriage.

As I realized that I was going to be divorced, I discovered many questions that the established legal, intellectual and emotional institutions did not address. And like many other people, I buried myself in books looking for answers.

With several friends (themselves divorced or working with divorce recovery ministries), I began the process of writing a service that would fill in some of the gaps. We worked within the guidelines of the United Methodist Church with an ordained minister administering the sacrament.

Only after we had begun the process of writing a service ourselves did we discover the obscure reference from the 1976 Abington publication, *Rituals for a New Day: An Invitation*, compiled by the Section on Worship of the Board of Discipleship and the Subcommittee on Alternative Rituals Editorial Committee. It explains much of the motivation and

283

process of ritualmaking for divorce and offers suggestions and examples of services. I want to share this information so that divorced Christians with similar needs will have a starting place to gain spiritual peace. Just as every person is unique, so is every marriage, and so is every divorce. I hope and expect that those who finds this service will adapt the scripture, rituals and prayers to their own situation.

The Recognition, Resolution and Renewal Service is available to download along with supporting material from the most complete divorce resource site, DivorceInfo at http://www.divorceinfo.com. This site is loaded with information about faith and divorce from all major religions, and it has well over 1,000 pages of information about most every aspect of divorce one could imagine. If you don't have a computer, you can contact the following number toll free 1-800-979-6960.

Service of Recognition, Resolution and Renewal

(Scott created a written program for the service to serve as a guide for the participants and witnesses. All that follows was both part of the service and also included in the program.)

A Brief Explanation of What This Service Is and Why It Has Been Written.

(This was printed on the fly leaf of the ceremony program.)

What It Is Not

It **is not** a religious ceremony to proclaim one person "right" and the other "wrong" in a divorce.
It **is not** to "trash" the ex-spouse in church.
It **is not** a pity party.
It **is not** a mandatory exit service required for all divorces.

What It Is

It is a voluntary service to be used at the request of individuals in need of spiritual closure of their marriage after a divorce.

It is intended to provide a Christ-centered ritualistic ceremony to formally address how we who are parting have come to this place in our lives, the burdens and joys we must accept, and where we will focus ourselves from this point forward.

It is an opportunity to say good-bye to who and what we cherished in the past, to embrace the good people and things that exist in the present, and to prepare for all that God blesses us with in the future.

It is a service full of forgiveness, thankfulness and loving kindness.

It is an opportunity for healing.

If anyone is in Christ, he is a new creation; the old is gone, the new has come. — 2 Corinthians 5:17

(What follows is the actual order of service as it was performed. Congregational responses appear in **bold**. Instructions as they appeared in the program are in [brackets]).

Welcome and Call to Worship

Dorothy: Brothers and sisters, welcome in the name of the risen Christ to this service of recognition, resolution and renewal. We gather to remember the marriage of Scott and M. Small. We gather to mourn their divorce. And we gather to celebrate the power of the Holy Spirit to bring about healing and new life. The grace of the Lord Jesus Christ be with you.

All: And also with you.

Dorothy: The Risen Christ is with us!

All: Praise the Lord.

285

Reading [Scott]

Prayer of Forgiveness

Alison/All: Merciful God, we confess that we have not loved You with our whole heart.
We have failed to be obedient members of Your church.
We have not done Your will.
We have not kept Your commandments.
We have broken Your laws.
We have broken Your covenants.
We have rebelled against Your love.
We have not loved our neighbors,
And we have not heard the cry of the needy.
Forgive us.
Forgive our families past, present and future.
Forgive us all, we pray.
Free us for joyful obedience, through Jesus Christ our Lord.
Amen

Offering [Ritual One — Recognition]

(The congregation was invited to write notes of things members wished to release from their lives.)

Scott: [Reads Ecclesiasties 3:1-3, 6]
It is now time to gather up our burdens to hand them over to God.
[The offertory plate is passed around to gather up everyone's notes and letters. Then the notes and letters are placed in the covered pot where they will be lit and burned.]

Allison: Hear the good news: "Christ died for us while we were yet sinners; that proves God's love toward us." In the name of Jesus Christ, you are forgiven!

286

All: In the name of Jesus Christ you are forgiven. Glory to God. Amen.

Scripture Readings

Lee: Hear what the Scripture says about marriage: 1 Corinthians 7:15-17

Hear what the Scripture says about perseverance: 2 Peter 1:2-11

Hear what the Scripture says about healing: Proverbs 3: 5-8 & James 5:13-16

Thoughts of Celebration, Regret and Affirmation

Scott: This is a time set aside for anyone who wishes to share briefly stories and testimonies of marriage, faith, love, growing, giving or God.
(People shared.)

Prayer of Thanks [Ritual Two — Resolution]

(Claude added extemporaneous remarks of love and support for his son, Scott.)

Claude: We have honored the past, we are learning to accept and be thankful for what we have in the present, we look forward to future blessings. Please join me in a few minutes of silent prayer focusing on those things we are thankful for. Think especially of things that, when they happen, we are not very thankful for. Know that by faith in God in His Truth, in His time, with His wisdom, we will come to understand, and be thankful for his gifts.
[Silent prayer]

Claude: Dear Lord of all life, we give You thanks that You and You alone are God. That You made each and every one of us in Your image to be like You, to live with You, to play with You, to work with You, and to grow in You.

All: Lord, we give You thanks.

Claude: That You, Gracious Creator, You gave us the gift of free will, self-determination, and the ability to make choices for ourselves.

All: Lord, we give You thanks.

Claude: That You, Loving Father, You made men and women to fall in love, marry and start their own families so they could enjoy sharing together all the wonders of this world you made.

All: Lord, we give You thanks.

Claude: That You, Yahweh, made a covenant with and blessed the union of Scott and M. Small with Your all-giving, all-knowing, unconditional, empowering love.

All: Lord, we give You thanks.

Claude: That through the power of the Holy Spirit You are now weeping with us at the breaking of Your covenant and the premature death of this holy marriage by divorce. Help us to always remember You are here with us to provide Your love, mercy, forgiveness and healing for Scott and for M., for our families, for our friends, and to all Your children who have only to call on Your name.

All: Lord, we give You thanks.

Claude: Lord, our Strength: When we fail to realize or appreciate all the many daily opportunities that you have blessed us with; When others we care about turn from us, from themselves, and from You; When we don't understand why You still love us or them; Or why this world is as it is; We give You thanks. For we are Your children, and You, Father, You are our loving master. You give us life.

All: Lord, we give You thanks. Amen.

Communion [Ritual Three — Renewal]

(Dorothy performed communion, assisted by Alison.)

Dorothy: The Lord be with you.

All: And also with you.

Dorothy: Lift up your hearts.

288

All: **We lift them up to the Lord.**

Dorothy: Let us give thanks to the Lord our God.

All: **It is right to give our thanks and praise.**

Dorothy: And so with your people on earth and all the company of heaven we praise Your name and join in their unending hymn;

All: **Holy, holy, holy, Lord God of power and might,**
Heaven and earth are full of Your glory.
Hosanna in the highest.
Blessed is He who comes in the name of the Lord.
Hosanna in the highest.

Dorothy: And so,
In remembrance of your mighty acts in Jesus Christ,
We offer ourselves in praise and thanksgiving
As holy and living sacrifice,
In union with Christ's offering for us,
As we proclaim the mystery of faith.

All: **Christ has died; Christ is risen; Christ will come again.**

Dorothy: All honor and glory is Yours, almighty Father (God), now and forever.

All: **Amen.**

The Lord's Prayer

Breaking of the Bread

Giving of the Bread and Cup

Benediction

Dorothy: Children of God, go forth in peace. The grace of the Lord Jesus Christ, the love of God, and the communion of the Holy Spirit be with you all.

All: **Amen.**

(The following statement appeared at the end of the ceremony program.)

289

Words honestly cannot express the appreciation and love I have for everyone who has supported me, listened to me whine, cried with me, prayed with me, and shared their time with me over the past six months. God has truly blessed me. I pray someday, with God's help, I am able to return the loving kindness you have given to me. Thank you. — Scott

Outline for a Ritual of Healing and Closure

This ritual was created by G. Margaret Downs and published as "Closing the Wound: A Ritual after Divorce" in *Festivals*, Vol. 6, No. 4, date and publisher currently unknown. Adapted by Ms. Downs from the Roman Catholic Liturgy of the Hours, it is reprinted here as it originally appeared. Instructions as they appeared in the article are in [brackets].

[I began with a welcome to all in attendance and a short explanation of the service and the reasons for it. I introduced those who would participate in the service and asked that we begin in silence and stillness.]

Opening Song

Opening Prayer

Psalmody   Psalm 103 (sung)
                  Psalm 139 (recited antiphonally)
                  Psalm 86 (sung)

[I chose the settings of these Psalms, the Psalms themselves and the readings because of personal preference. Whatever speaks to you should be your choice.]

Reading   "Desire for the Vision of God," from the *Proslogian* by St. Anselm, Bishop, Office of Readings, Friday of the first Week of Advent

Sung Response

Reading   2 Corinthians 5:17-20

Sung Response

Homily

291

[At the conclusion of the homily, all were invited to make some gesture of affirmation or blessing, a hug, a statement, whatever they felt appropriate to do.]

Blessing Cup

[A cup of wine was shared as a symbol of blessing each one present and of the unity that is part of this service. I took the cup to each person as my response to them. This was accompanied by a chant from the Taize monastic community.]

Intercessions

[All were invited to participate.]

The Lord's Prayer

Closing Prayer

Closing Song

Greeting of Peace

Service of Lamentation and Healing

This ritual was created by Rev. Julie E. Griffith, a pastoral intern at the Westminister Presbyterian Church in Minneapolis, Minnesota, for her friend, Kurt J., and performed in her home at 7:00 P.M., May 10, 1995. Some materials were adapted from *Liturgy in Learning Through Life* (Westerhoff, Willamon and Crouch, 1994).

A prayer from the *Iona Community Worship Book* (1988) graced the cover of the program for the service with a line drawing of wild geese flying over barren winter trees. It is used here by permission.

YOU
keep us waiting …
You, the god of all time
want us to wait
For the right time
in which to discover
who we are
where we must go, who will be with us
and
what we must do.

YOU
keep us …
Through hard questions
with no easy answers,
through failing where
we hope to succeed,
and
making an impact when
we felt we were useless;
Through the patience,
and dreams,
and love of others
You keep us —

293

(This is the actual order of service as it was performed. Congregational responses appear in **bold**. Instructions appear in [brackets]).

The Gathering

One: Blessed are those who mourn,
All: **For they shall be comforted.**
One: This evening, we come in mourning as a community to recognize the death of a marriage. Before God and one another, we lift up the pain, anger, guilt and loneliness that are a part of such a death and we look toward mercy and redemption. We are here to proclaim that death is not only an end but also a beginning — out of the ashes, out of pain, new life is born. So, tonight, we are witnesses to both death and resurrection, to both the limits of our human being and the limitless forgiveness that is ours through the graciousness of God. Also, we are here to be a reconciling community within which new life may be nurtured. Let us now commit ourselves to nurture Kurt — and L. — as they enter into new lives, separate from each other.

Reflective Music

Call to Prayer

One: Kurt, I ask that you pray now for faith and understanding in the face of the death of this marriage.

The Prayer

Kurt: O God, Creator and Sustainer of all life, I come before you trusting in your goodness and great love for every one of us. I feel now the pain of parting with one I have loved, but I rejoice that I was privileged to experience life with L.. I entrust L. to you in the death of this marriage. I entrust myself to you as I rest in and work through this complex and

294

difficult time of change. Have mercy on us, O God: in your compassion forgive us our sins, known and unknown, things done and left undone; and so uphold us by your Spirit that we may live and serve you in newness of life. Amen.

Responsive Psalm

One: I love the Lord, because God has heard my voice and my supplications.

All: **Because God inclined an ear to me, therefore, I will call on the Lord as long as I live.**

One: The snares of death encompassed me; the pangs of Sheol laid hold on me; I suffered distress and anguish.

All: **Then I called on the name of the Lord, "O Lord, I pray, save my life."**

One: For you have delivered my soul from death, my eyes from tears, my feet from stumbling.

All: **I walk before the Lord in the land of the living.**

One: For what shall I return to the Lord for all God's bounty to me?

All: **I will lift up the cup of salvation and call on the name of the Lord. I will offer you the sacrifice of thanksgiving and call on the name of the Lord. Praise the Lord!**

Reflective Music

Scripture Reading and Ritual Acts of Healing and Hope

Matthew 7:1-5: The Log and the Speck
(Kurt and L.'s proxy responded to the following questions.)

One: In relation to the death of this marriage, what one log was stuck in your eye that blinded you to the needs of your spouse or the marriage?

In relation to the death of this marriage, what one speck filled the eye of your spouse and blinded her/him to your needs or those of the marriage?

Have you now cleared your eyes of this log? If so, know that you go unjudged.

Look into the eyes of your former spouse ... Are they clear? Say to your spouse: Know you go unjudged.

May these logs and specks be removed forever and your eyes remain clear.

Matthew 7:7-12a: Ask, Knock, Seek ... and it shall be given.

One: In relation to the new life before you, what one thing do you ask and hope for your former spouse to receive?

(Kurt and L's proxy lit two candles from one unity candle and then extinguished the unity candle.)

In relation to the new life before you, what one thing do you seek and hope to find for yourself?

May you pass your hope for your former spouse to her/him in the light of this candle and say: In this new life, I hope you receive ....

May you illuminate your hope for yourself with the light of a second candle and say to yourself: In this new life, I hope to receive ....

Isaiah 43:1-3 (paraphrase)

One: But now God says: Fear not, I have redeemed you. I have called upon your name and you are mine! When you pass through the waters, I will be with you; When you walk through the fire, you will not be burned, For I am your God. I am your savior.

Responsive Prayer

One: In peace, then, let us pray:

For Kurt and L. and all others who have suffered the death of their marriage, that they may accept Your newness, and be blessed with your peace and freedom.

All: **God, grant our prayer.**

One: For their daughter, H., that she may continue to know the love of both her parents, which Kurt specifically would like to signify with the future gift of his wedding ring. Above all, may H. know Your immanent love, O God, so that she may also share in your recreative power.

All: **God, grant our prayer.**

One: For those people, both present and absent, who have strengthened and supported Kurt and L. in the past, and now undertake to support them in this new life, separate one from the other.

All: **Grant our prayer most merciful and gracious God.**

Reflective Music

Blessing and Dismissal

One: Dear God, our Creator and sustainer, accept these our prayers; in the multitude of your mercies, look with compassion upon us and on all others who turn to you for help and comfort; for you are most gracious. You love our bodies and our souls; you weep for our pain and laugh with our joy; for this we give you thanks. Amen.

Kurt, we now recognize the death of your marriage. We recognize, affirm and bless you as a single person among us, created in the image of God, and we pledge our support to you as you continue to seek God's care and guidance for the new life which, in courage and faith, you have undertaken.

May the peace which passes all understanding be with you — and with each of us — now, and ever more. Amen.

A Ritual in Which Only One Spouse Participates

This ritual is from a worship service created and performed in a United Methodist Church in 1971 by a woman who wishes to remain anonymous, here called Sandra. It appeared originally in *Rituals for a New Day: An Invitation,* created by The Task Force on the Cultural Context of Ritual (c)1976 by Abingdon Press and is used by permission.

(Congregational responses appear in **bold**. Instructions as they appeared in the program are in [brackets]).

Call to Worship

Minister: We are here to worship God. There is a centering on the life and events of a particular person, but most of all we are here to experience the presence of God, to acknowledge and worship him.

Responsive Reading   (Psalm 46): "God is our refuge and our strength. ..."

Concluding Reading by Sandra

[Sandra read an original poem reflecting on the meaning of the psalm which had sustained her through her difficult times. Portions are as follows:]

> God has been my refuge and my strength
> The Creator who formed the Rockies
> And brought forth the Pacific throughout centuries of time.
> ... Who quiets us in trouble.
> Who gave to me a sense of love and beauty at my mother's death bed
> The same God who gave me my birthright,
> Who created within me the will to learn and to love,

... This God — there is no other — rumbles in the midst
of us,
    meets us where we are:
    Where tragedy and joy share the same bed,
    Where senselessness and pain are even helpmates of
beauty and
    comfort and Love.
    ... And so we can hold within us the ambiguity —
    We can hold within us Death and Life together.
    And somehow the miracle that
    (it seems at times like these),
    Love abounds
    And lives forever, while Death has an end.

Prayer by the Minister

Statement by Sandra

[Sandra read a personal statement, sharing the circumstances
of the marriage and divorce. She explained why her three
children were not present, as well as offering an honest
confession of the difficulties of the decision and living with the
consequences. Portions are as follows:]

This service is important and meaningful to me in that it
allows me to relate my divorce within the context of faith. I
appreciate the No-Fault Divorce Law in that the only public
gathering witnessing to my divorce is this one which is a
worship of the Almighty God ... My emotions and feelings
have not been colored by a court of law, but rather I have
called upon brothers and sisters of the household of faith to
worship with me and in this context to feel with all my heart
and soul the meaning of the Act of Divorce. There is
strength in worshipping and praying together. I believe that
resources are being tapped which otherwise lie dormant.
I signed my divorce on Friday, July 12. I come from
years of a good marriage ... years that brought forth my
three children ... years I grew in. And through some mystery

I was brought where I am now. I believe that God was with the two of us before we encountered one another, that He was with us when we were married, and that now He is with each of us separately, and there is a purpose to our separation and divorce ....

There are ever-present ambiguities of a decision such as this. They are looming and made the decision long and difficult. Life is full of ambiguities: a mother dies when a baby is born, the arid desert is drenched with a flood ...

Song

[An original song written by a friend entitled, *The Sharing of Love Is Wrought with Ambiguities.*]

Minister: We come not to be flippant or to be in maudlin despair. We come with a suspicion that divorce has as many theological ramifications as does marriage. Wherever human life is broken or hurt there are theological responses and responsibilities. Historically, the church has celebrated the act of marriage but has left divorce in the shadows. The brokenness experienced in this event is like unto the brokenness to which our Lord Jesus alluded. We believe in the appropriateness of celebrating divorce at the Lord's Table.

Sharing in Holy Communion

A Symbolic Act of Shared Experience

[A candle was passed in brief ritual.]

Song

Words from Others to Sandra

[Here members of the congregation spoke words to her of memory and hope, asking for forgiveness and for a new life for her.]

Prayer Circle Hand-in-Hand

Shalom

A Ritual for the Congregation

This ritual is from a worship service created by Nancy F. and performed by Rev. David Maze for her and her husband, C. at the Wesley United Methodist Church, Toledo, Ohio, July 13, 1971. It first appeared in *Rituals for a New Day: An Invitation*, created by The Task Force on the Cultural Context of Ritual (c)1976 by Abingdon Press, and is used by permission.

[An announcement of the separation of two life-long members of the congregation was read on behalf of the couple by the pastor in the midst of the regular Sunday morning worship service.]

(Congregational responses appear in **bold**. Instructions as they appeared in the program are in [brackets]).

Pastor: Dear Fellow Christians:
After much prayer and soul-searching, it becomes necessary for us to share a difficult decision with you. On Wednesday of this past week we started legal action toward the dissolution of our marriage. This came not out of anger toward each other or in haste, but out of the realization that our lives have over the years not grown in the same direction, but in different directions.
Because you loved us yesterday, we ask for your continued love and support — that same support each of us has received all our lives here at this church. Please pray for us that our lives, now to be lived apart, might be as beautiful as they were when we were together and that each of us might continue to serve humankind, the church and Jesus Christ.

Litany of Hope

People: **We believe that God never gives up on us.**

302

Pastor: We believe that Jesus was God in human form who showed us the astounding steadfastness of God's love for us.

People: **We believe God's Holy Spirit is always with us, even in times of deep suffering and sorrow.**

Pastor: We know that God's love continues, and continues, and continues.

People: **Nothing, not even death, can separate us from this love.**

Pastor: We are a people of *koinonia.*

People: **We live in mutual love and support.**

Pastor: We are the sons and daughters of God.

People: **We live as a family with all boys and girls, men and women everywhere.**

Pastor: We believe that God is still creating and that we are called to join in this creation.

People: **We believe that God's love is something that will never give up on us, and so we approach the future with confidence.**

A Service of the Holy Eucharist and Healing: The Liturgy of Healing and Wholeness and Blessing of Singularity

This service was created by Dr. Kay Collier-Slone, the Director of Ministries with Single Adults in the Episcopal Diocese of Lexington, Kentucky, and is used here with her permission. Dr. Collier-Slone explains:

"It makes sense to most Episcopalians to ritualize things. I come from a sacramental, liturgical church and was raised to understand that there is an appropriate sacramental act for every important event in my life. It was a shock to find out that there were no services for divorce or the ending of relationships. Much of my teaching in the area of single adult ministry includes teaching people how to create rituals as needs arise. The Liturgy of Healing and Wholeness is a good example.

"The complete service is set in a format similar to a normal Episcopal service. We use the rite for healing and Eucharistic prayers from the *Book of Common Prayer*. It is offered in our diocese every Palm Sunday evening, usually at three different churches in three different areas of the diocese or geographical region. A priest who understands and supports our work celebrates the Eucharist or Holy Communion, and I assist him/her as the Lay Eucharistic Minister or Chalice Bearer. We ask people who have participated previously in this service to return as readers."

(The entire service is adapted from and includes standard liturgical text found in the *Book of Common Prayer*. It is printed on programs shared with all who participate. Congregational responses are in **bold** and instructions as they appear in the program are in [brackets].)

Hymn

"All Who Hunger Gather Gladly"

Priest: Blessed by God, Father, Son and Holy Spirit

All: **And blessed be God's kingdom, now and forever. Amen.**

Priest: Almighty God, to you our hearts are open, all desires known, and from you no secrets are hid: Cleanse the thoughts of our hearts by the inspiration of your Holy Spirit, that we may perfectly love you, and worthily magnify your holy Name, through Christ our Lord.

All: **Amen.**

The Collect

Priest: Almighty God, whose dear Son went not up to joy but first he suffered pain, and entered not into glory before he was crucified: Mercifully grant that we, walking in the way of the cross, may find it none other than the way of life and peace, through Jesus Christ your Son our Lord, who lives and reigns with you and the Holy Spirit, one God, for ever and ever. Amen.

The Word of the Lord

OLD TESTAMENT: A reading from Jeremiah 18:1-7

Priest: These are the words which came to Jeremiah from the Lord: Go down at once to the potter's house, and there I will tell you what I have to say. So I went down to the potter's house and found him working at the wheel. Now and then a vessel he was making out of clay would be spoilt in his hands, and then he would start again and mold it into a vessel of his liking. Then the word of the Lord came to me: Can I not deal with you, says the Lord, as the potter deals with his clay?
The word of the Lord.

THE PSALM: 116:1-3, 7-8, 10-11, 15 [read in unison]

I love the Lord because he has heard the
voice of my supplication,
                              because he has inclined his ear to me
                                    whenever I called upon him.
The cords of death entangled me;
                                    I came to grief and sorrow.
Then, I called upon the Name of the Lord:
                    "O Lord, I pray you, save my life"
For you have rescued my life from death,
            my eyes from tears, and my feet from stumbling.
I will walk in the presence of the Lord
                                    in the land of the living.
How shall I repay the Lord
                    for all the good things he has done for me?
I will lift up the cup of salvation
                        and call upon the Name of the Lord.
I will offer you the sacrifice of thanksgiving
                        and call upon the name of the Lord.

THE GOSPEL: Matthew 7:7-11

Priest: Ask, and you will receive; seek, and you will find; knock, and the door will be opened. For everyone who asks receives, he who seeks finds, and to him who knocks, the door will be opened.

   Is there a man among you who will offer his son a stone when he asks for bread, or a snake when he asks for fish? If you then, bad as you are, know how to give your children what is good for them, how much more will your heavenly Father give good things to those who ask him?

   The Gospel of the Lord.

All: **Praise to you, Lord Christ.**

The Homily   [by the Priest]

The Litany of Healing

[The prayers of the Litany will be read from the congregation by those who feel called to voice a particular prayer. If several voices begin to read, please be comfortable that all are called and welcome to read.]

God the Father, your will for all people is health and salvation;
We praise you and thank you, O Lord.
God the Son, you came that we might have life, and might have it more abundantly;
We praise you and thank you, O Lord.
God the Holy Spirit, you make our bodies the temple of your presence;
We praise you and thank you, O Lord.
Holy Trinity, one Lord, in you we live and move and have our being;
We praise you and thank you, O Lord.
Lord, grant your healing grace to all who are sick, injured or disabled, that they may be made whole;
Hear us, O Lord of Life.
Grant to all who seek your guidance, and to all who are lonely, anxious or despondent, a knowledge of your will and an awareness of your presence;
Hear us, O Lord of life.
Mend broken relationships, and restore those in emotional distress to soundness of mind and serenity of spirit;
Heal us, O Lord of life.
When wholeness is only possible with the unbinding of lives, let us believe that nothing shared that was good will be lost, and that all we were takes its honored place in our life's journey; that nothing is canceled but some things settled and concluded; that much that cannot be said or communicated nonetheless still abides and endures;
Hear us, O Lord of life.
Be especially present to all who live alone and feel alone, that they may know the strength and sufficiency of your eternal companionship;
Hear us, O Lord of life.

Bless the children of brokenness, that they may continue to know the love of both their parents, and above all to know your heavenly love, so that they may also share in your recreative newness;
Heal us, O Lord of life.
For the grace to assume new responsibilities, and to release those responsibilities which are no longer ours;
Hear us, O Lord of life.
For eyes to see, ears to hear, minds to know and spirit to live into the unique opportunities of singularity, bearing the model of Jesus Christ, single adult;
Heal us, O Lord of life.
For all those helpers who minister to the pain and sadness of our lives, granting them wisdom and skill, sympathy and patience;
Hear us, O Lord of life.
For the creation and extension of chosen households and "funny families" which offer us each the blessing of companionship and support on our journeys;
Hear us, O Lord of life.
Grant the dying peace and a holy death, and uphold by the grace and consolation of your Holy spirit those who are bereaved;
Hear us, O Lord of life.
You are the Lord who does wonders;
You have declared your power among the peoples.
With you, O Lord, the well of life;
And in your light we see light.
Hear us, O Lord of life;
Heal us and make us whole.

[A period of silence is kept.]

Priest: O Lord our God, accept the fervent prayers of your peoples; in the multitude of your mercies look with compassion upon us and all who turn to you for help. For you are gracious, O lover of souls, and to you we give glory, Father, Son and Holy Spirit, now and forever.

All: Amen.

Priest: Let us confess our sins against God and our neighbor.

[Silence may be kept.]

Priest/All: Most merciful God,
we confess that we have sinned against you
in thought, word and deed,
by what we have done,
and by what we have left undone.
We have not loved you with our whole heart;
we have not loved our neighbors as ourselves.
We are truly sorry, and we humbly repent.
For the sake of your Son Jesus Christ,
have mercy upon us and forgive us;
that we may delight in your will,
and walk in your ways,
to the glory of your name. Amen.

Priest: Almighty God have mercy on you, forgive you all your sins through the Lord Jesus Christ, strengthen you in all goodness, and by the power of the Holy Spirit keep you in eternal life.

All: Amen.

[The celebrant now invites those who wish to receive the laying on of hands and anointing to come forward.]

Invitation to the Altar [During healing sing "I Will Change Your Name."]

[Your presence here today indicates that you would like to ask for God's healing in this sacrament. Those who wish to either receive or to offer their support to others by laying their hands on them as the priest does may simply come forward to the chancel steps. As each person moves to stand before the priest, he/she may whisper to him/her the names of those, including yourself, whom you would like included in this sacrament of healing. The priest will then make the sign of the

309

cross on your forehead, anointing you with oil, and place hands on your head as he says the prayer for your healing, and healing of those whom you offer up.]

[When all have received the sacrament:]

Priest: The peace of the Lord be always with you.
All: **And also with you.**

Hymn
  "I Come with Joy"

Eucharistic Prayer C

[The people remain standing.]

Priest: The Lord be with you.
All: **And also with you.**
Priest: Lift up your hearts.
All: **We lift them to the Lord.**
Priest: Let us give thanks to the Lord our God.
All: **It is right to give thanks and praise.**
Priest: God of all power, Ruler of the Universe, you are worthy of glory and praise.
All: **Glory to you forever and ever.**
Priest: At your command all things came to be: The vast expanse of intersellar space, galaxies, suns, the planets in their courses, and this fragile earth, our island home.
All: **By your will they were created and have their being.**
Priest: From the primal elements you brought forth the human race, and blessed us with memory, reason and skill. You made us the rulers of creation. But we turned against you, and betrayed your trust; and we turned against each other.
All: **Have mercy, Lord, for we are sinners in your sight.**
Priest: Again and again, you called us to return. Through prophets and sages you revealed your righteous Law. And in the fullness of time, you sent your only Son, born of woman,

310

to fulfill your Law, to open for us the way of freedom and peace.

All: **By his blood, he reconciled us.**
By his wounds, we are healed.

Priest: And therefore, we praise you, joining with the heavenly chorus, with prophets, apostles and martyrs, and with all those in every generation who have looked to you in hope, to proclaim with them your glory, in their unending hymn:

Priest/All: **Holy, holy, holy Lord, God of power and might, heaven and earth are full of your glory.**
Hossanna in the highest.
Blessed is he who comes in the name of the Lord.
Hosanna in the highest.

Priest: And so, Father, we who have been redeemed by him and made a new people by water and by Spirit, now bring before you these gifts. Sanctify them by your Holy Spirit to the Body and Blood of Jesus Christ our Lord.

On the night he was betrayed he took bread, said the blessing, broke the bread and gave it to his friends and said, "Take, eat: This is my Body, which is given for you. Do this for remembrance of me."

After supper he took the cup of wine, gave thanks, and said, "Drink this, all of you: This is my blood of the new Covenant, which is shed for you and for many for the forgiveness of sins. Whenever you drink it, do this for the remembrance of me."

Remembering now his work of redemption, and offering to you this sacrifice of thanksgiving:

All: **We celebrate his death and resurrection, as we await the day of his coming.**

Priest: Lord God of our Fathers and Mothers: God of Abraham, Isaac and Jacob; God of Sarah, Elizabeth and Rebecca; God and Father of our Lord Jesus Christ: Open our eyes to see your hand at work in the world about us. Deliver us from the presumption of coming to the Table for solace only, and not

311

for strength; for pardon only, and not for renewal. Let the grace of this Holy communion make us one body, one spirit in Christ, that we may worthily serve the world in his name.

All: **Risen Lord, be known to us in the breaking of the bread.**

Priest: Accept these prayers and praises, Father, through Jesus Christ our great High Priest, to whom, with you and the Holy Spirit, your church gives honor, glory and worship, from generation to generation, Amen.

And now, as our Saviour Jesus Christ has taught us, we are bold to say,

The Lord's Prayer

The Breaking of the Bread

Priest: Christ our Passover is sacrificed for us.

All: **Therefore let us keep the feast.**

Post-Communion Prayers

Priest: Almighty and eternal God, so draw our hearts to you, so guide our minds, so fill our imagination, so control our wills that we may be wholly yours, utterly dedicated to you: and then use us, we pray, as you will, and always to your glory and the welfare of your people; through our Lord and Saviour, Jesus Christ.

All: **Amen.**

All: **Heavenly Father, you know our hearts, our souls, our minds.**

[Together] You are our constant and eternal companion, whatever our season of singleness. You walk with us in our daily tasks, in our joys and our sorrows, and in the grip of brokenness. We thank you that today, you loosen the bonds which have held us, that we may move forward, beyond disappointment, bitterness, frustration and grief to the fullness of life that you hold in store. We commit to you now the dreams which we hold in our

312

hearts, and unions once made in your name. With your help, we forgive those sins which were committed against us, and forgive ourselves for those sins which we have committed. Should we stray from the path of forgiveness, or feel moments of despair in our singularity, we ask that you set us on your path once again, blessing our intentions and commitments to that path. Amen.

Father, we ask your blessing on those friends and special helpers who have given unstintingly to us of their strength, their faith and their love in our times of brokenness, and who go with us in our healing and new life. And we ask the grace to transform our own struggles into compassion and service for others on their singular journey. Amen.

Heavenly Father, we come before you as you created us, singular men and women, whole and unique. We offer you these individual lives to use as you deem best, for the greater purpose in the community to which you call each one, and in the world. We give thanks that in our rebirth you take the broken clay of our life stories and mold it into creations of worth and dignity, made strong by the scars of the journey. We kneel in awe and wonder that your amazing love and grace wipes away all shame and claims us for your own, worthy and beloved.

[Then the celebrant faces the congregation and says ...]

Priest: We recognize, affirm and bless you, singular men and women among us, joining us as brothers and sisters, children of one God in the blessed company of all his faithful people.

May God the Father bless you, God the Son heal you, God the Holy Spirit give you strength. May God the holy and undivided Trinity guard your body, save your soul and bring you safely to His heavenly country, where He lives and reigns forever.

All: Amen.

Closing Hymn
    "Amazing Grace"

313

An Order for Recognition of the End of a Marriage

This model service is from the *Book of Worship United Church of Christ* (c) 1986, United Church of Christ, Office of Church Life and Leadership, New York, NY. It is used here by permission.

(Congregational responses appear in **bold**. Instructions are in [brackets].)

Introduction

This order is intended for those occasions when a man and a woman who have experienced a divorce wish to acknowledge responsibility for their separation, affirm the good that continues from the previous relationship and promise in the presence of God, family, and supportive friends to begin a new relationship. Great sensitivity to the particular circumstances of the couple will be needed on the part of those who assist them in planning the service. Considerable advance preparation may be necessary. The promises indicated within the order should be developed by the woman and man themselves, with whatever counsel they request.

The service is penitential in nature and cannot be construed to be an encouragement of divorce or a deprecation of marriage. It does not celebrate the failure of a relationship, but acknowledges that a divorce has occurred and that two human beings are seeking in earnest to reorder their lives in a wholesome, redemptive way. The service is a reminder that nothing can separate people from the love of God in Jesus Christ.

Elements of the service may be used during pastoral counseling when a public service seems inappropriate.

Hope and joy are appropriate in this service as a man and woman pledge goodwill to each other and responsibly arrange for continuing obligations they may share.

If there are children of mature age in the family of the divorced woman and man, they may wish to share in this service

314

in a supportive way. With great care, the one presiding may include them.

[A divorced woman and man may invite the pastor or another representative of the church to lead the service in a supportive gathering of members and friends.]

Greeting

[All may stand for one or more of the following or for other words of scripture.]

Leader: Let us remember these words from Jesus: Where two or three are gathered in my name,
People: **There am I in the midst of them.**
Leader: God is our shelter and strength, always ready to help in times of trouble.
People: **So we will not be afraid, even if the earth is shaken and mountains fall into the ocean depths;**
Leader: Even if the seas roar and rage, and the hills are shaken by the violence.
People: **God is our shelter and strength.**
Leader: God be with you.
People: **And also with you.**
Leader: Let us with confidence draw near to the throne of grace;
People: **That we may receive mercy and find grace to help in time of need.**

Introduction

[In these or similar words, a leader may explain the nature and purpose of the service. There are optional words for use if the man and woman are parents.]

Leader: We are here to witness an end and a beginning and to share the making of new commitments. [WOMAN] and [MAN] have decided, after much effort, pain, and anger, that

315

they will no longer be wife and husband, but they wish to respect and be concerned for each other.

Leader (for Parents): They are now, and will continue to be, parents to their child(ren), and they wish to be responsible for him/her/each of them.

Leader: [MAN] and [WOMAN] are grateful to you, who are family and friends, for your love and support, your efforts of healing, and your presence here. Those gathered may say in unison or repeat after the leader the following or other words of support:

People: **[WOMAN] and [MAN], in this difficult time, we join with you as your friends. We have been with you in your joys, in your struggles, and in your tears. We have not always known how to be helpful. Although we may not fully understand, we accept your decision. We care, and we give you our love.**

Prayers

[One or both of the following prayers or other prayers may be offered. The second prayer is a prayer of confession and is followed by words of assurance concerning God's mercy and grace.]

Leader: Let us pray. O God, make us aware of your presence. You have blessed us in all our moments: of joining, of relating, of intending, and of beginning. Be with us in our times of separating and of ending, releasing us from those vows we can no longer keep; we ask in Christ's name.

People: **Amen.**

Leader: Let us ask God for the forgiveness we need.

People: **God of all mercy, we know that you love us even when we are not sure we love ourselves. Embrace us**

when frustration and failure leave us hollow and empty. Forgive our sins, and grant us forgiving hearts toward others. In the confession of our lips, show us now the promise of a new day, the springtime of the forgiven; through Jesus Christ, who is able to make all things new. Amen.

Leader: God's love for us is shown in this: While we were yet sinners, Christ died for us.

Reading of Scriptures

[One or more lessons may be read. The man and woman, other family members, or friends may assist with the scripture reading.]

Psalms: Psalms 13; 31:1-2, 9-10, 14, 16; 91:1-6, 9-12; 130:1-7

New Testament: Mark 4:35-41; Mark 9:33-37 if children are involved; Romans 8:35; 37-39; 1 John 4:1-12, 19-21

Statement of Commitment

[In these or similar words, the leader may invite the woman and man to speak words leading to hope about the future.]

Leader: [MAN] and [WOMAN], some of us, your family and friends were present when you made your commitment to marriage. Before God, and all of us, we invite you to share the new commitments you are prepared to make.

[Here may follow personal words spoken by the woman and man. The words may express some of the agreements they have made with each other after much work, anguish, and counseling. Areas that may be included are:

Regret, apology, and confession related to unfulfilled intentions;
Mutual care and respect;

317

Support and care for their children;
The need for supportive friends;
Affirmation of good continuing from their life together.

The leader may invite words of support and love from those present or from a representative among them.]

Affirmation

[The leader or the entire gathering may say these or similar words of affirmation. There are optional words that recognize the presence of children from the relationship.]

Leader/All: **We affirm you in the new commitments you have made: commitments which find you separated but still concerned about each other and wishing each other good will, commitments which enable you to support and to love your child(ren), and commitments which help to heal pain you may feel. Count on God's presence; trust our support; begin anew.**

Benediction

Leader: Go in peace
People: **Amen.**
Leader: Go forth into the world in peace; be of good courage; hold fast to that which is good; render to no one evil for evil; strengthen the fainthearted; support the weak; help the afflicted; honor all people; and serve God, rejoicing in the power of the Holy Spirit.
People: **Amen.**

The End of a Marriage

We first found a variation of this ceremony posted on the Internet [The Global Ideas Bank home page at http://www.globalideasbank.org]. The full ceremony below appeared originally in *Celebrating Life : A Book of Special Services* (1993), edited by Andrew Hill and published by the Lindsey Press. It is used here by permission.

(Instructions appear in [brackets].)

PREPARATION

Opening Address

[Either the minister may use his or her own words *or* use other words *or* say ...]

Minister: _____ and _____ you have agreed, after much pain and heartache, to end your marriage. The love which formerly bound you together has died. Out of respect for one another, however, and before you finally part, you want to say "thank you" for the good times, forgive one another for the pain and the hurt, acknowledge your new freedom and accept your continuing responsibilities as parents. For these reasons you have come here today.

[Or he or she can say]

Minister: After much effort, pain and anger _____ and _____ have decided that they no longer wish to be husband and wife. They still wish to be friends and to respect each other and to care about each other. They are now and will continue to be responsible parents to their children.

Mutual Confession

[The couple may use their own words *or* use other words *or* say ...]

Man: I confess to God and to you, _____, that I have hurt you and caused you pain, and that I have not been able to fulfill my marriage promise to you. I ask your forgiveness and the forgiveness of God.

Woman: _____, I forgive you. May God also forgive you.

Woman: I confess to God and to you, _____, that I have hurt you and caused you pain, and that I have not been able to fulfill my marriage promise to you. I ask your forgiveness and the forgiveness of God.

Man: _____, I forgive you. May God also forgive you.

[Or the man and woman may say together ...]

Together: All that we ought to have thought and have not thought; All that we ought to have said and have not said; All that we ought to have done and have not done; All that we ought not to have thought and have yet thought; All that we ought not to have said and yet have said; All that we ought not to have done and yet have done; For thoughts, words and deeds, we pray O God for forgiveness, and repent with penance. Amen.

[Or they may say individually ...]

Man: _____, I am grateful for the good times we had together. I am sorry for the pain and the hurt I have caused you. Will you please forgive me?

Woman: _____, I forgive you.

Woman: _____, I am grateful for the good times we had together. I am sorry for the pain and the hurt I have caused you. Will you please forgive me?

Man: _____, I forgive you.

THE LIVING HERITAGE

Readings and Homily

[These may be introduced as appropriate.]

THE END OF THE MARRIAGE

Release from Promises

[Either the couple may use their own words or use other words or say ...]

Man: _____, I release you from your promise to be loyal to me as my wife. I will continue to respect and care for you as a person, [and] to be your friend [and to be a responsible parent to our children]. You are now a free person and may marry again if you wish. May you find peace and happiness.

Woman: _____, I release you from your promise to be loyal to me as my husband. I will continue to respect and care for you as a person, [and] to be your friend [and to be a responsible parent to our children]. You are now a free person and may marry again if you wish. May you find peace and happiness.

Return of Ring/Rings

[Some couples/women may choose to keep their ring/rings since marriage cannot be undone, only ended. Either the couple may use their own words *or* use other words *or* say ...]

Giver: I give you back the ring which was the symbol of our marriage.

Receiver: I receive back the ring which was the symbol of our marriage.

The Peace

[The man and woman greet each other in an appropriate way.]

Minister: It is to peace that God has called you.

Announcement of End of Marriage

[Either the minister may use his or her own words *or* use other words *or* say ...]

Minister: _____ and _____, we, your family and friends [as well as the law of the land], now recognize that your marriage is ended and that you are separate and independent people.

Blessing of the Separate Parties

[Either the minister may use his or her own words *or* use other words *or* say ...]

Minister: May God bless your separate lives and homes.

CONCLUSION

Prayer

[Either the minister may use his or her own words *or* use other words *or* say ...]

Minister: We pray for all people in relationship that they may honour and respect each other and treat one another with dignity. Where marriages are happy may there be renewal and enrichment for the common life. Where marriages are in turmoil and bondage may there be comfort and support.

Where marriages have waned of love may there be resolution with the least of conflict and misunderstanding.

We pray for _____ and _____ at this time of their parting. May they willingly accept those parts of their lives when they lived as husband and wife, and may they remember gratefully the good times together. May they continue to honor and respect one another in their separate and independent lives and may they find appropriate peace and happiness.

We pray for all people and all life in whatever condition. May every living being, forgetting none, be at peace. Amen.

Closing Words

Exit

[The man and woman leave in an appropriate way.]

Transformative Divorce Ceremony

This ceremony was created by Gay and David Williamson (authors of *Twelve Powers in You* (2000), Deerfield Beach, FL: Health Communications, Inc.). It appears in their earlier book *Transformative Rituals: Celebrations for Personal Growth* (1996), Deerfield Beach, FL: Health Communications, Inc., and is used here by permission of the authors.

(Couple responses appear in **bold**. Instructions are in [brackets].)

[Choose a musical selection or two that represent what the people involved are experiencing and would like to share with others.]

Leader: True marriage is more than the joining of two persons in the bonds of matrimony. It is a process of uniting two souls attuned to each other. True marriage is a path which kindred souls choose to walk and share together. In the course of this relationship, _____ and _____ have developed and shared love, trust and true intimacy with each other. Their souls have connected in a sacred bond. Their hearts and minds have become entwined and rooted in one another. When a separation takes place, these deep roots are pulled apart, often causing deep pain. This pain is often accompanied by questions that have no answers, and by feelings of guilt, doubt and fear. These feelings are real. These feelings don't need explanation; they need to be validated by providing comfort, support and, above all, love.

   And so we are gathered here to lovingly support _____ and _____ and their (son/ daughter/children). Divorce is neither a right nor a wrong decision. It is a choice. We are given not only the ability to choose, but truly the responsibility that will lead to our highest spiritual good and the full expression of our potential. We don't often choose a path that is free of pain, and we don't always remain on the path we chose. As our spiritual unfolding continues, we know that we are doing our best. We will make mistakes, but that only means we are choosing life and are willing to risk.

In the sixth chapter of Luke, Jesus taught us, "Judge not, and you will not be judged; condemn not, and you will not be condemned; forgive, and you will be forgiven" (Luke 6:37).

And so today we affirm our forgiveness. We let go of the past. We seek to release fear, doubt and guilt and fill spaces left between us with compassion. We wish each other well and desire only good for all concerned.

Although this ceremony commemorates the day of your divorce, your relationship does not end. There can never completely be a separation between you. For always there will be a past that is shared. And always there will be concerns of the present. Certain bonds remain between you. Let these ties call forth your wisdom and goodness; let them be ties that strengthen and support.

Please repeat after me:

I, _____ (husband's name)

Husband: I, _____

Leader: I, _____ (wife's name)

Wife: I, _____

Leader: Hereby affirm my place in the ending of our marriage.

Couple: **Hereby affirm my place in the ending of our marriage.**

Leader: Now I enter into a new relationship with you.

Couple: **Now I enter into a new relationship with you.**

Leader: I treasure the beautiful things we have shared.

Couple: **I treasure the beautiful things we have shared.**

Leader: I desire only good for you (and our children).

Couple: **I desire only good for you (and our children).**

Leader: Above all, I promise to respect you as an individual.

325

Couple: **Above all, I promise to respect you as an individual.**

Leader: This is my pledge.

Couple: **This is my pledge.**

Leader: (to wife) May I have your ring?

Let us pray. Let the return of this ring be the release from a pledge once undertaken and now outlived. As what you exchanged is now returned, so shall you be free to enter into a new life, a new marriage and a new love. May you separate now, not with regret for love unachieved, but with hope and belief in love yet possible. Amen.

[Repeat for husband, if double ring ceremony.]

Leader: (Returns ring to husband) And so, as you _____ and _____ have stated to one another your intention to live apart and create lives independent; as you have further declared your common commitment to the well-being of one another and to all whose lives you touch; a commitment to respect yourself and each other, I now pronounce your marriage dissolved. I summon society — family, friends and strangers — to honor the decision you have made and the separate paths you have chosen.

[The Leader asks the child/children to come forward and stand between the parents.]

Leader: This separation is in no way your responsibility; it is only that of your parents. Your presence in their lives remains most important. You brought joy to their marriage when you were born and you continue to bring them joy.

Husband: (To child or each child) _____, I am and always will be grateful for you. Nothing can ever erase my love for you, even though your mother and I have chosen to live apart. I give you this ring as a symbol of eternal love. It has no beginning and no ending. Such is my love for you. (Kiss)

Wife: (To child or each child) _____, I am and always will be grateful for you. Nothing can ever erase my love for you, even though your father and I have chosen to live apart. I give you this gold chain as a symbol of a happy and beautiful moment we have had together. (Kiss)

[The parents put the chain through the ring and fasten it around each child's neck. Or, as another option, give other symbolic gifts or just a gold chain without the rings.]

Leader: Let us pray. May all that is noble, lovely and true, all that is enriching and creative and all that is beautiful, be in your lives and abide in your homes, forever. Amen.

Ceremony of Dissolution

This ceremony was created by James Lancaster and is one of a number of creative, ecumenical ceremonies from *Equal Rites: Lesbian and Gay Worship Ceremonies and Celebrations* edited by Kittredge Cherry and Zalmon Sherwood. (c) 1995 Westminster John Know Press. It is used here by permission of Westminster John Knox Press.

(Congregational responses appear in **bold**. Instructions are in [brackets].)

[This ceremony is designed to be a simple dissolution of a marital bond between two women or two men. It is not designed to castigate them for any perceived or imagined failure, to elicit confessions, or to bestow forgiveness. Any hymns or prayers to that effect are inappropriate to this ceremony.

The vows will be discussed beforehand between the individuals and the minister as part of the counseling that should precede this dissolution ceremony, in the same way that counseling precedes a holy union. The ribbon symbolizing the dissolution may be of different colors or types if the participants so choose. Practicing the ritual untying is advised lest the ribbons knot embarrassingly during the ceremony.]

Hymn

Assisting Minister: Yahweh said to Abram, "Leave your country, your family, and your parents' house, for the land I will show you...." So Abram went as Yahweh told him ... Abram was seventy-five years old when he left Haran. Thanks be to God.

People: **Amen.**

Minister: Today we are called to witness the start of a journey. After great struggle, thought, and prayer, N. and N. have decided to dissolve their union. Each gives back to the other

328

the life that was shared, and henceforth they shall lead separate lives. Although their road to this day has been fraught with deep pain as well as great joy, they have chosen to end their relationship not in bitterness or in flight, but as *sisters/brothers*, in Christian love and the remembrance of love. Many of us have known and grown to love them as a couple. We gather here at the start of this new journey to celebrate their life together and bless them for their lives apart.

Assisting Minister: Let us pray. God of all people, we often leave what is familiar and safe and come to places strange to us, where friends are few and the horizon bleak. Yet in the wilderness you sent ravens with food for the prophet Elijah. You sent manna from heaven to feed the children of Israel. In the wilderness you sent angels to minister to your child, Jesus Christ. Strengthen us to be angels to our friends, N. and N., that we may comfort and sustain them through this painful time. In the love that you spread like light over all the earth, we pray.

People: **Amen.**

Silence for Individual Reflection and Prayer

Assisting Minister: A reading from …

[Suggested lessons are Matt. 12:1-8, Matt. 6:25-34, Luke 6:36-38, Luke 11:9-13, Isa. 11:6-9, and Psalm 121. These lessons should not be to punish but to strengthen all the congregation; they may warn against sitting in judgement of others.]

Homily

Hymn

Minister: [Motions for the participants to come before the altar]: N. and N., your journey has been long, and now, like Abram, like Sarah, you face another long journey. This

329

community has gathered to give thanks to God for your life together and for the life you have shared with us. Yet while that union has ended, you remain a part of this community, sheltered in its arms and loved in its hearts. We grieve for the sorrow of this loss, for it is a loss to us as well as to you. But just as the promise of resurrection follows the death of someone dearly loved and gives us hope and joy, so the promise of new life for each of you and for this community shines like dawn upon this day. The new lives we will share together shall be no less filled with grace and beauty than those that came before. We strengthen and uphold each other to be able to receive that grace and that beauty.

Will the congregation please rise?

[The congregation rises.]

Minister: When N. and N. were joined in holy union, they made vows and promises to each other. This congregation stood witness to their union. Today as we dissolve that union, we speak to responsibilities on this solemn occasion as well.

Minister: [Addressing one participant]: Do you, N., promise to forgive what needs to be forgiven, and to ask God to strengthen you for forgiveness? Do you promise to cherish the memory of this relationship, to reflect upon it, to learn and grow from the mistakes that were made, and to be heartened by the good things you gave to each other?

Participant: I do.

Minister: [Addressing the other participant]: Do you, N., promise to forgive what needs to be forgiven, and to ask God to strengthen you for forgiveness? Do you promise to cherish the memory of this relationship, to reflect upon it, to learn and grow from the mistakes that were made, and to be heartened by the good things you gave to each other?

Participant: I do.

Minister: [Addressing the congregation]: Does this assembled community promise to uphold these *sisters/brothers* in love and kindness? Do we promise to nurture our relationships

330

with each of them, sharing laughter as well as tears? Do we promise to reflect upon our own experiences and learn from them new ways of being ever more loving children of God?

People: **We do.**

[The Assisting Minister brings forth loosely tied ribbons and holds them between the participants. The minister may say the following words or the ritual may be performed wordlessly, in silence or accompanied by music.]

Minister: The ribbon symbolizes the union of your lives. Today you give those lives back to each other.

[The participants gently pull the ribbons apart, and then exchange the ribbons.]

Minister: [Raising hands in blessing and addressing the participants]: May the sweetness of your time together rise like fresh spring air in your memory. May the angry words and hurtful deeds fall away from you like ash that is blown away. May each day bring you solace and joy, and each night, comfort and rest. May you feel God's gentle hands beneath and about you, and may you know that you are loved.

Moment of Silence

Minister: You are free to live your lives in the fullness of God's gifts and in the mercy of life in Christ. This community affirms its love for you, even as we share that love with each other.

[After the sharing of the peace, the participants may return to their seats in the congregation.]

Assisting Minister: Let us pray. We thank you, Sovereign of the Ages, for your deep and abiding love for us. We ask that you carry us on your wings through times of trial, that we may not be caught in the tempter's snares. We pray that you guide us in your way of peace and catch us up in your robe of wonder, that we may know only your love, and nothing but your love, forevermore. In your holy name, we pray.

People: Amen.

Assisting Minister: Go in peace. Serve God.

People: **Thanks be to God.**

Hymn

Ceremony of Divorce

This ceremony was created by Marianne Williamson. It is from *Illuminata: Prayers For A Better World* by Marianne Williamson. Copyright (c) 1994 by Marianne Williamson. Reprinted by permission of Random House, Inc.

Ms. Williamson writes: "The purpose of this ceremony is to heal hearts, by forgiving the past and releasing the future. The rite is to be held in the presence of the couple's children, and one person chosen by the couple to be the officiant of the ceremony.

Like all ceremonies presented here, this one should not be taken lightly or done casually. I recommend that a spiritual counselor or therapist be the officiant, after having worked with the couple privately to ensure that both participants are ready to declare publicly their forgiveness and release."

OFFICIANT: We come together today not in joy, but in acceptance.

For yourselves and for your children, we ask God's help in this important transition. May you each release each other in love and forgiveness, that you may go on from this point healed and whole, no longer married but family still.

We join with you in God's presence, as you hereby let go the bond of marriage between you. We ask God's blessing on you, as you both seek and grant forgiveness. We join with you in the recognition that through the grace of God there are no endings but only the chance for new beginnings, and we pray this day for God to give that new beginning, to you and to your children.

I say to the children of this couple, whose souls are tried by the experience of this divorce, or have perhaps been tried still more by the condition of your parents' marriage: May the angels minister unto your hearts and free you from your pain. May you forgive your parents. In your hearts, may you accept and bless this decision.

333

(The officiant now asks the children, one by one, if there is any statement of feeling or intention that they would like to make. The children do so.)
And so it is. Let us pray.

Dear God,
We ask You to take these two dearly beloved souls into your hands.
Include in Your mercy and compassion their children.
May the golden cord that has bound these two in marriage be not violently severed, but carefully and peacefully laid aside, this act forgiven and granted meaning by God Himself.
May these two remain parents and sacred friends forever.
Never shall the bond of marriage be made meaningless, before God or humankind.
May these two beloved children of God remember that the love of their union was important, and honor it always.
Your experiences together were the lessons of lives lived searching for love.
God understands.
He asks you to remember the innocence in each other, now and forever.
May forgiveness wash you clean.
The love you gave and the love you received were real and will be with you always.
The rest, let us silently and willingly give to God, that He might heal your hearts and give rest to your souls.
You have suffered enough, in coming to this point.
With this prayer, may your family begin again, having released the past and sought from God Himself a new path forward.
We place both past and future in the hands of God.
You are still a family, blessed and held together by God.
May you remain so forever.
And so it is.
Amen.

(At this point, the couple may choose a ceremonial return of each other's wedding rings or some other symbolic gesture of loving release. In marriage ceremonies, a couple often chooses to light a single candle from two separate ones. In the divorce ceremony, a couple may choose to light two separate candles from one. This symbolizes that although they shall now lead two separate lives, the fire at the centers of their beings were blended by God and shall remain so forever.)

DIVORCING HUSBAND: *(To wife) (Name)*, I bless you and release you. Please forgive me; I forgive you. Go in peace. You will remain in my heart.

DIVORCING WIFE: *(To Husband) (Name)*, I bless you and release you. Please forgive me; I forgive you. Go in peace. You will remain in my heart.

OFFICIANT: Please repeat after me:
> Dear God
> Please help us now.
> Bless this decision.
> Bless our children.
> Thank You for what has been.
> Thank You for what shall be.
> Amen.

I now ask all those gathered here for two minutes of silent prayer for the healing and restoration of these wounded hearts.

(They do so.)

And so it is. *(Name)* and *(name)*, you are released from your commitment of marriage. You remain committed forever to the bonds of goodwill.
> God bless you and bless your children.
> Amen.

Ritual of Separation and Release

This ritual was created and is distributed by the Central Conference of American Rabbis. Original copies, which include the Hebrew text as well as the following English text, are available from the Central Conference of American Rabbis, 355 Lexington Avenue, New York, N.Y. 10017. It is reprinted here by permission.

(Instructions appear in [brackets].)

Version A: Both Parties Present

[It is understood that the following ritual will be conducted only after the rabbi has had the opportunity to counsel with one or, preferably, both of the parties involved, and only after the couple has received a civil divorce decree. The rabbi will explain to the participants that this ceremony and the accompanying document do not constitute a halachic *get*. The ceremony should take place in the presence of witnesses. Participants might invite their children, family, or close friends to be present.]

Rabbi
Since earlier times, Judaism has provided for divorce when a woman and a man, who have been joined together in *kiddushin* (sacred matrimony), no longer experience the sacred in their relationship. The decision to separate is painful, not only for the woman and the man (and for their children), but for the entire community. Jewish tradition teaches that when the sacred covenant of marriage is dissolved, "Even the altar sheds tears." (Gittin 90b)

[Woman's Name] have you consented to the termination of your marriage?

[Woman responds]

[Man's Name] have you consented to the termination of your marriage?

[Man responds]

Woman

I, _____, now release my former husband, _____, from the sacred bonds that held us together.

Man

I, _____, now release my former wife, _____, from the sacred bonds that held us together.

Rabbi

[Woman's and Man's Name], years ago you entered into the covenant of *kiddushin.* Now you have asked us to witness your willingness to release each other from the sacred bond of marriage, and your intention to enter a new phase of life.

What existed between you, both the good and the bad, is ingrained in your memories. We pray that the good that once existed between you may encourage you to treat each other with respect and trust, and to refrain from acts of hostility. (And may the love that you have for your children, and the love that they have for you, increase with years and understanding.)

[Personal words by the rabbi.]

This is your Document of Separation, duly signed by you both. It marks the dissolution of your marriage. I separate it now as you have separated, giving each of you a part.

[Woman's and Man's Name], you are both now free to enter into a new phase of your life. Take with you the assurance that human love and sanctity endure.

May God watch over each of you and protect you as you go your separate ways.

And let us say: Amen.

Version B: Only One Party Present

[It is understood that the following ritual will be conducted only after the rabbi has had the opportunity to counsel with one or, preferably, both of the parties involved, and only after the couple has received a civil divorce decree. The rabbi will explain to the participants that this ceremony and the accompanying document do not constitute a halachic *get*. The ceremony should take place in the presence of witnesses. Participant might invite his/her children, family or close friends to be present.]

Rabbi

Since earlier times, Judaism has provided for divorce when a woman and a man, who have been joined together in *kiddushin* (sacred matrimony), no longer experience the sacred in their relationship. The decision to separate is painful, not only for the woman and the man (and for their children), but for the entire community. Jewish tradition teaches that when the sacred covenant of marriage is dissolved, "Even the altar sheds tears." (Gittin 90b)
[Name], have you consented to the termination of your marriage?
[Person Responds]

Person

I, _____, now release my former husband/wife, _____, from the sacred bonds that held us together.

Rabbi

[Name], years ago you entered into the covenant of *kiddushin*. Now you have asked us to witness this ceremony, which formally breaks the sacred bonds that once united you, and which marks your entry into a new phase of life.

What existed between you and your former husband/wife, both the good and the bad, is ingrained in your memories. We pray that the good that once existed between you may encourage you to treat each other with

338

respect and trust, and to refrain from acts of hostility. (And may the love that you have for your children, and the love that they have for you, increase with years and understanding.)

[Personal words by the rabbi]

Rabbi

This is your Document of Separation. It marks the dissolution of your marriage. I separate its two parts now as you and [Name] are separated.

[Name], you are now free to enter into a new phase of your life. Take with you the assurance that human love and sanctity endure. "Let there be peace, peace for you, and peace for those who help you; truly, God is your Helper." (I Chron. 12:19)

And let us say: Amen.

Document of Separation

(The actual document is printed in Hebrew text and the following English text and is kept by the husband and wife as evidence of their separation and release.)

On _____, the _____ day of _____, in the year [date according to the Jewish calendar] __ (the _____ day of _____, in the year 20__ of the civil calendar), according to the calendar that we use here in the city of _____, state of _____, I, _____, release my former husband, _____, from the sacred bonds that held us together. He is free and responsible for his life, just as I am free and responsible for my life.

This is his Document of Separation from me.

or

I, _____, release my former wife, _____, from the sacred bonds that held us together. She is free and responsible for her life, just as I am free and responsible for my life.

This is her Document of Separation from me.

Signed: _____
Witnesses: _____
Rabbi: _____

A Ceremony for Divorce

This model for a ceremony was created by Rabbi Earl Grollman and published in his book, *Living Through Your Divorce* by Earl A. Grollman and Marjorie L. Sams Copyright (c) 1978 by Earl A. Grollman and Marjorie L. Sams. It is reprinted here by permission of Beacon Press, Boston.

A Ceremony for Divorce

For many there is a value in rituals.

"Ceremonials require each individual, however deep his or her grief or confusion, to reach out in a way that gives depth and meaning to the present."
— Margaret Mead

There are rites for momentous occasions:
A ceremony for birth,
the miracle of life;
A ceremony for marriage,
the consecration of love;
A ceremony for death,
the commemoration of memory.

A divorce ritual might help you to achieve a more positive ending of your marriage, balancing the cold brutality and psychic limbo of the courtroom; accept in a straightforward manner the severing of your life together; share with your children the knowledge that parental responsibilities continue; give your friends an opportunity to demonstrate their understanding and support.

The ceremony could take place in a home, a clergy member's study, or at a religious service.

Some divorce rituals have already been published.

341

Ask a minister, rabbi or friend to help you create a meaningful ceremony.

You might begin the ceremony with *Shalom.*
It is a Hebrew word,
Meaning "welcome,
farewell,
peace."

"To everything there is a season, and a time for everything under heaven — a time to be born, and a time to die, a time to break down, and a time to build up, a time to weep, and a time to laugh, a time to cast away stones, and a time to gather stones together, a time to embrace, and a time to refrain from embracing, a time to keep, and a time to cast away."

— Ecclesiastes

There was a season and a time, when you said *Shalom.* You entered your marriage with vows of love and permanence. The hopes and dreams of marital happiness have perished.

The relationship is ended.

Now the "season and a time" have come to say *Shalom* — farewell.

You publicly acknowledge that your vows cannot be kept. You will no longer live together.

You must face the future alone.

To remove part of the bitterness and start a life apart, you may promise that you will not be vindictive, but as forgiving as you can.

You may promise that even though you have failed as husband and wife, you will now attempt to succeed as father and mother.

You have "acted out" the crisis of separation.

The ceremony is a commitment to a new kind of relationship.

"To everything there is a season and
A time for every matter under heaven."

May you go forward to find *Shalom*, peace.

[Symbolically, the wedding ring may be placed upon a different finger.]

A Ritual for Saying *Shalom*

This ritual was created by Rabbi Jim Bleiberg and members of his congregation in Raleigh, North Carolina, to mark the occasion of their parting. While it is not strictly a "divorce ritual," in many ways the intention of the ritual is the same as others in this book: to end a relationship with truth, love, care and forgiveness — or, as Rabbi Bleiberg puts it, justice, truth and peace. We have included it because of its thoughtfulness and beauty, and because the ritual evokes themes and employs symbols in ways that could be helpful as you prepare a parting ceremony of your own. Although the ceremony is for the most part in English, those wishing text that includes Hebrew can contact Rabbi Bleiberg (see the contact list in the Appendix).

(Congregational responses appear in **bold**. Instructions are in [brackets].)

A RITUAL FOR SAYING *SHALOM*

Rabban Simeon ben Gamliel said: The world endures on account of three things:
on account of justice, truth and peace. (Avot 1:18)

Opening Song: Ya-ba-bim-bam

Reader: Jewish mystics have long taught that God created and destroyed many universes before creating our own. Similarly, throughout our lives, as we grow, change, and move on to new experiences, we say good-bye to old worlds and create new ones.

This is a ritual for saying Shalom, a means of honoring an old world as it is passing away and welcoming a new world as it is born. It is based on the teaching of an ancient Rabbi, Shimon ben Gamliel, who said: "The world endures

344

on account of three things: on account of justice, truth and peace," (Avot 1:18)

Rabbi: My time for serving as your Rabbi is drawing to a close. But we can find a permanent place in our hearts for this time by marking its end with justice, truth and peace. We also will firmly establish the new worlds that are just beginning for us when we build them on a foundation of justice, truth and peace.

You are welcome to join in all parts of this ritual that are meaningful to you. Feel free to refrain from participating when you prefer to do so.

Justice

Reader: The ancient rabbis told a story about the meaning of justice. Once there was a man who was clearing stones out of his land and throwing them into the public domain. A pious man, seeing him, said, "Wretch, why do you remove stones from a domain that *is not* yours to a domain that *is* yours?" The first man just laughed at him. After a time, he had to sell his field and, walking on the public domain, he stumbled over the stones he had thrown. He said, "How well that pious man put it: Why do you remove stones from a domain that is not yours to a domain that is yours?" (B. Bk 50b)

Rabbi: It is tempting to vent the stone of our anger on our neighbors if we think that we can do so without consequences.

People: It is tempting to set aside the stone of responsibility if we think others will bear the burden of our actions.

Rabbi: It is tempting to cast off the stone of blame if we think we can censure others without impugning ourselves.

People: Justice demands that we clear away the stumbling blocks that we placed in the path of our neighbors.

Rabbi: Justice demands that we accept others for who they are and not who we need them to be.

People: Justice demands that we care for the blessings that we enjoy and not squander privately what is acquired communally.

Reader: Justice demands that we engage in personal affirmations instead of recriminations.

Rabbi: Each of us now will have a chance to take a stone from a basket. When we do so, we will symbolically claim that which we have cast into the public domain but in all fairness belongs to us. We will take a stone to promise to serve as community stewards and models of tolerance; to promise that we will support those who wish to advance the well-being of the community.

[Participants take a stone and then the entire group says the following blessing.]

People: Holy One of Blessing, have mercy upon the righteous and faithful of all peoples, and upon all of us. Uphold all who faithfully put their trust in You, and grant that we may always be numbered among them. Praise be the Holy One of Blessing, the Staff and Support of the Righteous.

Truth

Reader: Take a look at these Hebrew letters: (Hebrew text). They spell the Hebrew word for truth, *emet*. The ancient Rabbis observed that each of these letters (Hebrew text) have two legs on which to stand. But, the Hebrew word for falsehood, pronounced *sheker*, looks like this: (Hebrew text). Each of the letters in *sheker* (Hebrew text) have only one leg on which to stand. The ancient Rabbis taught that the appearance of these words reminds us that "truth" rests on two legs and so is firmly based while what is done in falsehood is inherently unstable and will not endure.
(Based on *Yalkut Bereshit.* 3)

Rabbi: Let those who wish to speak their truth now stand up on their two feet. Now is the time to share precious memories and feelings and to speak the truths that are in our hearts. Thus we will firmly establish the worlds that we are creating for ourselves and honor the world we have shared in the past.

[After the last speaker, the group says this blessing.]

People: **Holy One of Blessing, You favor us with knowledge and teach us understanding. May You continue to favor us with knowledge, understanding and insight. Praised is the Holy One, Source of Truth.**

Song

Makor Ha-Emet, Source of Truth

Baruch attah adonai Makor Ha-emet
The spirit of wisdom and understanding
To be wise enough to know we don't know,
The spirit of insight and knowledge
To have the sparking curiosity to find out.
May our days and years increase,
May we find what we are looking for,
May our days and years increase,
May we find what we are looking for.
The spirit of wisdom and knowledge
To respect ourselves and the ones we love;
May we overcome trouble, pain and sorrow
May our days and years increase
May we find what we are looking for
May our days and years increase
May we find what we are looking for
Barusc attah Adonai Makor Ha-emet.
Blessed is the Lord our God, Source of Truth

Peace

Rabbi: Six years ago, when I began my service as Rabbi of Temple Beth Or, we greeted each other with *"Shalom."*

People: Now we say *Shalom* again to bid each other farewell.

Reader: But *Shalom* means more than hello and good-bye. It is a statement of our dreams and aspirations. It directs us toward a vision of the most exalted state in which people can live — whole, fulfilled and complete.

Rabbi: Though *Shalom* remains a dream and not a reality for us, there have still been moments when we tasted a hint of the great *Shalom* for which we yearn.

People: We have known a delicious peace basking in the presence of newborn children and an awesome peace, hearing the silence when death at last claimed our loved ones.

Reader: We have known a joyous peace when our *simchas* (celebrations) knit us together and a tear-filled peace when we embraced in the midst of tragedy.

Rabbi: We have known a gentle peace as a congregation united in prayer and a nurturing peace as we studied words of the Torah.

People: We have known a powerful peace when we spoke the truth to each other and a consummated peace when we labored to improve the world.

Reader: Six years ago, we wished each other *shalom*, and now we wish each other *shalom* again. The dream of *shalom* still moves us. The yearning for *shalom* still aches within us.

Rabbi: As Hillel taught: "Be of the disciples of Aaron, loving peace, pursuing peace, loving all people, and bring them near to Torah."

People: Rabbi Tarphon counseled: "It is not your task to complete the work, neither are you free to desist from doing it."

Rabbi: As a symbol of the sweetness and the peace we have shared together, we will dip apples in honey. As a sign of our hope to enjoy a sweet peace in the future, we will taste the apples and honey. As we go our separate ways may the taste of this sweetness sustain us.

[The apples are dipped in honey. Then the following blessing is said before eating.]

Holy One of Blessing, let Israel your people know enduring peace, for it is good in Your sight continually to bless Israel with Your peace. Praised be the Holy One of Blessing who blesses the people of Israel with peace.

Song
> *Shalom Rav*

People: *Sha-lom rav al Yis-ra-eil am'-cha ta-sim l'-o-lam* **(2 times)**

Rabbi: At Rosh Hashanah, we dip apples in honey to wish each other a sweet new year. Today we do so to say good-bye, to wish each other well and to thank God for bringing us to this sacred moment. We close this service by singing together.

Closing Song
> *She-he-che-ya-nu*

> Ba-ruch a-ta, A-do-nai, E-lo-hei-nu, me-lech ha-o-lam, she-he-che-ya-nu ve-ki-ye-ma-nu ve-hi-gi-a-nu la-ze-man ha-zeh.

A Prayer of Release

This is a modern version of an ancient Jewish prayer adapted by Rabbi Allen Maller of Culver City, California, and recommended by him to help those who feel guilty about breaking vows. It is part of his ministry to those who wish to ritualize their divorce in the Reform Jewish tradition (see Chapter 3). It is used here by his permission.

Dear God, we meant in all seriousness the vows we made to You, and to ourselves,
   Even as we mean the vows we seek tonight.
   We vow in order to be elevated.
   We want so much to rise above ourselves.
       But even as we vow, next time ...
       We are conscious how last time...
       We failed.
   The guilt of our failures weighs heavily.
   We sinned, we transgressed, we failed.
       It hurts so much, we fear to admit it.
       We chastise ourselves secretly
       Disparaging our efforts repeatedly,
       For the more committed we were to the ideal
       The greater is the guilt we feel.
   Yet how can we hope to renew
   When in our guilt we despair?
   Thus the vows unrealized of the past
   Prevent vows idealized of rebirth.
       Can a year really be new
       After all that we have been through?
       It is a cycle that takes us nowhere
       Until past guilt for human failure is
       Disavowed by Kol Nidre.

We do not annul these promises lightly.

We know that our failures cannot be simply left as a chain
dragging us down.

> *Kol Nidre has the potential to unburden us from
> perfectionism. May it help us transform the limits of
> our past into the possibilities of our future.*

May rebuke lead us to repentance
Reproach lead us to re-evalutation.

> *May regret lead us to repair*
> *Remorse lead us to renewal.*

Since we betrayed,
Are future vows
To be made in vain?
The answer lies in the human paradox:
We need to vow
To swear commitment
To future hopes, to higher ideals,
Knowing that our reach exceeds our grasp
And that some of our vows will be made in vain.
Nevetheless we pray:

> *All vows, promises and commitments we made since
> last Yom Kippur and in the years before —*
> *May we be given the strength to keep them.*

Our marriage vows — may they endure;

> *Through dark days and dull days*
> *Through fatigue and anger.*
> *May our love prove strong enough, and*
> *Our faith deep enough to last.*

Our vows for good health, to exercise, to diet;

> *May we take our own lives seriously enough to heed
> them.*
> *Keeping our vows each day as we eat, as we work,
> as we relax.*

The promises we made to study and to worship;

> *We meant them when we made them,*
> *And so many things got in the way.*
> *This time, may we be strong enough to let*
> *Our better selves prevail.*

Vows made by boys and girls standing on the bima,

Feeling what life as Jews might hold in store for them.
May idealism and vision be with them all their days.

> *Commitments to parents and to friends, pledges to charity and work for others. Help us be as compassionate and generous as we felt ourselves to be at those moments.*

Going of the Ways

We first found this ritual on the Internet. It's from Herman Slater: *A Book of Pagan Rituals* (York Beach, ME; Samuel Weiser, 1978). Material is used here by permission.

In the pagan tradition, marriage is called "handfasting" and divorce "handparting." (Instructions appear in [brackets].)

Not every couple will desire to remain wedded forever. Each person is an individual, and sometimes the differences will be too great for them to remain together. The decision to part should not be taken lightly, but if all else fails, this ritual should be performed to help the couple part as cleanly as possible.

The couple should spend as much time as needed with the priest and priestess to work out a fair distribution of properties, arrange for raising and support of children, if any, etc. This agreement should be signed and witnessed and notarized, with copies for each. (Or this part may be done with a lawyer, if preferred.)

The altar should be set up in the western edge of the ritual area. The altar should be set up as usual, with two candles, a sharp knife, and a picture of the couple to be parted. The Priest and Priestess should light the candles and incense, then turn to those gathered.

Priest: May the place of this rite be consecrated before the Old Ones, for we gather to perform that which must be done. _____ and _____, come before us.

[The couple comes forward and stands before the Priest and Priestess, husband in front of Priestess, wife in front of Priest.]

Priestess: You both know fully well the import of the step you are about to take. So now, for the very last time, do you, _____ , wish to part?

[wife answers]

So do you, _____ , wish to part?

[husband answers]

[If one or both say "no" the ritual will be halted, and an attempt will be made at reconciliation. If the reconciliation does not work, and both say "yes", the ritual continues as follows.
The priestess takes the picture from the altar and places it in the incense smoke for a moment. She then gives it to the couple saying:]

Priestess: Here in this place and before the eyes of the old ones and the creatures of the elements I bid you destroy this symbol of your life together.

[The couple will then tear and shred the picture, handing the pieces to the Priest. He will place them in the incense brazier, and set them afire.
Meanwhile, the Priestess will tie a soft cord (the Handfasting cord if one was used and kept) about the right wrists of each partner, leaving a handbreadth space between them. The Priest takes the knife from the altar and stands with it in salute before the couple. He says:]

Priest: We ask you, O Blessed Goddess, And Most Revered God, to heal the wounds of parting and to comfort the hearts of those who feel pain. When both have gone their ways, let love and not bitterness remain within.

[The Priest quickly cuts the cord binding their wrists.]

Priest: You are free.
Priestess: Go now, and go to peace, for this rite is ended.

354

[If one partner is unavailable, but all agree that a parting is necessary, a Priest or Priestess from another group can play the part of the missing person for the ceremony.]

Rory's Two Healthy Parting Rituals

We found these personal/neo-pagan rituals on the Internet (posted in early 1999 by Rory at geocities.com/Athens?Forum/ 9402/s_rites.html). Since then we have been unable to find them again, or to locate the author, presumably someone named Rory. (**Note**: if you know Rory and how to contact him, please let us know.)

1. Having had relationships break up with ritual and without ritual, I strongly recommend some sort of ceremonial closure.

The simplest one I've done involved sitting down in a beautiful place with a blank piece of paper and two pens with differently colored inks. Starting at opposite corners of the paper, each person drew a line and then we made a pattern in the center of the paper, the lines crossing and mixing like our lives. After doing this for a short while, we each disengaged the lines from the mix and went to our respective, remaining corners of the paper.

Next came the scissors. We cut the paper into three pieces, those parts with single-colored lines (our individual lives, before and after), then the center, mingled section. We each took our respective parts and split the shared portion evenly between us, rising quietly to walk away.

2. A second, more involved "unfasting" I once heard of involved the couple meeting again at the place where they'd first met, talking for a long while with words of appreciation, followed by stepping backwards back over their handfasting broom and untying their marriage cord. From there, they each went on their separate ways. (I assume one took the broom and the other the cord.) This is the ceremony I think I would use, were I to choose again.

The Divorce Ritual

This ritual was created and self-published by James Gamble in 1994. It was originally designed for an individual but can be adapted for a couple. It has been edited here for clarity and length. It is available in its original, bound booklet form from the Tanro Company, P.O. Box 20472, Castro Valley, CA, 94546.

(Instructions appear in [brackets].)

Introduction

It is suggested that you have at least three people at your ceremony: A family member (who might also have been at the wedding), a friend and a witness who will sign the documents afterwards. However, it is acceptable, if you want, to do the whole procedure by yourself. The clothing you wear is whatever you feel is appropriate. It is suggested that you don't wear any jewelery connected with the marriage either during the ceremony or for at least one year after the ceremony. It is permissible, but not required, to have a "Holy Book" on the table during the ceremony. You may stay with the original simplicity or you may make the setting for the ceremony as elaborate as you wish with printed invitations or other celebrations. The Ritual stays the same.

It is permissible to have a religious person as "Master of Ceremonies" to officiate and prompt you with your lines. It is suggested that you do not embellish the anger part of the ceremony. The purpose of the ceremony is to acknowledge the anger and happiness you felt, and to let it go.

At the end of the ceremony, it is suggested that you place the wedding band or marriage memento in storage and do not look at it again for at least a year.

357

Props and Preparations

The following things are needed before proceeding with the ceremony:

A black or white candle in a candle holder; matches or lighter, a plate or pie-tin, and a pen.

Your wedding band, or a memento of the marriage, a black cloth or black scarf, and a large butcher knife. (No, you are not going to use the knife for "that.")

A wedding picture of just you and your ex-spouse or another picture of just you two.

A dining room table or picnic table.

A Holy Book, if you want.

A bottle of champagne for a toast, as an option.

Before the ceremony begins, light a candle and place it in the center of the table. The plate or pie tin is placed in front of the candle. The Holy Book, if used, is placed behind the candle. The black cloth or scarf is placed to the right of the candle. The ring or memento is placed on top of the cloth. The knife is placed in front of the cloth. The wedding picture is placed to the left of the candle. Fill in the names and dates on the Ritual and the Certificate of Divorce.

The initiate stands in front of the table, facing the room, and may be assisted by another person. The friends and witness are placed in a semicircle around the front of the table. The following pages are read and/or recited by the initiate while facing the guests.

The Ritual [To be read out loud by one or both participants]

Participant: The purpose of this ritual is for me to acknowledge that my marriage has ended and to make the transition back to being a single person. I understand that I am responsible for what happens to me in my life. I understand that I want to get the negative feelings and

358

experience behind me and it is my responsibility to make that happen.

It is my intention to dissolve this marriage in Fact as it is now being dissolved legally by the court.

I was married on: _____

To: _____

I acknowledge that I took an Oath to be married in front of witnesses and friends which included the phrase: "Until Death Do Us Part." I regret that I have chosen to break that Oath. Having done so does not make me a bad person.

I acknowledge that I have felt hurt and angry in response to the actions of my former spouse towards me.

I acknowledge that there are parts and memories of that marriage that I will always cherish in my mind.

I acknowledge that my spouse had some admirable qualities and that some part of me will always love him/her and the good times that we had together. We had some wonderful experiences. We created a warm place to live. (Where appropriate) We created some beautiful and special children.

While there may be some connections, our marriage as man and wife is over. I acknowledge the good parts and the bad parts of that marriage, but it's over!

[The participant then performs the following symbolic acts while repeating "I Divorce Thee."]

Tears a wedding picture of the two of you in half and drops the pieces. "I divorce thee!"

Places a wedding band or memento inside of black scarf or cloth and waves the butcher knife in a cutting motion over cloth once from life to right. "I divorce thee!"

Turns a candle upside down and smashes out the flame in the plate or pie tin. "I divorce thee!"

Participant: I divorce thee and I declare in my heart and my mind that this marriage is null and void.

359

[The Participant faces the witnesses and holds his hands chest high in a prayerful manner.]

Participant: I was married but now I am single once more!

[The Participant pushes his hands outwards so the palms face the witnesses.]

Participant: The circle is complete. I release myself from this marriage. And it is so!

[The Participant claps his hands once.]

The Heart of Parting

Since we found this outline for a ritual on Alan Cohen's webpage in 1998 (www.alancohen.com), he has published a book, *Happily Even After*, which includes another model ceremony and suggestions for how you can do a ceremony of your own. This is from his column "From the Heart" (October 1995) and is used here with Mr. Cohen's permission.

[NAME], I join with you to celebrate the good and beauty of our relationship, and to acknowledge you for all the blessings you have brought into my life. My heart is truly grateful for all the gifts you have bestowed upon me. [Describe the most important gifts.] You have enriched me with your love and invited me to grow. For this I will always cherish you.

Now, as our paths take us in different directions, we mark this important moment by declaring that we are letting go of all that has been, to make way for all that is to be. With full love and appreciation, I release you to live the life God directs you to live, and I release myself to be all that I can be.

We hereby declare that our marriage (or relationship) as it was is complete, and each of us is now free to take our next step as spirit appoints us.

I will always hold you in my heart and bless you. May our love continue to grow, no matter what form our lives take.

May peace be with you always, my beloved friend.

A Ritual Incorporated into a Service of Remarriage

This ritual is from a worship service created and performed in the First University United Methodist church, Minneapolis, Minnesota, June 27, 1971, for Philip M. and Susan G. It appeared originally in *Rituals for a New Day: An Invitation*, created by The Task Force on the Cultural Context of Ritual (c)1976 by Abingdon Press, and is used by permission.

While more a marriage ceremony than a divorce ritual, we have included this here because if offers an example of how one couple facilitated the transition from divorce to remarriage. Like "A Ceremony for the New Family" that follows, it offers an honest acknowledgement of life's realities, especially the couple's responsibility for children from a previous marriage, as well as hope for the future of a new relationship and family.

(Congregational responses appear in **bold**.)

Processional Hymn

Welcome
[A personal statement by the bride and groom.]

Statement of Intentions

Groom: In a marriage like ours, people are bound to have some misgivings because of the difference in our ages, because I have been married before and am now divorced and because I have responsibility for two children by my first marriage.

Bride: We know we cannot make these problems disappear, but in spite of them, we choose each other. We have become each other's best friend. We feel the commonness of our roots, and we wish to share the direction of our futures.

Groom: So I choose you, S., to be my wife.

Bride: And I choose you, P., to be my husband.

Moment of Silent Meditation

Congregational Response

All: No marriage is without its own problems, for we are all human and we all make mistakes. Lift up your heads and be thankful for the love you share! Your lives and our lives can be still filled with joy.

Hymn

A Ceremony for the New Family

Obviously, this is not a divorce ritual. It is, however, a ritual that may follow a divorce. We offer it here because we think it is a particularly graceful example of how to include the children of a divorce in a second wedding and a remarriage. It was created by Roger Coleman and appeared in an article by Mary Beth Gordon in *The Witness* (December 1988), reprinted here by permission of The Episcopal Church Publishing Company, Detroit, Michigan. The article describes "a family-oriented wedding ceremony designed to make children an integral part of the marriage celebration. It differs from traditional wedding rites in only one respect: after the newlyweds exchange rings, their children join them at the altar for a special family service. During the five minute ceremony, the couple places a sterling silver medal — known as the Family Medallion — around the neck of each child as they pledge their love to all the children either spouse brings to the marriage."

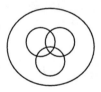

PRESENTING THE FAMILY MEDALLION

[An appropriate place for acknowledging the importance of children is following the pronouncement of the couple as husband and wife.]

Introduction

Minister: Often marriage is viewed as a union of two individuals. In reality, marriage is much broader.

As we give thanks to God for the love which brings
_____ and _____ together, so too, we

recognize the merging of families here represented and the additional love and responsibility they bring to this relationship.

We are, in fact, all members of one family, of God's family, a relationship established in the New Testament *Letter to James* (adapted from the Living Bible):

"And it was a happy day for God when we received our new lives through the truth of God's Word, and we became, as it were, the first children in God's new family."

[Also Gal. 3:28 may be read and Mk. 10:13-16 included when younger children are present.]

Presentation of the Medallion

[The child or children may be brought forward by grandparents or others if they are too young to stand with parents during the ceremony.]

Minister: As part of the family nature of God's creation we recognize _____ and the significant role he/she/they play(s) in this marriage today celebrated.

_____ and _____ present to _____ this/these Family Medallion(s) created as a symbol of family relationships and in recognition of the potential for a more just and loving world which God presents us through the gift of each child.

[The following may be repeated by the minister or by one or both parents.]

Parents: In the placing of this/these medallion(s) we pledge to you, _____, our continuing love and protection even as we surround you now with our arms of support and protection.

[Other comments or readings may be included by the minister.]

Prayer for the Family

Minister: Creator God, you have made us in your own image, male and female, that together we may live as members of your one family.

As you surround us with never-ending love, strengthen us that we too might reflect your love, becoming ever
supportive of one another in times of sorrow,
forgiving of one another in times on anger,
patient in those moments when we seek to rebuild out of the pain of broken trusts and shattered dreams.

We give thanks, O Lord, for this family. In your presence we are humbled by the recognition that, today, we face a new future, one which love has unfolded and is unfolding before our very eyes.

May we ever respect the sanctity of this gift.

As you have filled our cup with joy, may we share the strength of our deepening love for each other, including, in ever-widening circles, those who wait without hope and live without love's shelter. Amen.

Appendix
Bibliography

Ahrons, Constance 1994. *The Good Divorce: Keeping Your Family Together When Your Marriage Comes Apart*. New York: Harper Perennial.

Beck, Rene and Metrick, Sydney Barbara 1990. *The Art of Ritual*. Berkeley: Celestial Arts.

Bennett, Amanda and Foley, Terence B. 1997. *In Memorium: A Practical Guide to Planning a Memorial Service*. New York: Fireside.

Blair, Pamela D. Winter 1998/1999. "Divorce Ceremonies." *Divorce*, pp. 24-27.

Brener, Ann, et. al. 1993. *Mourning and Mizvah: A Guided Journal for Walking the Mourner's Path Through Grief to Healing.* Woodstock: Jewish Lights.

Bridges, William 1980. *Transitions: Making Sense of Life's Changes*. Reading: Perseus.

Brown, L. and Brown, M. 1986. *Dinosaur's Divorce: a Guide for Changing Families*. Boston: Joy Street Books-Little Brown.

Burns, Bob, and Smalley, Gary 1992. *The Fresh Start Divorce Recovery Book: A Step-by-Step Program for Those Who Are Divorced or Separated*. Nashville: Thomas Nelson.

Cherry, Kittredge, and Sherwood, Zalmon [eds.] 1995. *Equal Rites: Lesbian and Gay Worship, Ceremonies and Celebrations*. Louisville: Westminster John Knox.

367

Childs-Gowell, Elaine 1992. *Good Grief Rituals: Tools for Healing*. Barrytown: Station Hills.

Clements, Marcelle 1998. *The Improvised Woman*. New York: Norton.

Cohen, Alan 1999. *Happily Even After*. Carsbad: Hay House.

Colgrove, Melba, and Bloomfield, Harold, and McWilliams, Peter 1991. *How to Survive the Loss of a Love*. Los Angeles: Prelude Press.

Collier-Slone, Kay 1992. *Single in the Church*. New York: Alban Institute.

Desteian, John 1989. *Coming Together — Coming Apart: the Union of Opposites in Love Relationships*. Boston: Sigo.

Ferguson, Bill 1990. *How to Heal a Painful Relationship: And If Necessary, Part as Friends*. Houston: Return to the Heart.

Frankel, Valerie and Tiem, Ellen 1994. *The Heartbreak Handbook*. New York: Fawcett Columbine.

Ford, Debbie 1998. *The Dark Side of the Light Chasers:Reclaiming Your Power, Creativity, Brilliance and Dreams*. New York: Riverhead Books.

Gamble, Douglas James 1994. *The Divorce Ritual*. Castro Valley: Tanro Company.

Giampolo, Carlino 1997. *The Art of Letting Go: the Journey from Separation in Love to Fulfillment in Life*. Honolulu: Carlino and Company.

Gordon, Mary Beth December 1988. "A Ceremony for the New Family." *The Witness*.

Gottman, John 1990. *Why Marriages Succeed or Fail ... and How You Can Make Yours Last*. New York: Fireside.

Gray, John 1998. *Mars and Venus Starting Over*. New York: Harper Collins.

Grollman, Earl and Sams, Marjorie L. 1978. *Living Through Your Divorce*. Boston: Beacon Press.

Harris, Lynn 1996. *He Loves Me, He Loves Me Not*. New York: Avon Books.

Harvey, Donald 1993. *When the One You Love Wants to Leave: Guidance and Comfort for Surviving Marital Crisis*. Grand Rapids: Baker Books.

Hazen, Barbara S. 1978. *Two Homes to Live In: A Child's-Eye View of Divorce*. Human Sciences Press/Plenum.

Hendricks, Gay and Hendricks, Kathlyn 1990. *Conscious Loving: the Journey to Co-Commitment*. New York: Bantam Books.

Hendricks, Kathlyn and Hendricks, Gay 1997. *The Conscious Heart: Seven Soul Choices That Inspire Creative Partnership*. New York: Bantam Books.

Hill, Andrew (ed.) 1993. *Celebrating Life; a Book of Special Services*. London: The Lindsey Press.

Hollis, James 1993. *The Middle Passage: From Misery to Meaning in Midlife*. Toronto: Inner City Books.

Houston, Jean Winter, 1998. "Ritual as a Passage." *Quest*, pp. 23-25.

Hudson, Pat 1998. *You Can Get Over Your Divorce: The 7-Step Guide to Speed the Healing and Get on with the Rest of Your Life*. Rockland: Prima Publishing.

Imber-Black, Evan 1988. *Rituals in Families and Family Therapy*. New York: W.W. Norton and Company.

Imber-Black, Evan and Roberts, Janine 1998. *Rituals for Our Times: Celebrating Healing, and Changing our Lives and Our Relationships*. London: Jason Aronson.

Joselow, Beth 1994. *Life Lessons: 50 Things I learned from My Divorce*. New York: Avon Books.

Kaganoff, Penny and Spano, Susan [eds.] 1995. *Women on Divorce: A Bedside Companion*. New York: Harcourt Brace.

Kingma, Daphne Rose 1987. *Coming Apart: Why Relationships End and How to Live Through the Ending of Yours*. New York: Ballantine Books.

Kingma, Daphne Rose 1998. *The Future of Love: The Power of the Soul in Intimate Relationships*. New York: Doubleday.

Klein, Charles 1997. *How to Forgive When You Can't Forget: Healing Our Personal Relationships*. New York: Berkeley Books.

Klein, Issac 1979. *The Guide to Jewish Religious Practice*. New York: The Jewish Theological Seminary of America.

Koman, Aleta 1997. *How to Mend a Broken Heart: Letting Go and Moving On*. Chicago: Contemporary Books.

Kramer, Peter, D. 1997. *Should You Leave: A Psychiatrist Explores Intimacy and Autonomy - and the Nature of Advice*. New York: Charles Scribner.

370

Kuster, Elizabeth 1996. *Exorcising Your Ex: How to Get Rid of Demons of Relationships Past.* New York: Fireside.

Larson, Hal and Larson, Susan 1993. *Suddenly Single: A Lifeline for Anyone Who Has Lost a Love.* San Franciso: Halo Books.

Levine, Stephen and Levine, Ondrea 1995. *Embracing the Beloved: Relationship as a Path of Awakening.* New York: Doubleday.

Maller, Allen 1979. "Is Divorce a Mitsvah?" Culver City: Temple Akiba.

Metrick, Sydney Barbara 1994. *Crossing the Bridge: Creating Ceremonies for Grieving and Healing from Life's Losses.* Berkeley: Celestial Arts.

Miller, D. Patrick 1995. *A Little Book of Forgiveness.* New York: Viking - Fearless Books.

Moseley, Douglas and Moseley, Naomi 1994. *Dancing in the Dark: the Shadow Side of Intimate Relationships.* Georgetown: North Star Publications.

Nave, Yolanda 1985. *Breaking Up: From Heartache to Happiness in 48 Pages.* New York: Workman Publishing.

Nelson, Scott 1991. *Lost Lovers, Found Friends: Getting Over a Romance Without Losing a Friend.* New York: Fireside.

Netzer, Carol 1995. *Cutoffs: How Family Members Who Sever Relationships Can Reconnect.* Far Hills: New Horizon Press.

Pierrakos, Eva and Saly, Judith 1993. *Creating Union: The Pathwork of Relationship.* Madison, VA: Pathwork Press.

Rilke, Ranier Maria and Mitchell, Stephen [trans.] 1984. *Letters to a Young Poet.* New York: Random House.

Royko, David 1999. *Voices of Children of Divorce.* New York: Golden Books.

Sargent, Denny 1994. *Global Ritualism: Myth and Magic Around the World.* St. Paul: Llewllyn Publications.

Schnarch, David 1998. *Passionate Marriage.* New York: Henry Holt.

Searl, Edward 1993. *In Memorium: a Guide to Modern Funerals and Memorial Services.* Boston: Skinner House.

Sherman, Ed 1994. *Practical Divorce Solutions.* Occidental: Nolo Press.

Shideler, Mary. 1971, May 5. "An Amicable Divorce." *The Christian Century*, pp 553-555.

Simons, Ronald L. and Lin, Kuei-Hsiu and Gordon, Leslie. C. and Conger, Rand D. and Lorenz, Frederick O. 1999, November. "Explaining the Higher Incidence of Adjustment Problems Among Children of Divorce Compared with Those in Two-Parent Families." *Journal of Marriage and the Family*, pp. 1020-1033.

Slater, Herman [ed.] 1978. *A Book of Pagan Rituals.* New York: Samuel Weiser.

Smoke, Jim 1995. *Growing Through Divorce.* Eugene: Harvest House.

Snow, John. H. 1974. "Christian Marriage and Family Life." *Christianity and Crisis,* pp. 279-83.

Spong, John Selby 1990. *Living in Sin: a Bishop Rethinks Human Sexuality.* San Francisco: Harpercollins.

Talia, M. Sue 1997. *How to Avoid the Divorce from Hell and Dance Together at Your Daughter's Wedding.* Danville: Nexus Publishing.

Teyber, Edward 1992. *Helping Children Cope with Divorce.* San Franciso: Josey-Bass.

The Task Force on the Cultural Context of Ritual 1976. *Rituals for a New Day: An Invitation.* Nashville: Abingdon Press.

Trafford, Abigail 1992. *Crazy Time: Surviving Divorce and Building a New Life.* New York: Harper Perennial.

United Church of Christ Office of Church Life and Leadership 1986. *Book of Worship United Church of Christ.* New York.

Van der Hart, Onno 1988. *Coping with Loss: the Therapeutic Use of Leave-Taking Rituals.* New York: Irvington Publishers.

Vaughn, Diane 1986. *Uncoupling: Turning Points in Intimate Relationships.* New York: Vintage Books—The Oxford University Press.

Wall, Kathleen and Ferguson, Gary 1994. *Lights of Passage: Rituals and Rites of Passage for the Problems and Pleasures of Modern Life.* San Francisco: Harper San Francisco.

Wall, Kathleen and Ferguson, Gary 1998. *Rites of Passage: Celebrating Life's Changes.* Hillsboro: Beyond Words.

Wallerstein, Judith and Blakeslee, Susan 1996. *Second Chances: Men, Women and Children a Decade After Divorce.* New York: Houghton Mifflin.

Ward, Hannah and Wild, Jennifer (ed.) 1995. *Human Rites: Worship Resources For an Age of Change.* London: Mobray-Wellington House.

373

Westerhoff, John H. III, Willamon, William H. and Crouch, Timothy, J. 1994. *Liturgy and Learning Through the Life Cycle*. Akron: OSL Publications.

Whitehead, Barbara Dafoe 1996. *The Divorce Culture*. New York: Alfred Knopf.

Williamson, Gay and Williamson, David 1996. *Transformative Rituals: Celebrations for Personal Growth*. Deerfield Beach: Health Communications, Inc.

Williamson, Marianne 1994. *Illuminata: Prayers for a Better World*. New York: Riverhead Books.

Winther-Rassmussen, Anne 1998. *Divorce Ritual: Your Personal Guide to a Healthy Closure to Your Marriage*. Unpublished Masters Thesis Project. California State University, Northridge.

Wymard, Ellie 1994. *Men on Divorce: Conversations with Ex-Husbands*. Carlsbad: Hay House.

Young, James J. April, 1985. "Ministering to Divorced Catholics." *Catholic Update,* pp. 1-3.

Zweig, Constance and Abrams, Jeremiah [eds.] 1991. *Meeting the Shadow: The Hidden Power of the Dark Side of Human Nature*. New York: G.P. Puttnam.

Recommended Reading

We think these are some of the best books on divorce and related fields. We readily acknowledge that our list is far from complete. Indeed, we've continued to find books right to the date of publication. If you would like a greater choice of books, we recommend Essential Divorce Books which can be found on the Internet at www.oxfordbooks.com or www.divorceinfo.com.

Complete references for each book can be found in the bibliography. Many, but not all, have also been mentioned in the text. A number of these books deal with multiple subjects; we've listed them where we think they belong, but there's a lot of overlap. Also, many have excellent bibliographies of their own.

Marriage and Relationship

The Conscious Heart: Seven Soul Choices That Inspire Creative Partnership by Kathlyn Hendricks and Gay Hendricks.

> This wise and accessible book discusses many issues of relationship, including taking 100% responsibility for yourself — your feelings, your issues and your life.

Creating Union: the Pathwork of Relationship by Eva Pierrakos and Judith Saly

> You've probably never heard of Pathwork or this book, but you may find it as insightful and helpful as we have.

Passionate Marriage by David Schnarch

> This excellent and sophisticated book focuses on problem-solving in relationship, especially in sexuality, the area of the author's expertise.

375

Why Marriages Succeed or Fail... and How You Can Make Yours Last by John Gottman

> Based on years of research, this is one of the most comprehensive, practical and down to earth books about marriage we've ever read.

Embracing the Beloved: Relationship as a Path of Awakening by Stephen and Ondrea Levine

> We are unabashed fans of the Levines and believe that this book offers insights about relationship that you will not find elsewhere. It also discusses and describes a parting ceremony.

Experience of Separation and Divorce

Coming Apart: Why Relationships End and How to Live Through the Ending of Yours by Daphne Rose Kingma

> This book puts the end of relationships in a larger life context and has some excellent exercises and vizualizations that can help you sort through your feelings as you prepare for a ritual. A new 2000 edition also includes a ceremony.

Crazy Time: Surviving Divorce and Building a New Life by Abigail Trafford

> There are a lot of books out there with similar content, but we like this one the best for its command of the psychology of divorce and its direct, no-nonsense style.

The Dark Side of the Light Chasers:Reclaiming Your Power, Creativity, Brilliance and Dreams by Debbie Ford

> This is a particularly accessible bestseller about a difficult subject—how to identify, embrace and transform the shadow.

The Good Divorce: Keeping Your Family Together When Your Marriage Comes Apart by Constance Ahrons

> Though a bit academic for some, this book is one of the finest discussions we know of about the process of divorce and the changes in society involving divorce and bi-nuclear families.

How to Heal a Painful Relationship: And If Necessary, Part as Friends by Bill Ferguson

> By a lawyer who renounced adversarial law, this book presents a sophisticated and compassionate take on divorce and relationship in a down home, straightforward style.

How to Survive the Loss of a Love by Melba Colgrove, Harold Bloomfield and Peter McWilliams

> This little classic has been reprinted forever and is wonderful help when working with loss and grief.

A Little Book of Forgiveness by Patrick Miller

> This book is little only in form. In content, it's immense in wisdom about the problems, paradoxes and promise of forgiveness.

Meeting the Shadow: The Hidden Power of the Dark Side of Human Nature edited by Constance Zweig and Jeremiah Abrams

> We recommend this book because it's one of the most comprehensive collections of material available on the shadow.

Men on Divorce: Conversations with Ex-Husbands by Ellie Wymard

> In the service of empathy, we recommend this book to both women and men because it gives voice to men's points of view.

The Middle Passage: From Misery to Meaning in Midlife by James Hollis

> Perhaps it's just because we're older and admire the psychology of Carl Jung, but this is one of the best book we've ever read about working with the inevitable changes and challenges of midlife.

Transitions: Making Sense of Life's Changes by William Bridges

> Another "little" book that offers a lot of informed common sense about how we can manage change in our lives.

Uncoupling: Turning Points in Intimate Relationships by Diane Vaughn

> Though academic, this book is well worth reading if you want to understand more about the sociology of the divorce process.

Women on Divorce by Penny Kaganoff and Susan Spano

> In the service of empathy, we recommend this book to both men and women because it gives voice to women's points of view.

You Can Get Over Your Divorce: The 7-Step Guide to Speed the Healing and Get on with the Rest of Your Life by Pat Hudson

> We found this book just before we went to press. We wish we'd found it sooner. It's a practical and user friendly guide to the divorce experience. It includes a chapter on using ritual with divorce. It also describes a unique process of using a ritual at different stages of divorce.

Practical Matters

Divorce Info (www.divorceinfo.com)

> This Internet site, operated by Lee Borden, a non-adversarial lawyer and one of the contributors to this book, has everything you need or want to know about divorce. It can also link you to many other helpful sites.

How to Avoid the Divorce from Hell and Dance Together at Your Daughter's Wedding by M. Sue Talia

> Here's another lawyer who tired of adversarial law and wrote a book on the practicalities of divorce that is psychologically sophisticated and full of hard headed yet compassionate insights and advice.

Practical Divorce Solutions by Ed Sherman

> This accessible and easy to read book is what we used when working out legal and financial issues.

Ritual, Religion and Divorce

Some of the most helpful writing on the subject of religion and divorce, including the use of ritual, can be found in articles and essays published in a variety of periodicals. These are not always easy to find. We have referenced some in the text of the book and recommend an Internet search for others.

Liturgy and Learning Through the Life Cycle by John Westerhoff, William Willamon and Timothy Crouch

> This book includes a discussion of theological issues and examples of Christian rituals for many of life's transitions, including divorce (and served as the basis for two of the rituals in this book).

Living in Sin: a Bishop Rethinks Human Sexuality by John Selby Spong

> This book deals with many important theological issues, including divorce, from an Anglican point of view.

Single in the Church by Kay Collier-Slone

> While this book focuses on ministry to singles, it also touches on themes to do with the aftermath of separation and divorce and includes divorce rituals.

Rituals for a New Day: An Invitation by the Task Force on the Cultural Context of Ritual (Out of Print)

> We list this book because of the impact it had on the development of (and our thinking about) alternative liturgy. Maybe if enough people make requests, the publishers will reprint it.

Children and Divorce

Dinosaur's Divorce, a Guide for Changing Families by Marc Brown and Laurence Brown

One of many excellent books about divorce for kids 6-12.

Helping Children Cope with Divorce by Edward Teyber

A down to earth book that's accessible, practical and hopeful.

Second Chances: Men, Women and Children a Decade After Divorce by Judith Wallerstein and Susan Blakeslee

Based on a longitudinal research study, a haunting evocation of the effects of divorce on children.

Two Homes to Live In: A Child's-Eye View of Divorce by Barbara Shook Hazen

A good book for kids under 6 years old.

Friendship After Divorce

Happily Even After by Alan Cohen

This book takes a wonderfully affirmative psychological and spiritual approach to friendship after the end of any relationship. Also for a free catalogue of Alan Cohen's books, tapes and seminar schedules call 1-800-462-3013, write to hay House, P.O. Box 5100, Carlsbad, CA 92018-5100 or visit www.alancohen.com.

Lost Lovers, Found Friends: Getting Over a Romance Without Losing a Friend by Scott Nelson

Based on research, this book is down to earth, practical and well worth reading for anyone trying to work out a friendship with an ex-partner.

Ritual

These books and one article include a model divorce ritual.

The Art of Ritual by Rene Beck and Sydney Barbara Metrick

A bit abstract, it's still one of the best books we've found about the theory and practice of ritual.

A Book of Pagan Rituals by Herman Slater

Rituals from the neo-pagan tradition.

Celebrating Life; a Book of Special Services by Andrew Hill

A book of Unitarian rituals and ceremonies.

Crossing the Bridge: Creating Ceremonies for Grieving and Healing from Life by Sydney Barbara Metrick

This book covers some of the same ground but is more accessible and specifically focused than *The Art of Ritual*.

"Divorce Ceremonies." *Divorce* by Pamela Blair.

Divorce is a new magazine and this winter 1998-1999 article describes some helpful vizualizations.

Divorce Ritual: Your Personal Guide to a Healthy Closure to Your Marriage by Anne Winther-Rassmussen

Except for our book, this is the only attempt we know to address the subject of rituals for divorce. Written as a Master's Thesis, it's got a lot to recommend it, including practical advice and a literature review about divorce rituals that is the most complete we've found. (Also, see the Contact List.)

Equal Rites: Lesbian and Gay Worship, Ceremonies and Celebrations edited by Kittredge Cherry and Zalmon Sherwood

The best book we found on this particular subject.

Illuminata: A Return to Prayer by Marianne Williamson

This book is justifiably popular for its spirit, intelligence and compassion (and was used as a source for several rituals in this book).

Lights of Passage: Rituals and Rites of Passage for the Problems and Pleasures of Modern Life by Kathleen Wall and Gary Ferguson

We really like the combination of theory and practice found in this book.

Living Through Your Divorce by Earl Grollman and Marjorie Sams

A book by one of the first rabbis to create modern divorce ceremonies.

Rites of Passage: Celebrating Life's Changes by Kathleen Wall and Gary Ferguson

> We really like the combination of theory and practice found in this book, too.

Rituals for Our Times: Celebrating Healing, and Changing Our Lives and Our Relationships by Evan Imber-Black and Janine Roberts

> A solid, practical and accessible book about all kinds of ritual.

Transformative Rituals: Celebrations for Personal Growth by Gay and David Williamson

> A graceful and practical book.

People Who Can Help You Create A Ceremony

    Some lay and clergy contributors to this book volunteered to talk about their experience with a parting ceremony or a divorce ritual, and to offer counsel and guidance. We have listed them with the contact information they have provided. As you will know from your reading, all can speak to you from their personal experience. Some also have considerable professional experience working with ritual and ceremony. If you desire hands-on assistance in creating and performing a ceremony or ritual, however, this is something you will have to discuss with the person you contact.

Barbara Penningroth
www.healingdivorce.com

Phil Penningroth
www.healingdivorce.com

Scott Small
4905 Sims Road
Knoxville, TN. 37920
(865) 609-8187
smallguy@icx.net

Anne Winther-Rasmussen
Grønnevej 41
2830 Virum
Denmark
phone: (45) 4585-9021
anne.winther@mail.tele.dk

Colette van Praag
P.O. Box 295
Sonoma, CA. 95476
(888) 431-1154
epiphany53@aol.com

Carolyn Elizabeth Dyche
Carolyn@grapevine.net

Marcy Harmon
harmony@cdsnet.net

Lee Borden
3280 Morgen Drive
Birmingham, AL. 35216
divorceinfo.com

Rev. William Barnes
1023 Battlefield Drive
Nashville, TN. 37204
(615) 297-3973

Rev. Jim Robey
7072 Dickey Springs Road
Bessemer, AL. 35022
(205) 425-5772
JAROBEY@aol.com

Rev. Jeanne Audrey Powers
4000 Groveland Ave. #1107
Minneapolis, MN. 55403
(612) 872-9744
japowers1@aol.com

Rabbi Allen Maller
Temple Akiba
5249 Sepulveda Blvd.
Culver City, CA. 90230
(310) 398-5783

Dr. Kay Collier-Slone
Solo Flight: Catch the Vision
P.O. Box 27
Paris, KY. 40362
(606) 252-6527
diolex@alo.com

Rev. Julie Griffith
4449 44th Avenue South
Minneapolis, MN. 55406
shepherdess@uswest.net

Rabbi James Bleiberg, Psy.D.
1600 Powder Mill Lane
Wynnewood, PA. 19096
JimBlei@aol.com

Rabbi Earl Grollman,
D.H.L., D.D.
79 Country Club Lane
Belmont, MA. 02478
FAX (671) 484-3927

Gay Lynn and
    David Williamson
2750 Van Buren Street
Hollywood, FL. 33020
(954) 922-5521
www.12powers2000.org

VISIT OUR WEBPAGE AT
www.healingdivorce.com

About The Authors

Phil and Barbara Penningroth have lived what they write about in **A Healing Divorce**. Together, they created and performed a parting ceremony to end their 25 year marriage. Since then, they have remained good friends and co-written this book. It is based on their own experience and informed by their many years as mental health professionals, as well as by the inspiring stories of others who have used the transforming power of ritual and ceremony to bring healing to the end of their relationships.

Barbara is a Registered Nurse and a Marriage and Family Therapist. She currently lives in Carmel, California.

Phil is a freelance writer with articles, stories, plays and screenplays to his credit. He currently lives in Boulder, Colorado.